BASICS OF
LEGAL DOCUMENT
PREPARATION

Legal Writing, 2d ed., Steve Barber, 1997

Administration of Wills, Trusts, and Estates, 2d ed., Gordon W. Brown, 1997

Basics of Legal Document Preparation, Robert R. Cummins, 1997

Constitutional Law: Cases and Commentary, Daniel E. Hall, 1997

Criminal Procedure and the Constitution, Daniel E. Hall, 1997

Survey of Criminal Law, 2d ed., Daniel E. Hall, 1997

California Estate Administration, Zella Mack, 1997

Torts and Personal Injury Law, 2d ed., Cathy J. Okrent and William R. Buckley, 1997

The Law of Corporations, Partnerships, and Sole Proprietorships, 2d ed.,
    Angela Schneeman, 1997

Texas Legal Research, 2d ed., Pamela R. Tepper, Peggy N. Kerley, 1997

Legal Research, Steve Barber, Mark A. McCormick, 1996

Wills, Estates, and Trusts, Jay H. Gingrich, 1996

Criminal Law and Procedure, 2d ed., Daniel E. Hall, 1996

Introduction to Environmental Law, Harold Hickok, 1996

Civil Litigation, 2d ed., Peggy N. Kerley, Joanne Banker Hames, Paul A. Sukys, 1996

Client Accounting for the Law Office, Elaine M. Langston, 1996

Law Office Management, 2d ed., Jonathan S. Lynton, Terri Mick Lyndall,
    Donna Masinter, 1996

Foundations of Law: Cases, Commentary, and Ethics, 2d ed., Ransford C. Pyle, 1996

Administrative Law and Procedure, Elizabeth C. Richardson, 1996

Legal Research and Writing, David J. Smith, 1996

Legal Research and Writing, Carol M. Bast, 1995

Federal Taxation, Susan G. Covins, 1995

Everything You Need to Know About Being a Legal Assistant, Chere B. Estrin, 1995

Paralegals in New York Law, Eric M. Gansberg, 1995

Ballentine's Legal Dictionary and Thesaurus, Jonathan S. Lynton, 1995

Legal Terminology with Flashcards, Cathy J. Okrent, 1995

Wills, Trusts, and Estate Administration for Paralegals, Mark A. Stewart, 1995

The Law of Contracts and the Uniform Commercial Code, Pamela R. Tepper, 1995

Life Outside the Law Firm: Non-Traditional Careers for Paralegals,
    Karen Treffinger, 1995

An Introduction to Paralegal Studies, David G. Cooper, Micheal J. Gibson, 1994

Administrative Law, Daniel E. Hall, 1994

Ballentine's Law Dictionary: Legal Assistant Edition, Jack G. Handler, 1994

The Law of Real Property, Michael P. Kearns, 1994

Ballentine's Thesaurus for Legal Research and Writing, Jonathan S. Lynton, 1994

Legal Ethics and Professional Responsibility, Jonathan S. Lynton,
    Terri Mick Lyndall, 1994

Criminal Law for Paralegals, Daniel J. Markey, Jr., Mary Queen Donnelly, 1994

Family Law, Ransford C. Pyle, 1994

Paralegals in American Law: Introduction to Paralegalism, Angela Schneeman, 1994

Intellectual Property, Richard Stim, 1994

BASICS OF LEGAL DOCUMENT PREPARATION

Robert R. Cummins

Delmar Publishers

I(T)P   An International Thomson Publishing Company

Albany • Bonn • Boston • Cincinnati • Detroit • London • Madrid • Melbourne
Mexico City • New York • Pacific Grove • Paris • San Francisco • Singapore • Tokyo
Toronto • Washington

NOTICE TO THE READER

Delmar Staff

Acquisitions Editor: Christopher Anzalone
Editorial Assistant: Judy A. Roberts
Developmental Editor: Jeffrey D. Litton

Project Editor: Eugenia L. Orlandi
Production Manager: Linda J. Helfrich
Art & Design Coordinator: Douglas J. Hyldelund

COPYRIGHT © 1997
By Delmar Publishers Inc.
an International Thomson Publishing Company

The ITP logo is a trademark under license.

Printed in the United States of America

For more information, contact:

Delmar Publishers
3 Columbia Circle, Box 15015
Albany, New York 12212-5015

International Thomson Publishing–Europe
Berkshire House
168-173 High Holborn
London, WC1V 7AA
England

Thomas Nelson Australia
102 Dodds Street
South Melbourne, 3205
Victoria, Australia

Nelson Canada
1120 Birchmount Road
Scarborough, Ontario
Canada, M1K 5G4

International Thomson Editores
Campos Eliseos 385, Piso 7
Col Polanco
11560 Mexico D F Mexico

International Thomson Publishing GmbH
Königswinterer Strasse 418
53227 Bonn
Germany

International Thomson Publishing Asia
221 Henderson Road
#05-10 Henderson Building
Singapore 0315

International Thomson Publishing–Japan
Hirakawacho Kyowa Building, 3F
2-2-1 Hirakawacho
Chiyoda-ku, Tokyo 102
Japan

17 XXX 07

Library of Congress Cataloging-in-Publication Data

Cummins, Robert R.
    Basics of legal document preparation / Robert R. Cummins.
       p.   cm.
    Includes bibliographical references and index.
    ISBN 13: 978-0-8273-6799-9
    ISBN 10: 0-8273-6799-6
    1. Legal documents—United States. 2. Pleading—United States.
3. Legal composition. I. Title.
KF250.C83   1997
808'.06634—dc20   96-17180
                                       CIP
                                       AC

"So great moreover is the regard of the law for private property, that it will not authorize the least violation of it; no, not even for the general good of the whole community."

Sir William Blackstone,
***Commentaries on the Law of England* (1783)**

CONTENTS

PREFACE

Introduction

The field of paralegal and legal assistant studies has long been without a textbook devoted solely to the legal document and its place in the field of law. I taught a course in legal documents without a textbook of any kind for some time. Students benefited greatly from the material after starting their careers, but the course demanded the structure and reference offered only by a textbook. This textbook is an attempt to present the legal document as an essential tool of the legal profession.

My premise in writing this textbook is to present the legal document in its duality as both an instrument and a pleading, each having a different function. I feel that it is essential to the production of any legal document that the preparer have a fundamental understanding of the basic principles of substantive and procedural law behind the document. Therefore, I have chosen what I believe to be the key areas of law from the standpoint of legal document preparation. Each chapter provides a section called Ballentine's Review that defines essential terminology, followed by an analysis of the basic documents supporting the area discussed in the chapter. The documents are reviewed for both form and content, in most cases, paragraph by paragraph.

Although no single textbook can provide coverage of every document for all areas of the law or for each state, I have attempted to present the law and its documents from the standpoint of general American jurisprudence. The student is encouraged at each juncture to consult the substantive and procedural law of the particular state, as frequently there are differences to be found in both the form and the content required. Also, at no point do I intend to suggest that the documents presented are anything more than a *suggested* manner of preparation. In addition to the specific requirements dictated by local court rule, statute, and case law, the client will have individual needs and constraints that compel a deviation from any general structure. It is the task of the preparer of the legal document, be it instrument or pleading, to tailor the general format to the specific needs of the individual client in conformity with state law. This textbook is designed to teach the paralegal student that process.

Organization

Chapter 1 presents the fundamentals of legal documents and the mechanical knowledge required to produce the documents in conformity with the generally accepted rules of format and appearance. Chapters 2 through 7 provide the fundamental law and basic documents for the areas of contracts, real estate, corporations, partnerships, wills, and trusts. Chapters 8 through 12 offer the paralegal student an analysis of the pleading. These chapters provide the substance of the law of bankruptcy, federal and state procedure, discovery, domestic relations, and appeals—all areas of litigation involving extensive use of pleadings. Each chapter presents the basic pleadings for litigation in that area, along with an analysis of the sections of each document. Perhaps conspicuous by its absence is the area of criminal law. Since the practice of criminal law involves much in the way of substantive law and little in the way of pleadings, in the interest of space, I have left instruction in that area to local court rules.

Each chapter provides an epigram related to the content of the chapter. The quotes are designed to elevate the student's thought and orient attention to the subject. The Objectives section of each chapter presents my concept of what I hope the paralegal student will be able to accomplish after a careful consideration of the content of the text. The text presents an overview of the substance of the area concerned, followed by the documents related to that area. Each chapter also provides marginal notes defining the terms used in the text. The purpose here is twofold: (1) to offer a convenient reference for the meaning of each term, and (2) to emphasize terminology. I believe that if the paralegal student can master the terminology of the law, he or she can master the law.

At the end of the chapters are review questions designed to give the student a convenient review of the materials. The Putting It All Together section that follows will, I hope, occasionally amuse the student as well as provide practical, hands-on experience in the preparation of legal documents. Many of these scenarios are taken from factual settings found in actual case law.

Acknowledgments

This book is the product of the efforts of many individuals, without whose contribution the completion would not have been possible. My loving and supportive wife, Margaret Ann Cummins, has provided the love, encouragement, and technical support needed from inception to completion. My proofreaders and critics, Rosalind Beck and Donna Simmerson, have proved that former students may reward their instructors with more than they were given.

I am especially grateful to Delmar Publishers for offering me the opportunity to put this effort into print. My editors, Mary McGarry, Robert Nirkind, Christopher Anzalone, and Jeffrey Litton, have provided the writing talent and vision to make this textbook a reality. I also would like to acknowledge the following reviewers for their contributions:

Alix Popkin
Paralegal Solutions
Orlando, FL

Shellie O'Hara
Orlando College
Orlando, FL

Janice Mersinger
Cochise College
Sierra Vista, AZ

Joe F. Monroe
North Harris Montgomery Community College
Houston, TX

CHAPTER
1
Fundamentals of Legal Document Preparation

Originality is nothing but judicious imitation. The most original writers borrowed from one another. The instruction we find in books is like fire. We fetch it from our neighbor's, kindle it at home, communicate it to others, and it becomes the property of all.

———

VOLTAIRE (1694–1778)

OBJECTIVES

After completing this chapter, you will be able to:

1. Describe the nature of legal instruments and pleadings
2. Develop a checklist to obtain the preliminary background information to prepare a legal instrument
3. Create a legal document utilizing the correct paper, typeface, margins, and spacing
4. Identify the sections of a legal document and discuss the general rules for presentation
5. Detail the mechanics of legal document preparation concerned with capitalization, grammar, spelling, numbers, pagination, and preprinted forms
6. Prepare actual legal documents using *all* the applicable rules of preparation

BALLENTINE'S REVIEW

document—Anything with letters, figures, or marks recorded on it. EXAMPLES: printed words; photographs; pictures; maps.

instrument—Any formal legal document evidencing an agreement or the granting of a right. EXAMPLES: contract; deed; mortgage; will.

pleadings—Formal statements by the parties to an action setting forth their claims or defenses. EXAMPLES: complaint; cross-complaint; answer; counterclaim.

§ 1.1 THE LAW AND THE LEGAL DOCUMENT

A foundation in the nature of the law is essential to an understanding of the development of a legal document. The preparer of any document must have a basic knowledge of the rules of law that apply to a particular document and its individual components.

The **law** is a body of rules, standards, and principles enacted by the government to control its citizens and have a binding legal effect. These principles are rooted in every aspect of the development of humankind: nature, philosophy, custom, religion, and history. The principles of law have not remained static but have changed constantly through the ages, evolving into their current expression through the application of the legal system of government and justice in the United States. The law of the land comes from the government in the form of statutes and judicial decisions.

A **legal document** is the written, physical embodiment of information conforming to the principles of law enacted by the government through the legislative process and reviewed by the judicial system. The legal document stands at the juncture between the rule of law and its practical application in our daily lives. It is the legal document, as an instrument or a pleading, that brings the black letter of the law into physical existence to accomplish a stated result consistent with that law. In the written document, the law finds its most meaningful expression.

The purpose of this text is to present the basic elements necessary to create the appropriate legal document consistent with the rule of law that governs the situation. The coverage of any single area of the law must be brief. Only those principles of law necessary to the generation of the specific elements of a legal document will be addressed.

§ 1.2 INSTRUMENTS AND PLEADINGS

Legal documents can be classified as either **instruments** or **pleadings.** The distinction between the two categories of documents is in both their nature and their function.

The function of a legal instrument is to serve as an expression of the intention of the maker of the document. The primary focus is on providing written evidence of one's intent rather than serving some role in the litigation process. Although the contents of an instrument may become the object of litigation, it is not created as a part of the litigation process.

§ 1.3 NATURE OF LEGAL INSTRUMENTS

The nature of a legal instrument is best defined through its fundamental character as expressed by its:

- written form
- formal execution
- intent regarding a legal right

law: The entire body of rules of conduct created by government and enforced by the authority of government. EXAMPLES: constitutions; statutes; ordinances; regulations; judicial decisions.

legal document: The written, physical embodiment of information conforming to the principles of law enacted by the government through the legislative process and reviewed by the judicial system.

instrument: Any formal legal document evidencing an agreement or the granting of a right. EXAMPLES: contract; deed; mortgage; will.

pleadings: Formal statements by the parties to an action setting forth their claims or defenses. EXAMPLES: complaint; cross-complaint; answer; counterclaim.

The written form of a legal instrument is one element of its central nature that distinguishes it in American law. The writing may contain text, drawings, figures, photographs, blueprints, plans, or marks. It may be handwritten, typed, printed, engraved, or photocopied. Regardless of the form the writing takes, it is the writing itself, that identifies its character.

Another element defining the nature of a legal instrument is its formal execution. Although federal and state statutes often require certain forms or procedures to be followed to give an instrument enforceability, most legal instruments do not require any specific procedure to make them valid. The formality that defines its nature comes from its execution. **Execution** is the legal term for the completion of some act or conduct that brings a document into operation and effect. No instrument will have any legal standing without some form of execution. The execution may take the form of a signature, witnessing, delivery, filing, or recording. The type of instrument determines the formality required to execute it.

The third element of a legal instrument that defines its elementary nature is its expression of intent regarding a legal right. **Intent** refers to the state of mind of an individual in seeking a specific result through his or her actions. Inherent in the nature of all legal instruments is the idea that the individual creating the document intends the consequences of his or her acts. Thus, the legal instrument stands as an expression of the maker's state of mind as to the result sought. It is the maker's specific, stated intent that is central to the nature of the legal instrument.

§ 1.4 TYPES OF LEGAL INSTRUMENTS

While the *nature* of a legal document is found in its formal written expression of the intention of the maker of the document, the *type* of legal instrument refers specifically to the purpose the document is to fulfill.

Contractual Document

A contractual document is the formal written expression of the intent of the parties to the agreement. Chapter 2 provides an in-depth view of the preparation of the *contract* as a legal instrument. As a legal document, the contract stands as the stated expression of the intent of its parties and is intended to be enforceable in its executed form.

Real Estate Document

The change in ownership of property is the subject of the formal real estate instrument. In a transaction involving a transfer of property rights, it is the real estate document, formally executed, that expresses the intent to pass ownership. The object of the real estate transaction is to transfer ownership in some form that is enforceable against all claims to the contrary. As Chapter 3 discusses, this is accomplished through the contract for sale, the deed, the mortgage and promissory note, and the closing documents.

execution: The signing of a document or instrument; the completion of any transaction.

intent: Purpose; the plan, course, or means a person conceives to achieve a certain result.

Corporate Document

A separate, distinct, and artificial person is created by the formation of a *corporation*. The corporate entity has status in the law as a person, yet it is an entity separate from its individual owners. The legal instruments that create this unique legal *person*, once formally executed, allow the declaration of its intention to function as a legal entity. This is accomplished through documents such as its articles of incorporation, bylaws, corporate minutes, and stock subscriptions. Chapter 4 provides an in-depth look at the preparation of the legal instruments that create this legal entity and allow it to act.

Partnership Document

The legal instrument used to define the intentions of persons doing business together, without having formed a separate corporation, is the *partnership* agreement. As a contract to be formally executed to have legal effect, the agreement stands as the written expression of the intent of those persons who are parties to it. Chapter 5 presents the fundamental structure of the partnership agreement and describes its preparation.

Estate Document

The *will* stands as the basic legal instrument communicating the formal written intent of an individual property owner regarding the distribution of his or her property at death. Chapter 6 provides a detailed discussion of the will and its separate components along with guidelines for its preparation. No legal document has received more statutory attention than the will and its related documents. Thus, its preparation requires preliminary legal research to comply with those regulations.

Trust Document

An alternative means of property distribution is provided by the *trust*, the subject of Chapter 7. As a legal instrument, the trust document is similar in function to the will in its expression of the intended distribution of property. Once formally executed, a separate legal being is created whose sole function is to carry out the express written intentions of the creator of the trust.

§ 1.5 PRELIMINARY BACKGROUND INFORMATION

The ultimate goal in the preparation of a legal instrument is to create an enforceable document that satisfies its stated purpose. To accomplish this result, the document must be meticulously prepared within the boundaries of the common law and state statutes. The preparer of the instrument should draw enough information from the client to adequately present his or her intentions. A *checklist* is an aid that helps to ensure that enough information is gathered to satisfy the requirements of diligence and precision. The individual drafter may want to develop his or her own checklists, since not every situation lends itself to a generic checklist and not every item in such a check-list will apply to a given circumstance. The basic concerns for a general check-list should include:

- the client conference
- introductory information
- family information
- health information
- employment information
- financial information
- family advisors
- important documents

Depending upon the type of instrument to be created, one or more items in the checklist will have greater relevance. For instance, if an individual is solely concerned with a contract for the sale of a summer cottage in the Catskills, then the information concerning that individual's health may not have the significance it would if a person were seeking to have a last will and testament prepared.

The Client Conference

The first step in the preparation of a legal instrument is the client confer-ence. It is here that the client provides the information necessary to develop the requisite documents to serve the client's interests. If the client has been given a copy of an information checklist before the conference, he or she will have the vital information at hand for the conference. Each item in the check-list should be discussed in detail with the client to ensure complete disclosure of all relevant information.

The client conference should commence with a record of the date, a file number if available, the name of interviewer, and the general purpose in the caption of the checklist (as shown in Figure 1–1, Exhibit 1).

Introductory Information

The introductory information should include basic facts such as full names, addresses, and phone numbers of any participants to the transaction. The type of instrument to be drafted may require greater detail regarding the identity of the parties. For general purposes, the facts can be obtained as shown in Figure 1–1, Exhibit 2.

Family Information

While the marital and family status of an individual is more relevant to a last will and testament or trust than to a simple contract, complete back-ground information will help to advise the client of the best course of action. Therefore, a thorough investigation into the family status of a client will sat-isfy the need for diligence and care in prescribing the appropriate legal instru-ments. The family information section of a checklist should include the areas of investigation shown in Figure 1–1, Exhibit 3.

CLIENT CONFERENCE CHECKLIST

CLIENT: DATE:

INTERVIEWER: FILE #:

CONSULTATION PURPOSE:

INTRODUCTORY INFORMATION

Client's full name:
Spouse's full name:
Current address:
Home telephone #:
Fax #:
Other addresses (if any):
Date of birth:

FAMILY INFORMATION (if applicable)

Date of marriage (attach copy of certificate):
Place of marriage:
Type of ceremony:
Names/dates of birth of children:
Prior marriage of client:
Names/dates of birth of children by prior marriage:
Prior marriage of spouse:
Names/dates of birth of children of spouse:
Antenuptial contract between spouses (attach):
Support obligation for children of prior marriage:

HEALTH INFORMATION

State of client's health:
State of spouse's health:
State of children's health:
Nature of current medical treatment:
Current medication:
Name of physician(s):
Health insurance coverage:

FIGURE 1–1 A sample client conference checklist

EMPLOYMENT INFORMATION

Client

    Social security #:
    Name of employer:
    Address:
    Length of employment:
    Job description:
    Salary (attach pay stub):
    Insurance:
    Prior employment history:

Spouse

    Social security #:
    Name of employer:
    Address:
    Length of employment:
    Job description:
    Salary (attach pay stub):
    Insurance:
    Prior employment history:

EXHIBIT 5
A sample employment information section

FINANCIAL INFORMATION

Monthly income:	Amount
Client:	_____
Spouse:	_____
Children:	_____
Total:	_____

Monthly household expenses:

	Amount
Mortgage or rent:	_____
Taxes:	_____
Insurance:	_____
Utilities:	_____
Telephone:	_____
Maintenance:	_____
Food:	_____
School:	_____
Clothing:	_____
Child care:	_____
Transportation:	_____
Medical:	_____
Pets:	_____
Entertainment:	_____
Church:	_____
Clubs:	_____
Charity:	_____
Total:	_____

EXHIBIT 6
A sample financial information section

FIGURE 1–1 (continued)

FINANCIAL INFORMATION (continued)

Property:

Real estate:
  Residence:
      Property description:

      Date of purchase:
      Cost/value:
  Other:

Personal (auto, boat, trailer, personal effects, jewelry):
Stocks, bonds, mutual funds, CDs:
Bank accounts:
Retirement accounts:
Estate interests or expectancies:
Pending litigation:
Life insurance policies:
Safe deposit boxes:

FAMILY ADVISOR INFORMATION

	Name	Address	Telephone #
Attorney:			
Accountant:			
Physician:			
Clergy:			
Broker:			
Other:			

IMPORTANT DOCUMENTS

Document	Location
Stock certificates, etc.:	
Deeds, mortgages, leases:	
Titles:	
Contracts:	
Insurance policies:	
Tax returns:	
Divorce decree:	
Antenuptial agreements:	
Notes:	
Other:	

FIGURE 1–1 (continued)

Health Information

The facts surrounding the health of a particular client are important if life expectancy or ability to perform an obligation are factors in the transaction to be accomplished by the legal instrument. An instrument must be drafted with the state of health and the ability of the parties to perform in mind. (See Figure 1–1, Exhibit 4.)

Employment Information

Information concerning the employment of all participants to a legal instrument is relevant with most types of legal instruments. Employment reflects upon earning potential, professional skills, and the ability to perform as required by the transaction requiring a legal instrument. Whether the instrument is a real estate contract, trust, will, or stock subscription, the parties' employment information should be obtained (as shown in Figure 1–1, Exhibit 5).

Financial Information

The importance of obtaining as much information as possible concerning the financial status of an individual participant to a legal instrument should be emphasized. Not only is the information material to the instrument itself, it may be relevant to the advisability of the underlying transaction. The extent of the detail required will vary with each circumstance. A thorough inquiry into an individual's financial picture should be made. (See Figure 1–1, Exhibit 6.)

Family Advisors

Information concerning the identity of all family advisors is relevant to the client's total position. It forms the background necessary to decision making on the transaction underlying a document as well as providing a source of information for the actual production of the instrument itself. (See Figure 1–1, Exhibit 7.)

Important Documents

An individual's property and financial interests are represented in many documents. Many of them should be attached to the checklist, depending upon their relevance. If not attached, their whereabouts should be known for provision if necessary. An example of this section of the checklist is shown in Figure 1–1, Exhibit 8.

§ 1.6 PLEADINGS

Pleadings are legal documents used by the parties to a lawsuit to convey notice of their intentions to the court and to their opponents. Pleadings are the written statements of participants in the litigation process that produce issues for resolution. They differ from instruments in that they further the cause of the litigation process as opposed to being the subject matter of it.

The function of pleadings has not changed since the English common law, but individual state procedural codes have defined the content required in specific types of pleadings. The exact nature of legal pleadings and their function is the focus of Chapters 8 through 12.

§ 1.7 SOURCES OF FORMS

Comprehensive and reliable form books serve as an invaluable aid in the preparation of instruments and pleadings. There are excellent general form books available for all areas of the law consisting of multivolume sets with annotations to each form and some editorial commentary. These books are general in nature. Care must be exercised to ensure their suitability for a particular circumstance and client.

For legal documents in the form of instruments, the major legal publishers provide multivolume sets detailing carefully selected forms for most areas of the practice of law. The two major sets are:

American Jurisprudence, Legal Forms 2d
West's Legal Forms, 2d

For coverage of the areas concerning pleadings, the major sets are:

American Jurisprudence, Pleading & Practice Forms
West's Federal Forms

Most states have general form books available for both instruments and pleadings from commercial publishers and the state bar association. In addition to the general form books, there are also subject-related form books addressing legal documents required in a specialized area of the law such as bankruptcy or real estate. Most large law firms and legal institutions have a bank of legal documents to be used by their members for the clients' needs. As with the general forms, care must be taken to ensure that they are appropriate for a specific client.

The chief disadvantage of most general forms is a lack of suitability. Every client has certain wishes and circumstances that are unique. It is virtually impossible to have one general legal document for a specific transaction that will suffice. If it is not properly adapted to the purpose, the client will find his or her document to be unenforceable, resulting in a violation of the canons of professional responsibility. The duty owed to the client must not be sacrificed in exchange for the convenience of a generic form.

§ 1.8 THE LEGAL DOCUMENT AND THE COMPUTER

The computer has become an essential tool in the modern legal setting. When first introduced, computers were not widely accepted. Today, computers are used for almost every facet of a law practice, including document preparation and legal research. While computers are used extensively for legal research purposes through access to national databases and CD-ROM technology, the focus of this text is their use in word processing for the development of legal documents.

The electronic generation of legal documents has become an invaluable tool to the legal professional. The ease of use and time-saving functions of computers have revolutionized document production in the law office. Attorney, paralegal, and secretary alike benefit from word processing capabilities, which ultimately benefits the client.

§ 1.9 FOUNDATIONS OF LEGAL DOCUMENT PREPARATION

Before considering the substantive areas of the law pertinent to the preparation of legal documents, an understanding of the general rules for keyboarding and formatting legal documents must be gained. No one particular style of legal document preparation is better than another, but there are certain principles that must be considered in serving the goals of uniformity, neatness, and presentation of information. Although the form of the documents can vary due to local custom and usage, the concepts presented in this text may serve as a guideline for any situation. The model documents provided throughout this book are preferred formats. However, local rules and variations should be considered when creating official documents.

The foundation of all legal documents begins with the paper to be used and the typeface selection. Formatting the document with regard to the margins and spacing completes that foundation.

Selecting Manuscript Paper

Selecting the paper to be used in the preparation of any legal document involves knowing not only what is preferred but also what is prohibited. Historically, legal documents were presented on 8 1/2 x 14 inch paper known as **legal size,** with the liberal use of the thinner "onion skin" for the second and subsequent pages as well as copies. Today, the required choice of paper is quality 8 1/2 x 11 inch white bond.

All federal courts, and most state courts, now require the submission of pleadings on 8 1/2 x 11 inch paper and no longer allow dual sizes. Uniformity has become the standard and has been adopted by most state court rules. Paper with a red preprinted left margin, known as **legal cap,** has been specifically prohibited by many court rules that require the paper to be "plain."

legal size: Paper that measures 8 ½ x 14 inches; the paper on which legal documents have historically been presented.

legal cap: The preprinted left margin of paper that was once used for legal documents; paper with a legal cap is now prohibited by many court rules.

There is one exception to the rule on the size of paper used in generating legal documents. Many law firms continue to use 8 1/2 x 14 inch paper in drafting and executing a will. Nonetheless, it is now preferred that even wills be prepared on 8 1/2 x 11 inch paper, a requirement expressed by some local probate rules.

Selecting the Appropriate Typeface

Most offices use some form of word processing equipment that provides variable type in the form of a **font,** or typeface, selection. The font should match standard **pica** typeface, which is ten characters per inch or a 12-point font in most word processing software. (See Figure 1–2.) Care should be taken to avoid choosing a typeface that is too small, such as an **elite** format. The key is to maintain uniformity and neatness in the presentation of the information in the documents.

Setting Text Margins

The **margin** in a legal document refers to those areas of each page that are outside the body of the document. The rules regarding the four dimensions remain standardized for any instrument or pleading. The margins on word processing equipment may be set electronically by the inch, while on a typewriter they are set manually with ten spaces to the inch.

font: An assortment or set of type all of one size and style; a typeface.

pica: Twelve-point type; a typewriter type providing ten characters to the linear inch and six lines to the vertical inch.

elite: A typewriter providing twelve characters to the linear inch.

margin: A border; a boundary ("the margin of the page").

Helvetica

Arial

Bookman

Courier

New Century Schoolbook

Palatino

In the matter of   (8 point)

In the matter of   (10 point)

In the matter of   (12 point)

In the matter of   (14 point)

In the matter of   (18 point)

In the matter of   (24 point)

In the matter of   (36 point)

FIGURE 1–2 Different typefaces and point sizes used in word processing

The top margin, that portion of each page from the heading or text to the top of the paper, should be two inches for the first page and one and one-half inches for each subsequent page. (See Figure 1–3, Exhibit 1.)

The left margin for the first and subsequent pages should be one and one-half inches from the left side of the paper. (See Figure 1–3, Exhibit 2.) An exception occurs for those items such as headings and titles that are centered on the page. The beginning of each paragraph should be indented one inch, or ten spaces, from the left margin.

The right margin of any legal document will vary depending upon word usage and length. As a general rule, the right margin should be between three-quarters to one inch, with the exception of the end of a paragraph. (See Figure 1–3, Exhibit 3.) **Justification** of the right margin is available on some word processing equipment and software and consists of a right margin aligned from the right side of the paper at a preset dimension. This preset selection should be one inch for all pages.

The bottom margin of each page of a legal document should be at least one inch from the bottom of the paper. This will vary depending upon document length, since many documents end short of a full page. Care must be taken to allow space for the insertion of page numbers, or **pagination,** and signatures.

Spacing Legal Documents

The general rule for the spacing of legal documents is that all pleadings and instruments should be double-spaced. There are several exceptions to that rule. Triple spacing should be used between the *caption* and the designation of the court. Triple spacing should also be used before the identification of the parties and before the *heading* or the title of the document preceding the body. Single spacing is used for quotes indented within the body of a document and for addresses and telephone numbers following the name of an individual or organization. (See Figure 1–3, Exhibit 4.)

§ 1.10 SECTIONS OF A LEGAL DOCUMENT

Each legal document may have one or more sections pertaining to the identification of the document, its purpose, and its completion with the required signatures.

Caption

The **caption** of a legal document is that portion of a pleading, that provides the necessary identification of the court and parties for the proper filing of that document. The court designation in the caption should be centered on the page and should always be capitalized. (See Figure 1–3, Exhibit 5.)

The caption must also include the names of the parties and the party designations, listing the plaintiff (petitioner) and defendant (respondent). The names of the parties and the party designations should extend from the left margin to the center of the page. The plaintiff is distinguished from the defendant by the

justification: The process or result of justifying lines of text so that the right margin is aligned from the right side of the paper at a preset dimension.

pagination: The numbers or marks used to indicate the sequence of pages.

caption: A heading or title; in legal practice, it generally refers to the heading of a court paper.

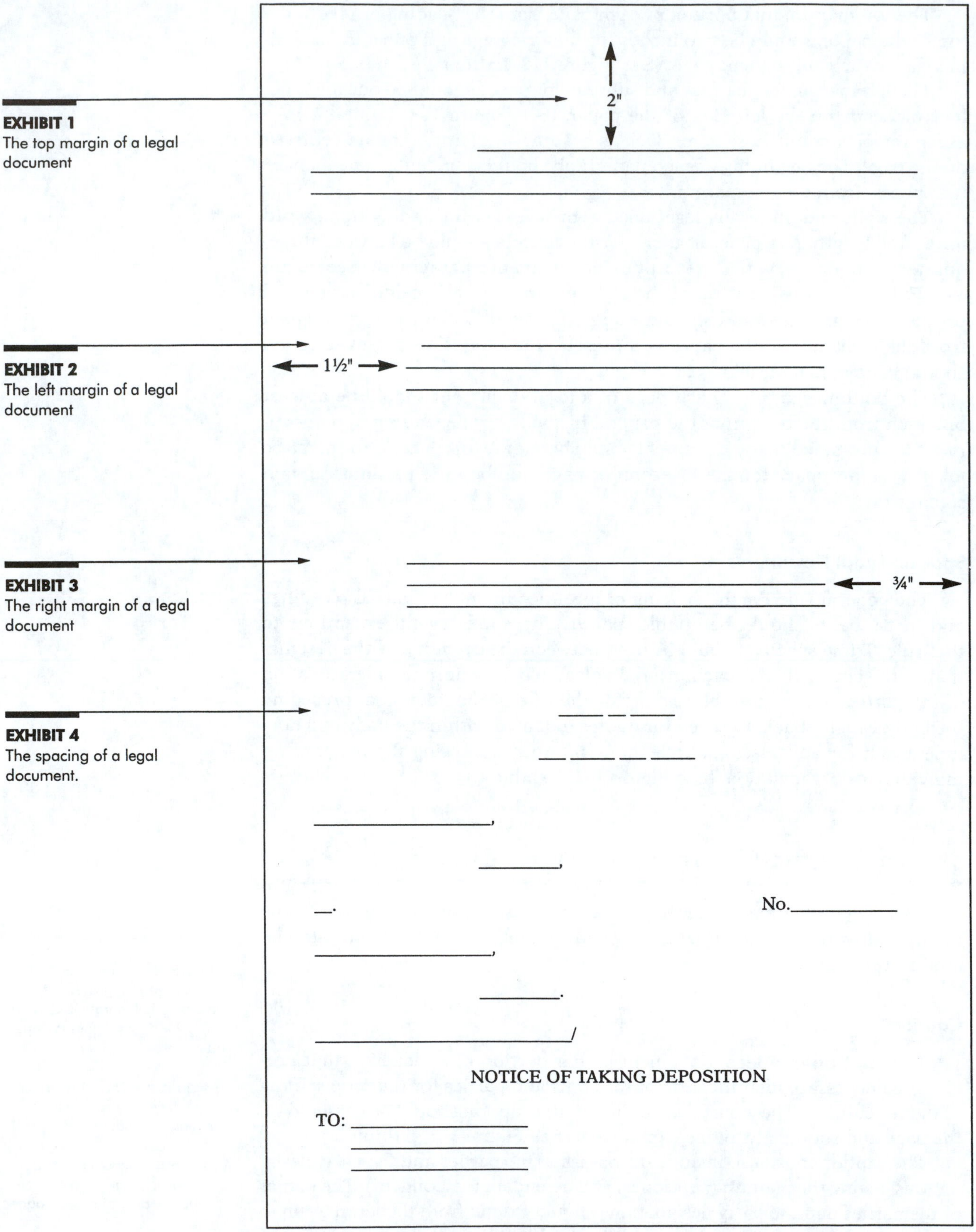

EXHIBIT 1
The top margin of a legal document

2"

EXHIBIT 2
The left margin of a legal document

1½"

EXHIBIT 3
The right margin of a legal document

¾"

EXHIBIT 4
The spacing of a legal document.

No._____

NOTICE OF TAKING DEPOSITION

TO: _____

FIGURE 1–3 Margins, spacing, and pagination of a legal document

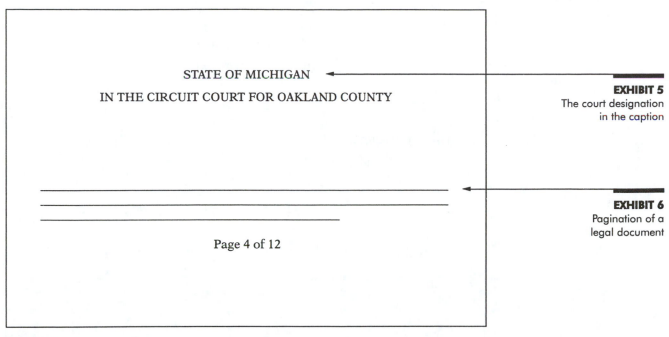

STATE OF MICHIGAN ←

IN THE CIRCUIT COURT FOR OAKLAND COUNTY

EXHIBIT 5
The court designation
in the caption

EXHIBIT 6
Pagination of a
legal document

Page 4 of 12

FIGURE 1–3 (continued)

use of the abbreviation for the word *versus: vs*. Names of the parties listed in the caption must be capitalized, while the party designations should be in lowercase letters. The case number issued by the court should appear to the right of the names and party designations, beginning at the center of the page with "No. _____." (See Figure 1–4.)

Heading

The **heading,** whether for a pleading or an instrument, is the title of the legal document indicating exactly what the document claims to be. Headings should be capitalized and centered two inches from the top of the first page and three spaces below the caption. (See Figure 1–5.)

Signatures

Since legal documents require a signature of either a client, party, or attorney, there must be space allotted for the accurate presentation of that individual's signature reflecting his or her name and capacity, or title.

All signature lines are placed at the end of the document beginning at the center of the page. A solid line should be provided for the actual signing, with the name of the signer in capital letters immediately below the line. If the individual is signing on behalf of a corporation or other organization, the name of that entity should be placed three spaces above the signature line and the individual's capacity should be reflected following the name. (See Figure 1–6.)

heading: The title of a legal document that indicates exactly what the document claims to be.

STATE OF MICHIGAN

IN THE CIRCUIT COURT FOR OAKLAND COUNTY

JOHN J. JONES,

       Plaintiff,

vs   No._____

SAMUEL S. SMITH,

       Defendant.

_____/

FIGURE 1–4 The names and party designations in a complete caption

LAST WILL AND TESTAMENT

OF

JOHN J. JONES

FIGURE 1–5 A sample heading

ABC CORPORATION

BY: _____

      JOHN J. JONES, President

FIGURE 1–6 The signature line of a party

Where a pleading or other document calls for the signature of an attorney, the signature line should reflect the name of the individual attorney immediately below the line along with the address, telephone number, and in some states, the local state bar number of that attorney. The name of the attorney's law firm, along with an identification of the party represented, should appear three spaces above the signature line. (See Figure 1–7.)

In preparation of a legal document, a situation frequently occurs where the text of the document ends at the bottom of a page, resulting in the final page consisting of only the signatures. To prevent speculation that the document has been altered, it is essential that some portion of the text of the document be continued onto the final page containing the signatures. This can be accomplished by an extension of the bottom margin or an alteration of the right margin from three-fourths to one inch, thus extending the length of the document.

Acknowledgment

The **acknowledgment** on a legal document is the certification of an authorized official that the person signed the document as a free act and deed. (See Figure 1–8.) This acknowledgment can occur in many forms including an attestation clause, notarization, or verification. The statement appears at the end of the document following the signature certified. The acknowledgment is preceded by a heading at the left margin reflecting the county and state, termed the **jurat.**

Following the jurat is the specific language certifying the signature as required by local state law. The law governing notaries public varies slightly from state to state, requiring a review of individual state requirements. Generally, no signature can be notarized without the notary public having had the opportunity to witness the actual act of signing the document. When preparing a legal document requiring notarization, it is necessary to leave the date and identity of the notary public blank to be filled in at the time of acknowledgment. Many states also require the signer to produce some proof of identity if not known to the notary public. The nature of the identification should be made part of the acknowledgment.

§ 1.11 MECHANICS OF LEGAL DOCUMENT PREPARATION

The production of any legal document requires that certain mechanics be addressed. The goals of an accurate presentation of the material and uniformity require that these mechanical concerns be consistent with each document.

Capitalization

Uppercase letters, termed **solid caps,** in a legal document are used to give certain words and names emphasis. All proper names should be solid caps, including the names of individuals, corporations, and businesses. Within the caption of a document, the court designation must be in solid caps along with the names of the parties involved.

acknowledgment: The signing of a document, under oath, whereby the signer certifies that he or she is, in fact, the person who is named in the document as the signer; the certificate of the person who administered the oath. EXAMPLES: clerk of court; justice of the peace; notary.

jurat: The certification that an affidavit has been duly sworn by the affiant before a duly authorized person. EXAMPLES: notary public.

solid caps: Uppercase letters used in a legal document to give certain words and names emphasis.

JONES & JONES, P.A.
Attorneys for Plaintiff

BY: _____
JOHN J. JONES, Esq.
555 N. Main Street
Metropolis, FL 32888
407/222-3000
Florida Bar No. 12345

FIGURE 1–7 The signature line of an attorney

STATE OF FLORIDA

COUNTY OF ORANGE

I HEREBY CERTIFY that . . .

WITNESS my hand and official seal in the County and State aforesaid this _____ day of _____, 199__.

_____

My commission expires:

FIGURE 1–8 The acknowledgment section

All **titles,** that portion of an instrument or pleading designating its identity and purpose, must be in solid caps and centered as well. Underlining of titles is not necessary for emphasis but may be added for style.

Within the body of certain pleadings there are particular words of importance that traditionally receive emphasis and need to be in solid caps. Such words vary depending on local usage, so local rules must be reviewed to determine which words or phrases, such as "ORDERED AND ADJUDGED" or "SUBSCRIBED AND SWORN TO," should be capitalized.

Grammar and Spelling

The preparer of a legal document is responsible for not only the accuracy of the information presented but also ensuring that there are no spelling or grammatical errors. An error in a legal document not only detracts from its professionalism but also may expose the preparer to legal liability. For example, if there is an obvious correction of a typographical error in the body of a will, upon its admission to probate, that will may be subject to being contested as having been altered at some point in time after it was signed by the maker.

Where the preparer of a legal document fails to express the intent of the client in a clear and unambiguous manner, the client's interests may be adversely affected by any error or omission, resulting in a loss or some other harm. In such a circumstance, it is necessary that the client be reimbursed for his or her loss by the preparer's law firm or organization. Therefore, it is ultimately the responsibility of the individual preparing the legal document to avoid any errors of spelling or grammar.

Numbers

The general rule is that any numbers used in legal documents should be written in word form followed by the **numeric designation** in parentheses, for example, "thirty (30) days." The rule for proper form when referring to amounts of money is similar. A specific sum of money is written in words with the numerical equivalent in parentheses, for example, "Five Hundred Twenty-five Dollars ($525.00)." Keep in mind that the decimal point in amounts of money is referred to as *and*. Therefore, $525.50 is written thus: Five Hundred Twenty-five Dollars and Fifty Cents ($525.50).

Pagination

Pagination refers to the process of numbering pages within a legal document. The first page of any instrument or pleading is not numbered. All subsequent pages should be numbered in a **footer,** which is the insertion of a page number one-half inch from the bottom of the paper and centered.

The specific number of each sequentially numbered page is designated with its numeral, for example, "-2-." Some documents traditionally reflect the total number of pages contained in the document along with the individual

titles: Portions of a legal instrument or pleading designating its identity and purpose.

numeric designation: Numbers that express amounts that can also be expressed with words; used in legal documents along with word forms to further clarify text.

footer: A line containing page numbers that appears at the bottom of each page of a legal document.

page number. These instruments, typically wills or contracts, reflect the page number as follows: "Page 2 of 8." Such pagination is also centered one-half inch from the bottom of the paper. (See Figure 1–3, Exhibit 6.)

Preprinted Forms

Periodically, a preprinted form will need to be prepared by filling in certain blank spaces. This must be done on a typewriter as opposed to word processing equipment, which is not well suited to such forms. The principle consideration in preprinted forms is the legibility of the inserted information. The general rule is that the typed letters should not touch the line of the blank space with the exception of those letters that extend downward. The "g" and "y" may touch the line but not extend below.

To eliminate confusion and avoid an inference that some information was missed, all blank spaces should be filled with a hyphen or the letters **N/A** (not applicable), signifying that the space was considered and the information is not available or does not exist.

N/A: Not applicable; used in legal documents to signify that the space has been considered and the information that should go in that space is not available or does not exist.

SUMMARY

- The preparation of a legal instrument begins with an understanding of its nature, type, and function. Regardless of whether the instrument takes the form of a contract, deed, mortgage, article of incorporation, partnership agreement, will, or trust, the fundamental character of the legal instrument remains unchanged.

- To provide a high level of precision and thoroughness in the creation of a legal document, the checklist becomes an invaluable tool.

- The greater the detail obtained regarding a client's marital status, employment information, financial condition, and any other relevant matters, the greater the level of accuracy that can be provided in the preparation of the legal instrument.

- While no single checklist can pretend to meet the unique needs of a given client and his or her current situation, a general format will provide the basis for addition and expansion as needed.

- The foundation of the preparation of a legal document begins with the selection of the appropriate manuscript paper and typeface to ensure uniformity.

- The presentation of the body of the legal document begins with the setting of the margins for the text and then requires adherence to the rules for the proper spacing of that text.

- In addressing the specific sections of the legal document, care must be taken to provide the required information for the caption and the heading in a uniform manner.

- All legal documents conclude with a signature of at least one individual or party, and many legal documents require the acknowledgment of a notary public.

- The signature and acknowledgment sections must be provided in a uniform manner at the close of the legal document in order to give the document legal effect.

- The actual mechanics of the preparation of a legal document must include adherence to the rules regarding capitalization, numbers, and pagination.

- Final responsibility for the content and accuracy of the information contained in the legal document is with the preparer, thus requiring attention to the elimination of any errors of grammar or spelling.

IN REVIEW

1. What is the definition of a legal document?
2. What purpose is served by expressing the intentions of a client in writing?
3. What is the difference between instruments and pleadings?
4. What are the three basic characteristics that make up the nature of a legal instrument?
5. What are the best sources for legal documents?
6. What are the basic areas of a general checklist that the preparer of a legal instrument should consider?
7. What margin is set for the top of the first page of a legal document? Each subsequent page? What margins are to be set for the left, right, and bottom of each page?
8. What information is to be provided in the caption to a pleading?
9. Where are titles placed on a legal document?
10. How are numbers expressed in the body of the text of a legal document?

PUTTING IT ALL TOGETHER

Your office represents Mr. Thomas Wilson, President of Acme, Inc., in an action against Eastern Moving & Storage Co., of which Mr. Stuart Green is president, for damage to certain property of Acme sustained in a recent relocation.

Exercises

1. Show proper spacing, placement, and capitalization for the caption and heading of the Stipulation for Judgment to be prepared by your office and reflecting the following information:

   Court: Calhoun County Circuit Court for the State of Michigan
   Case No. 93-12345

2. In preparing the agreement reflecting the Stipulation for Judgment, you find that the text ends at the bottom of the page, leaving inadequate space for the signatures of the parties. What would be your solution and how would it appear?

Contracts

The law is not a "light" for you or any man to see by; the law is not an instrument of any kind. The law is a causeway upon which so long as he keeps to it a citizen may walk safely.

—

ROBERT BOLT, *A MAN FOR ALL SEASONS* (1967)

OBJECTIVES

After completing this chapter, you will be able to:

1. Define a contract

2. Identify the preliminary considerations in the preparation of a contract

3. Detail the provisions of a contract that make up its basic content

4. Identify the need for any of the optional provisions that a contract may contain

5. Summarize the formalities required for the execution of the contractual agreement

BALLENTINE'S REVIEW

contract—An agreement entered into, for adequate consideration, to do, or refrain from doing, a particular thing. In addition to adequate consideration, the transaction must involve an undertaking that is legal to perform, and there must be mutuality of agreement and obligation between at least two competent parties.

§ 2.1 NATURE OF A CONTRACT

Contracts play a vital role in our personal lives and occupy an integral role in the typical business relationship. Any agreement between two or more persons or companies involves some form of a contract. In drafting a contract that adequately represents the intentions of the parties and fully sets forth the agreement reached, it is essential that the objectives are clearly expressed in language that is easily understood. The focus of this chapter will be to present this expression of intention in its simplest form.

The extent of the subject matter forming the basis of a contract is virtually unlimited. Just as any person or legal entity may be a party to a contract, so may any legally enforceable matter be the subject of the parties' agreement. An agreement may call for the sale or manufacture of goods, for personal service such as an employment contract, or for the sale or lease of property. A contract may call for one party to actively perform an act, and it may also require that a party refrain from performing an act.

The law recognizes the existence of a contract that is created by the action of the parties but not reflected in a writing. Such an agreement inferred by law is called an **implied contract.** This chapter will focus on its counterpart in the law, the **express contract.** An express contract is an actual agreement between the parties stated in distinct terms, and it may be either written or oral.

§ 2.2 ELEMENTS OF A CONTRACT

Traditionally, an agreement that creates a legally enforceable obligation between the parties must satisfy certain basic requirements before it will be considered enforceable. For a contract to be legally enforceable, the following five elements must exist:

- The parties must have the *capacity* to enter into a contract.
- There must be an *offer* and an *acceptance* of that offer.
- *Consideration* must support the contract.
- The subject matter of the contract must be *legal* and not against public policy.
- Under certain circumstances, the contract must satisfy the *statute of frauds* with a written instrument.

No contract will be enforceable if a single element is not satisfied.

implied contract: A contract that the law infers from the circumstances, conduct, acts, or the relationship of the parties rather than from their spoken words.

express contract: A contract, whether written or oral, whose terms are stated by the parties.

§ 2.3 PRELIMINARY CONCERNS IN FORMATION OF A CONTRACT

Before the actual agreement is reduced to a writing, there are certain preliminary concerns without which the agreement may not fully represent the intention of the parties. Those considerations involve:

- An identification and participation of all essential parties to the contract
- A determination of the existence of any property interests that may be the subject matter of the agreement
- The applicability of all federal and state laws
- Those matters affecting the mutuality of the agreement
- Performance of any conditions precedent

Initially, identification and participation of all parties to the contract are essential. To ensure its enforceability, the contract must reflect the identity of parties by naming each party to be bound by the agreement. Fundamental contract law requires that no contract be enforced against an individual who is not identified in the document as a party and who did not affix his or her signature reflecting that he or she has agreed to be bound by the terms and conditions of the agreement.

While representation by legal counsel is not a prerequisite to the formation of an enforceable contract, if the agreement involves substantial rights and duties, it is advisable that the parties obtain advice and counsel of one skilled in such matters. The complexities of a contract, along with the adverse interests of the parties, dictate a need for professional representation.

A second preliminary concern in the formulation of a contract is to find the existence of any special property interests that may be the subject of the agreement. If the focus of the agreement pertains to any property, whether real or personal, a determination must be made initially about the interests of each party in that property at the time of execution of the agreement.

The third preliminary concern requires a review of applicable federal and state statutes pertaining to the subject matter of the contract. This must be done to ensure that the agreement will not fail for a lack of statutory compliance. If the agreement is going to affect the tax liability of one or more of the parties, that result should be taken into account as a preliminary step in identifying the intentions of the parties. Other statutory concerns that may arise include such concerns as the Federal Truth in Lending Act or the Consumer Protection Act in most states. In addition, state statutes governing the form and content of certain types of contracts, such as a contract for the sale and purchase of real estate, must be considered.

A fourth preliminary consideration concerns those matters that affect the validity or legality of the transaction because of the lack of a "meeting of the minds." The validity of the agreement can be materially affected by such matters as:

- Conflicts of interest of either party
- Mistake of fact, either mutual or unilateral
- Ignorance of any material fact by one or both parties
- Fraud in any material element of the agreement
- Duress in the formulation of the contract
- Undue influence of one party to the agreement over any other party

Such matters go to the heart of the question of the existence of any meeting of the minds of the parties. Questions concerning the existence of any of the above conditions should first be resolved or the agreement may fail for a lack of mutuality.

Finally, many contracts involve the performance of certain **conditions precedent** preliminary to the execution of an agreement. A condition precedent requires that a specified event occur to give rise to the existence of an obligation. If a party to a potential agreement is required to deliver certain property in escrow, provide an abstract or title, secure title insurance, obtain a license or permit, or provide a release of a special property interest, then that event must occur before the contract can take place.

For example, assume hypothetically that Leonard Loveless found himself in the throes of an unfortunate divorce. The terms of the divorce judgment provided that he was to pay his soon-to-be ex-wife a certain sum of cash, and to do so, he had to sell his most prized possession, the Bass Slayer 5000. Elrod Bream had offered to pay $8,500 for the boat, but title to the boat had been in the name of both Leonard and his wife, Luanne. Before Leonard could enter into the agreement to sell the boat to Elrod, he had to obtain title to the boat in his name from the court. Such a condition precedent exists if there is an event that makes the effect of an agreement conditional upon its occurrence.

It is important to remember that each state has its own set of statutes governing the form and content of certain types of contracts. Those statutes must be consulted before the drafting of any instrument to ensure its effectiveness.

§ 2.4 CONTENTS OF AN INSTRUMENT

The preparation of any contract centers around the dual purposes of (a) *communication of the intention of the parties* in (b) *clear and concise language.* The order of presentation of the suggested areas of concern is a matter of style and in no way reflects upon the degree of importance of any paragraph. Consider the following topics when drafting a contract, although they may not apply to all documents. Each topic must be tailored to the specific needs of the parties to the agreement.

Title

Each contract should have a title that in some concise manner reflects the nature of the subject matter of the agreement. If the contract is for the sale of goods, it may be titled "CONTRACT FOR SALE OF MACHINERY." A consultation agreement may be titled "CONSULTATION AGREEMENT." (See Figure 2–1, Exhibit 1.)

Parties

The initial paragraph of any contract should reflect the date of the agreement and fully identify the parties to the agreement. The parenthetical references suggest the terms to be used throughout the agreement to identify the parties. If the status of the parties is relevant, such as marital status or corporate office, that status also may be reflected in the first paragraph, as shown in Figure 2–1, Exhibit 2.

conditions precedent:
Conditions that must first occur for a contractual obligation (or a provision of a will, deed, or the like) to attach.

CONTRACT OF EMPLOYMENT

EXHIBIT 1
A sample title

THIS AGREEMENT ("Agreement") is made this __ day of _____, 199_, by and between _____, a Delaware corporation, having its principal office at _____ (the "Company") and _____, (the "Employee"), as follows:

EXHIBIT 2
A sample beginning paragraph

CONSIDERATION. The Company hereby agrees to employ the Employee, and the Employee, in consideration of such employment, hereby accepts employment upon the terms and conditions set forth herein.

EXHIBIT 3
A sample consideration clause

PROPERTY. The lathe to be conveyed pursuant to the terms and conditions herein set forth is a Smith & Williams, Type D, 1982 upright center bore, serial number KC6378239, located at the Seller's place of business.

EXHIBIT 4
A sample property description

TERMINATION OF AGREEMENT. This Agreement will terminate two (2) years from the date hereof, unless terminated sooner as provided herein. Either party may terminate this Agreement upon thirty (30) days written notice of termination to the other party, at which time the Agreement shall terminate immediately.

EXHIBIT 5
A sample duration of agreement clause

DEFINITIONS. It is the intention of the parties that for purposes of this Agreement, the meaning accorded terminology used herein shall be as follows:

EXHIBIT 6
A sample definitions clause

Bond: an interest-bearing security
Broker: person who acts as intermediary
Conversion: exchange of bond into stock

COMPENSATION. In consideration for such consultation services, the Company agrees to pay the Consultant an amount equal to two percent (2%) of the purchase price of said property, said amount to be paid at the time of the closing of the sale of said property.

EXHIBIT 7
A sample compensation clause

FIGURE 2–1 A sample contract of employment

ENTIRE AGREEMENT. This Agreement constitutes the entire Agreement of the parties and supersedes all prior agreements, understandings, and negotiation, whether written or oral, between the parties. This Agreement may not be changed orally but only by an agreement in writing signed by both parties and stated to be an amendment hereto.

NONPERFORMANCE. Should the Employee, for any reason, become physically or mentally incapacitated from the performance of his or her duties as set forth herein, this agreement shall be considered null and void and shall terminate immediately.

SECURITY. It is understood and agreed that this contract is not to be binding upon either party until it is endorsed by some person, firm, or corporation as security for the execution of the promises and conditions thereof, or until a satisfactory surety bond is furnished that the parties will carry out all the promises and conditions of the contract.

ASSIGNMENT. This agreement shall not inure to the benefit of the heirs, successors, and assigns of the respective parties hereto.

ACCOUNTING. The Company agrees to keep complete and accurate books or accounts and to furnish monthly statements of receipts, disbursements, and such additional information as may be requested.

REMEDIES. The parties recognize that a breach of any of the restrictive covenants herein set forth may cause irreparable harm and that actual damages may be difficult to ascertain and in any event may be inadequate. Accordingly, the parties agree that in the event of such breach, the parties may seek to enforce their remedies through binding arbitration or any court of competent jurisdiction.

ATTORNEY FEES AND LITIGATION COSTS. If any legal action or other proceeding is brought for the enforcement of this Agreement, the successful or prevailing party shall be entitled to recover reasonable attorney fees and other costs incurred in that action or proceeding, in addition to any other relief to which that party would be entitled.

LIQUIDATED DAMAGES. In the event that either party to this Agreement should breach this contract, the parties hereby agree that the breaching party shall pay to the other party the sum of _____ Dollars ($_____) as liquidated damages.

NOTICES. All notices herein shall be in writing and may be delivered personally or by mail, postage prepaid. Any notice sent by mail, postage prepaid, will be deemed received three days after it is mailed.

FIGURE 2–1 (continued)

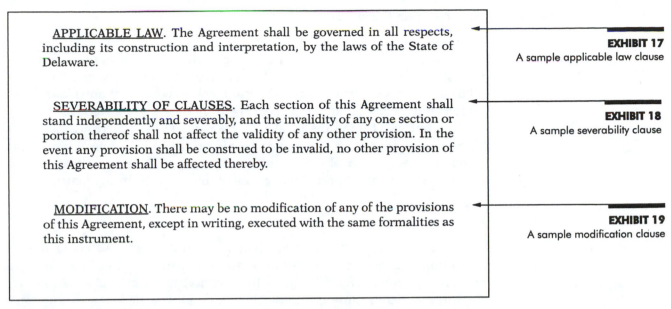

APPLICABLE LAW. The Agreement shall be governed in all respects, including its construction and interpretation, by the laws of the State of Delaware.

EXHIBIT 17
A sample applicable law clause

SEVERABILITY OF CLAUSES. Each section of this Agreement shall stand independently and severably, and the invalidity of any one section or portion thereof shall not affect the validity of any other provision. In the event any provision shall be construed to be invalid, no other provision of this Agreement shall be affected thereby.

EXHIBIT 18
A sample severability clause

MODIFICATION. There may be no modification of any of the provisions of this Agreement, except in writing, executed with the same formalities as this instrument.

EXHIBIT 19
A sample modification clause

FIGURE 2–1 (continued)

Consideration

A statement of the consideration that forms the basis of the contract should be included following the identification of the parties. The nature of the consideration will vary depending upon the subject matter of the agreement. The statement must be specific in its identification of the terms of the consideration, as illustrated in Figure 2–1, Exhibit 3. The agreement may then go on to a full description of the terms of the employment including salary, benefits, and responsibilities as agreed upon by the parties.

Description of Property

A detailed description of any property that is the subject matter of the agreement is another requisite paragraph necessary to accurately reflect the parties' intentions. If the subject matter of the contract is a particular piece of property, either real or personal, that property should be identified in as much detail as possible regarding its location and description (see Figure 2–1, Exhibit 4). If the property involved is real property, in addition to the postal address, a full legal description of the property should be included. The legal description of a parcel of land is the official description by governmental survey, metes and bounds, or a plat map.

Duration of Agreement

Since most contractual agreements are for a specified period, the agreement should reflect that fact under a paragraph titled "Term" or "Termination of Agreement," as shown in Figure 2–1, Exhibit 5. If the term of the contract is to be for an indefinite period that ends upon the occurrence of some event, then the exact nature of the event should be clearly identified.

Definitions and Terminology

The subject matter of a contract may involve technical terms that are familiar to the parties but not to the average individual. In order for the intention of the parties to be interpreted by anyone, the agreement should define all technical words, terms of art, or custom and usage so that any reader may understand the parties' intention (see Figure 2–1, Exhibit 6).

The purpose behind the inclusion of a detailed list of terminology is to eliminate the chance for either party to misconstrue any technical terms that are the subject matter of the agreement. It is also of benefit to both parties should litigation occur over some breach of the terms of the agreement.

Payment

Many contracts call for some form of payment of money, either in one lump sum at an agreed upon date or in periodic payments of set amounts over time. Any paragraph referring to such payments must accurately and fully set forth the understanding of the parties concerning such items as time and place of payment, amount, terms, method, interest, and security if contemplated (see Figure 2–1, Exhibit 7). The reference to the terms and conditions for payment of any monies is a particularly sensitive area of any contractual agreement and is the part of the agreement in which the accurate presentation of the parties' intention is most critical.

Entirety of Agreement

In most contractual settings, it is the intention of the parties that the written agreement fully represent the complete understanding between them. It is preferable to state in the agreement itself that it is the entire understanding, as shown in Figure 2–1, Exhibit 8. This avoids any later claim that there exists certain material terms that are the subject of another agreement, either oral or written.

The idea of having the written agreement encompass the entirety of the understanding between the parties means that the parties may refer to the agreement should any questions arise about their respective rights, duties, and obligations. No unresolved matters outside the written agreement should remain to be negotiated.

Excuses for Nonperformance

The parties to a contract may reasonably contemplate circumstances beyond either's control that would make performance of a particular condition or term impossible. Excuses for nonperformance may be such things as an act of God, a labor dispute, an illness, or death. If such an occurrence is a part of the negotiated understanding between the parties, the agreement should so state (see Figure 2–1, Exhibit 9).

The situation to be avoided would be an impossibility of compliance by one party through no fault of his or her own and an expectation of satisfaction by the other party. If the situation is addressed in the agreement, future misunderstanding can be avoided.

§ 2.5 OPTIONAL PROVISIONS

Each written contract is intended to contain the complete understanding between the parties as to the exact nature of their agreement. To adequately reflect that total agreement, there are a number of purely optional provisions that a well-drafted document should contain to eliminate any uncertainty as to the parties' intention.

Passage of Title

If the subject matter of the contract involves property, either real or personal, then title to that property will be conveyed at some point during the term of the contractual relationship. The written agreement should specify when that passage may occur and under what conditions.

Risk of Loss

Any contract with property as its subject matter should address the question of which party must bear the burden of risk of some form of loss to that property. As a rule, that risk is borne in the form of insurance by the party controlling the use of the property. If the risk has been the subject of negotiation, then the agreement should state which party pays for the insurance.

Warranties

In a contract for the sale of personal property or goods, the transaction usually involves a warranty. A **warranty** is a representation made by the seller about the quality, fitness, or title to goods, assuring the purchaser that certain facts are as represented. An **express warranty** arises if there is any affirmation of fact in writing by the seller. The Uniform Commercial Code governs transactions involving express warranties. If the agreement is silent concerning any express warranties made by the seller, there still may be an **implied warranty** created by the operation of law with respect to fitness for a particular purpose. The Uniform Commercial Code and other state and federal laws must be consulted for the applicable law concerning express and implied warranties.

warranty: With respect to a contract for sale of goods, a promise, either express or implied by law, with respect to the fitness or merchantability of the article that is the subject of the contract.

express warranty: A warranty created by the seller in a contract for sale of goods, in which the seller, orally or in writing, makes representations regarding the quality or condition of the goods.

Insurance and Bonds

Commercially available insurance covering the risk of any loss, as well as bonds governing the performance of a party, may be contemplated in the negotiation between the parties. The document should reflect the provisions concerning the levels of coverage, the risks contemplated, and the party that is expected to bear the burden of the cost (see Figure 2–1, Exhibit 10). It is incumbent upon one or both parties to secure the necessary surety before the existence of any enforceable obligation.

implied warranty: In the sale of personal property, a warranty by the seller, inferred by law (whether or not the seller intended to create the warranty), as to the quality or condition of the goods sold.

Transfer/Assignability of Rights

If there is to be some limitation on the transferability of the rights of a party, the contract should reflect the terms and conditions for assignability (see Figure 2–1, Exhibit 11). Frequently it is the intention of the parties to a contract that rights are not assignable to any third party. Such prohibited transfers might include selling the right to receive payments to another entity or passing the interests of one of the parties through his or her estate. If the contract does not address such contingencies, an interest may be transferred or assigned as permitted by law.

Subrogation

The parties to certain agreements may wish to reserve the right of **subrogation.** This occurs where one person, who has paid an obligation that should have been paid by another person, retains the right to be indemnified by the other. Technically, subrogation is the substitution of one person in the place of another concerning a certain right. **Indemnification** refers to reimbursement for some loss. Not all agreements lend themselves to either a reservation or release of any right of subrogation or indemnification, but if such has been the subject of the negotiation between the parties, the document should reflect the parties' intention.

Accounting

The need for an accounting of a party's compliance with the terms of a contract will occur with many types of contracts. The recording of information and the retention of records, if done on a formalized basis, should be addressed in the written instrument, as shown in Figure 2–1, Exhibit 12. The information may be as simple as the record of a few periodic payments or as complex as a full set of accounts for an elaborate commercial enterprise. The needs will vary depending on the nature of the contractual relationship. A well-drafted agreement will provide for the maintenance of records and will address the question of retaining an independent accounting service if necessary.

Confession of Judgment

The term **confession of judgment** refers to a practice at common law by which a debtor, by the terms of an agreement, allowed a judgment to be entered against him or her without the necessity of resorting to the courts. Such agreements are void in many states today. Local laws should be consulted to determine if such a provision in a written agreement will be considered enforceable. If so, and if contemplated by the parties, such a provision can result in the elimination of the expense and delay that occurs with litigation over a breach of the agreement.

Arbitration

An alternative process of dispute resolution by a neutral third party, known as an **arbitrator,** can be used to avoid the expense and delay ordinarily associated with litigation. Such a process is termed **arbitration,** and agreements to arbitrate are valid in all states provided there is consent of the

---

subrogation: The substitution of one person for another with respect to a claim or right against a third person; the principle that when a person has been required to pay a debt that should have been paid by another person, he or she becomes entitled to all of the remedies that the creditor originally possessed with respect to the debtor.

indemnification: Payment made by way of compensation for a loss.

confession of judgment: The entry of a judgment upon the admission and at the direction of the debtor, without the formality, time, or effort involved in bringing a lawsuit.

arbitrator: A person who conducts an arbitration; primary considerations in choosing the person are impartiality and familiarity with the type of matter in dispute.

arbitration: A method of settling disputes by submitting a disagreement to a person (an arbitrator) or a group of individuals (an arbitration panel) for decision instead of going to court.

parties. As long as the process is agreed upon by the parties, arbitration provides a convenient means of resolving any conflict within the confines of the agreement by an arbitrator skilled in such matters. The language of the contract expressing the arbitration agreement should state that the agreement is mutual and based upon a recognition of the possibility of failure of a party to perform (see Figure 2–1, Exhibit 13). The purpose of such a clause is not to prevent the parties to the contract from having their day in court but merely to avoid the expense and delay of ordinary litigation.

Costs and Attorney Fees

Should a dispute arise surrounding the contract or any of its provisions, legal expenses and related costs may be incurred. The agreement may anticipate such an occurrence by the inclusion of a paragraph that provides for the payment of such expenses by stipulation of the parties (see Figure 2–1, Exhibit 14). Most agreements provide that such costs are born by the party who defaults.

Liquidated Damages

The legal term **damages** applies to the recovery of money by a person who has sustained a loss through the acts or omissions of another. The sum that a party to a contract agrees to pay if he or she fails to perform as promised is called **liquidated damages** and is frequently the subject of consideration by the parties to an agreement. The contractual agreement should contain a clause that states the circumstances that constitute a breach and the cost of that breach in a specified dollar amount (see Figure 2–1, Exhibit 15). The purpose is to ensure performance by fixing the amount to be paid in lieu of performance.

Notice

The method and necessity of the conveyance of any information called for by the terms of the contract is called **notice.** Notice required by the contract may be oral or written and generally is required within a specified period to be effective. The notice clause should state the circumstances under which it applies and provide for the specific notice period (see Figure 2–1, Exhibit 16).

The time and circumstances under which notice must be given are a matter of agreement between the parties in most situations. Local state statutes should be consulted, however, to determine the effect statutory regulation may have on certain types of agreements.

Choice of Law

In contemplation of the potential for litigation over some term of the contract, it is advisable for the parties to identify the state laws that are to be applied to interpret the terms of the contract. The contract may establish the body of state law to be applied in the event of a dispute as long as there is some rational basis for the selection of a particular state. The selection of the state, while a matter of negotiation, must have some basis in fact. The choice

damages: The sum of money that may be recovered in the courts as financial reparation for an injury or wrong suffered as a result of breach of contract or a tortious act.

liquidated damages: A sum agreed upon by the parties at the time of entering into a contract as being payable by way of compensation for loss suffered in the event of a breach of contract; a sum similarly determined by a court in a lawsuit resulting from breach of contract.

notice: The method and necessity of the conveyance of any information called for by the terms of a contract.

is generally determined by the residence of one or both parties to secure the jurisdiction of a particular court (see Figure 2–1, Exhibit 17).

Severability

The separate clauses of an agreement should be independent of each other. This is called **severability,** meaning that the terms of a contract are divisible. The severability clause should be drafted to reflect that the breach of one clause does not affect the validity of another—it does not mean that the entire agreement is breached (see Figure 2–1, Exhibit 18). A severability clause in an agreement may serve to maintain, upon the breach of one portion of the agreement, the validity of the remainder of the agreement.

Modification

In the performance of a contract, circumstances beyond the contemplation of the parties at the time of the execution of the agreement may arise. A material change or **modification** in the terms of the agreement may be necessary. If the introduction of a new element or the elimination of some existing element will not clearly change the basic purpose of the agreement, then the procedure for modification of the agreement may be set forth. It is typical of most contracts that the parties agree that no modification may take place without the written consent of the other party (see Figure 2–1, Exhibit 19).

Breach of Contract

Any failure to act or perform in a manner called for by the contract without legal excuse constitutes a **breach of contract.** There is a significant body of law surrounding the question of the nature of a breach of contract. Applicable federal and state laws should be consulted as to the effect of any breach beyond that stipulated within the agreement itself in the form of liquidated damages.

severability: The divisibility of the terms or clauses in a contract, with the result that a breach of one promise is not a breach of the contract as a whole.

modification: A change, alteration, or amendment.

breach of contract: Failure, without legal excuse, to perform any promise that forms a whole or a part of a contract, including the doing of something inconsistent with its terms.

§ 2.6 FORMAL REQUIREMENTS OF INSTRUMENTS

The specific formalities of certain types of contractual agreements may be governed by either federal or state law. Several matters should be considered to formally execute the document regardless of any individual state regulation. Those considerations are:

- *Number of copies:* The original document should be maintained by one party with copies distributed to all remaining signatories.
- *Incorporation of documents:* Any documents incorporated by reference or attached to the agreement as exhibits should be attached to the original document and each copy.
- *Date of execution:* The date of the signing of the document should be reflected in the opening paragraph as well as on the signature page.

The date of execution may differ from the date the agreement is to take effect or be performed.

- *Signatures:* All parties to the contract must sign the document either personally or through a legal representative.
- *Attestation:* The witnessing of the signing of a written instrument, termed **attestation,** is frequently preferred by the signatories to an agreement.
- *Acknowledgment:* The authentication by a notary public should be attached to the document where required as a formality in the execution of such agreements.
- *Seal:* A **seal** is an impression made upon the original copy of an agreement to authenticate an act such as that performed by a corporation. Documents required to be sealed are prescribed by law in many states.
- *Filing or recordation:* Federal and state laws require that certain documents, such as a financing statement, be filed with a particular governmental agency. These requirements must be complied with before such agreements can be enforced.
- *Designation of custodian of records:* If the agreement requires the maintenance of any form of records, the procedure for such maintenance should be agreed upon prior to the document's signing.

It is the act of the formal execution of the contract that gives rise to its legal existence and the applicability and enforceability of its terms. As seen, the five basic elements of capacity, offer and acceptance, consideration, legality, and the statute of frauds are necessary for the existence of a legal and enforceable contract. It is the function of the preparer to further develop the actual understanding of the parties and reduce that understanding to writing.

attestation: The act of witnessing the signing of a document, including signing one's name as a witness to that fact.

seal: An imprint made upon an instrument by a device such as an engraved metallic plate, or upon wax affixed to the instrument; symbolizes authority or authenticity.

SUMMARY

- A contract is the written expression of the agreement between the parties. Its preparation and drafting must focus on the intention of the parties in a clear, concise, and simple manner. The basic elements of capacity, offer and acceptance, consideration, legality, and the statute of frauds must be met before an enforceable agreement exists.

- Once the contract satisfies the five basic elements, any other provisions are optional. It is the responsibility of the preparer of the contract to include any optional provisions that have been the subject of negotiation between the parties. Where those provisions have not been considered by the parties in their negotiations, it is advisable that the preparer recommend their inclusion. It is only through a full presentation of all the options available that a party may have his or her interests fully protected. Each provision of the contract must fully comply with federal and state laws where applicable. Therefore, it is the function of the preparer of the contract to not only provide for the basic elements of a contract but also consider any of the optional provisions as well as the applicable law.

IN REVIEW

1. What is a contract?
2. What are the various general types of contracts?
3. What are the five basic elements of a contract?
4. What information is necessary to identify the parties to a contract?
5. What are the preliminary concerns in the drafting of a contractual agreement?
6. What are the basic contents of a contract?
7. Why should the preparer of a contract consider certain optional provisions?
8. What are five optional provisions considered the most important to any contract?
9. What is a breach of contract?
10. What are the formal requirements of a contract?

PUTTING IT ALL TOGETHER

Wayne Wannabe, president and sole employee of Discount Legal Services, Inc., located at 100 N. Navel Ave., Osceola, __, has been contracted by I. M. King of the law firm of King & Queen, P.A., located at 100 S. Navel Ave., Osceola, __, with reference to the provision of paralegal services for an upcoming trial in the matter of the State of _____ v. Sprinkle. The firm believes that the trial will be lengthy and will require Discount Legal Services for research and document preparation as well as any other consultation services that may be necessary. Wayne is to be paid his usual consultation and service fee of $40.00 per hour and will bill the firm monthly.

Exercises

1. Prepare a detailed checklist of the necessary elements and provisions that should be contemplated by Wayne before his entry into an agreement with the firm.

2. Prepare a draft agreement on behalf of Wayne summarizing his contractual relationship with the firm.

CHAPTER

3

Real Estate Law and Its Documents

As a man is said to have a right to his property, he may be equally said to have a property in his rights.

———

JAMES MADISON (1792)

OBJECTIVES

After completing this chapter, you will be able to:

1. Outline the requirements of a contract for the sale of real property and prepare the document
2. Distinguish between the types of deeds and prepare the documents
3. Prepare a mortgage and promissory note
4. Prepare the documents relating to a real estate closing transaction
5. Prepare the necessary documents to reflect the leasehold relationship

BALLENTINE'S REVIEW

deed—A document by which real property, or an interest in real property, is conveyed from one person to another.

personal property—All property other than real property, including stocks, bonds, and mortgages. EXAMPLES: money; goods; evidence of debt. Personal property can be further categorized as tangible or intangible property.

real property—Land, including things located on it or attached to it directly (EXAMPLE: buildings) or indirectly (EXAMPLE: fixtures). In the technical sense, the interest a person has in land.

title—The rights of an owner with respect to real or personal property, *i.e.*, possession and the right of possession. A document that evidences the rights of an owner. EXAMPLES: deed; bill of sale.

§ 3.1 CONTRACTS FOR SALE

The modern real estate transaction involves the transfer of title to real property through a sale of that property. The transaction commences with the decision of the owner to place the property for sale and proceeds through the negotiation of a contract for the transfer of title for a stated price to be paid by a willing buyer. A contract for sale and purchase of real property is a separate and distinct document from a deed. The function of the contract for sale and purchase of real property is to commence a process that results in the subsequent execution and delivery of the deed. This section addresses the basic elements of a contract and analyzes the requirements for a contract for sale and purchase of real property. The form and nature of the deed are considered separately.

Essential Elements of the Contract

Although Chapter 2 examines the law of contracts in detail, for purposes of a discussion of the contract for sale and purchase of real property, some repetition is necessary. When the subject of the contract is the sale of real property, the contract becomes an agreement between the owner, or *seller*, and the purchaser, or *buyer*, to transfer title to a particular piece of land pursuant to the terms of the contract.

As seen in Chapter 2, the statute of frauds in virtually every state requires that where the subject of the contract is real property, the contract must be in writing. The essence of a contract is to express that "meeting of the minds" necessary to establish an agreement. For any contract to be valid and enforceable, it must satisfy four main elements:

- Capacity
- Offer and acceptance
- Consideration
- Legality

To illustrate a typical real estate transaction concerning the basic requirements of a contract, assume that Milton, age 50 and of sound mind, owns a piece of property that he has offered to sell to his cousin Norwood for $25,000. Norwood, age 38 and of sound mind, agrees to the purchase price and gives Milton $1,000 as a down payment. The contract is drafted for the purchase and sale of the property, following which Milton conveys title to Norwood and receives the balance of the purchase price. All of the basic elements of a contract—capacity, offer and acceptance, consideration, and legality—have been satisfied in this transaction resulting in a valid contract for sale.

Preparation of the Contract

The modern contract for sale and purchase of real property must address multiple issues and, consequently, may be detailed and lengthy. Many states have simplified the procedure and now require that a standard form be used for all transactions. Whether a standard form is used, as shown in Figure 3–1,

CONTRACT FOR SALE OF RESIDENTIAL PROPERTY

This agreement is made in the County of Jay, State of Fremont, on July 30, 1999, by RUFOUS S. TOWHEE, of 14 Nest Egg Lane, Osceola, Fremont, hereinafter referred to as seller, and FULVOUS GADWALL, of 919 Water Creek Rd., Osceola, Fremont, hereinafter referred to as purchaser.

In consideration of the covenants made each to the other, as herein set forth, the parties agree as follows:

SECTION ONE
PREMISES

Seller shall sell and convey and purchaser shall purchase, on the terms and conditions hereinafter set forth, the real property, together with improvements thereon, consisting of a dwelling house, and all appurtenances thereto, situated in the City of Osceola, County of Jay, State of Fremont, at 919 Water Creek Rd., more particularly described as Lot 22, Block Q, Audubon Preserve Estates, in the official records of the County of Jay, State of Fremont.

SECTION TWO
PURCHASE PRICE; TERMS OF PAYMENT

The full purchase price for the property is One Hundred and Twenty Thousand Dollars ($120,000), payable as follows: in cash or its equivalent at the time of closing.

SECTION THREE

DELIVERY OF DEED is assurance of its payment and satisfactory to seller, seller shall execute and deliver a deed describing the property and conveying the same to purchaser or his nominee.

SECTION FOUR
TITLE

(a) Seller shall furnish for purchaser's examination within thirty (30) days from this date a complete abstract of title or preliminary title report issued by Northern Gannet Title Company showing condition of the title of the property as of the date of issuance of the Abstract of Title. The Abstract of Title shall remain the property of seller pending completion of this transaction.

(b) Title to the property shall be good and marketable, free and clear of all encumbrances, liens, restrictions, easements, defects, and burdens, except unpaid taxes not delinquent and acceptable matters affecting title, if any.

(c) If any title restrictions, defects, or burdens appear on the Abstract of Title to which purchaser objects, such objection shall be stated in writing to seller who shall be allowed a reasonable time, but not to exceed thirty (30) days, in which to correct the same. If seller is unable or unwilling to do so, purchaser at his option may either terminate this contract and recover his deposit and costs, or pursue any other remedy available to purchaser in law or equity.

FIGURE 3–1 A model contract for sale of real property

**SECTION FIVE
CLOSING; TIME OF ESSENCE**

Unless extended by written agreement of the parties, this contract shall be completed and the transaction closed on or before September 1, 1999. Time is of the essence of this contract.

**SECTION SIX
TRANSFER OF PROPERTY**

Possession of the property shall be delivered within ten (10) days after closing. Purchaser has inspected the property, including the improvements thereon, and accepts the same in their present condition. Seller shall maintain the improvements, including the plumbing, heating, and electrical systems therein, in good working order to the time of transfer of possession, but all obligation of seller with respect to maintenance shall terminate at the date of transfer. Risk of loss by fire or other casualty prior to closing shall be seller's.

**SECTION EIGHT
BINDING EFFECT**

This contract shall inure to the benefit of and bind the heirs, personal representatives, and assigns of the respective parties.
Executed in duplicate on the day and year first above written.

_____
FULVOUS GADWALL, Purchaser

_____
RUFOUS S. TOWHEE, Seller

_____
Notary Public
My Commission Expires:

FIGURE 3–1 (continued)

or whether an original custom agreement is drafted, there are certain basic issues that must be addressed. The following checklist is designed to assist in the preparation of the contract by illustrating the primary considerations:

A. The parties
  • Name and address of seller(s) and purchaser(s)
  • Agent or broker
  • Corporate status
  • Marital status
  • Ownership interest of multiple sellers
  • Ownership interest of multiple buyers

B. Property description
   - Legal description
   - Encumbrances
   - Improvements
   - Personal property included

C   Purchase price
   - Amount
   - Down payment or earnest money
   - Balance due
   - Method of payment
   - Time and place of payment of balance

D. Acceptance
   - Time
   - Form

E. Closing
   - Date
   - Location
   - Parties required/power of attorney
   - Right to extend date
   - Proration of taxes, utilities, interest, rent
   - Possession
   - Documents required
     a. deed
     b. leases
     c. affidavits
     d. bonds
     e. escrow

F. Title
   - Evidence
   - Examination
   - Abstract
   - Defects and objections
   - Insurance policy
   - Method of conveyance

G. Warranties of the parties

H. Conditions of closing
   - Inspection
   - Financing
   - Condition precedent
   - Risk of loss/casualty insurance
   - Possession
   - Time of essence

I. Default
   - Specific performance
   - Liquidated damages
   - Alternative dispute resolution

J. Mortgage
   - Identity of mortgagor
   - Type of mortgage

- Broker
- Commission
- Claims
K. Miscellaneous provisions
    - Survival
    - Assignability
    - Existing tenancies
    - Notice
    - Severability
    - Entirety of agreement
    - Acknowledgment of notary public

The contract for sale and purchase of real property represents the entire agreement between the parties and forms the basis for the transaction. Care and prudence in every detail must be taken in its preparation.

§ 3.2 DEEDS

A deed is an important document in a modern real estate transaction because it is the formal written instrument through which title to real property is conveyed. Once that transfer has been completed, the deed becomes the manifestation of ownership of real property. Each deed is subject to the law of the state in which the property is located.

Types of Deeds

There are three types of deeds used to convey real property: (1) a general warranty deed, (2) a special warranty deed, and (3) a quitclaim deed. The three are distinguished by the degree of the **covenant**, or promise, of the grantor to the grantee that he or she may enjoy the property free of the claims of others.

A **general warranty deed** is one in which the *grantor*, or seller, guarantees the title against any defects. The traditional covenants warranted by the grantor to guarantee good, clear title are:

- The covenant of *seisin*, the right of possession
- The covenant of quiet enjoyment, the right to use the land without fear of some adverse claim
- The covenant of the right to convey ownership
- The covenant of the freedom from encumbrances
- The covenant of defense of title

Thus, the preparer of a general warranty deed would include language containing each of the general covenants, stating as follows:

AND grantor hereby covenants with said grantee that it is lawfully seized of said land in fee simple; that it has good right and lawful authority to sell and convey said land; that it hereby fully warrants the title to said land and will defend the same against the lawful claims of all persons whomsoever; and that said land is free of all encumbrances.

covenant: In a deed, a promise to do or not to do a particular thing, or an assurance that a particular fact or circumstance exists or does not exist.

general warranty deed: A deed in which the grantor, or seller, guarantees the title against any defects.

The language necessary to achieve a valid warranty deed may be set by statute in many states. With the provision of these warranties, the grantor has guaranteed that he or she is conveying a clear title to the property to the *grantee*, or buyer, and will undertake to compensate the grantee for any loss. It is the general warranty deed that is most commonly seen in the modern real estate transaction.

Similar to a general warranty deed is a **special warranty deed**. This type of deed is used where the grantor only covenants to defend the title against people making a claim or demand by, through, and under the grantor. For instance, if the grantor had given an easement against the property and had warranted against any encumbrances, he or she would be responsible for any claims by the recipient of that easement against the property.

A **quitclaim deed** is merely a covenant by the grantor to release any claim that he or she may have had in the property. The grantor makes no guarantees as to the title or any encumbrances on the property. The effect of the quitclaim deed is to transfer only that title which the grantor had in the property, however limited. Quitclaim deeds are commonly used to settle estate and divorce claims as opposed to the sale and purchase of real property.

In the modern real estate transaction, the purchaser is seeking to negotiate a price for the best deed possible, the general warranty deed. It is this form of deed that provides the greatest degree of guarantee from the grantor to the purchaser.

Preparation of the Deed

Statutory forms for deeds exist in many states as the instrument to convey title to real property, while in other states, the bar association, title companies, real estate companies, or law firms have prepared forms that comply with the state requirements for the preparation of a deed. Local statutes and forms should be consulted in the preparation of deeds. Most deed forms include (1) a caption, (2) a preamble, (3) language of conveyance, (4) a property description, (5) a warranty clause, and (6) proper execution.

Caption. The caption to the deed form is merely the entitlement portion indicating the type of deed that the document represents. The caption should appear at the top margin, in capital letters and centered, as in Figure 3–2, Exhibit 1.

Preamble. The preamble of the deed sets forth the date of the execution of the document and the identity of the grantor and grantee. (See Figure 3–2, Exhibit 2.)

The preamble may represent that not only are the parties to the instrument bound, but their successors, heirs, and assigns are also bound.

Language of Conveyance. The language of conveyance contained in the deed is that operative portion stating that it is the intention of the grantor to convey an interest in the property. This clause of the deed may also be the appropriate place to recite the consideration. (See Figure 3–2, Exhibit 3.)

The specific language may vary depending upon the extent of the interest conveyed by the grantor. If the deed is merely a quitclaim deed releasing only the grantor's interest, the language will indicate that.

special warranty deed: A deed in which the grantor only covenants to defend the title against people making a claim or demand by, through, and under the grantor.

quitclaim deed: A deed that conveys whatever interest the grantor has in a piece of real property, as distinguished from the more usual deed which conveys a fee and contains various covenants, particularly title covenants.

QUITCLAIM DEED

THIS QUITCLAIM DEED, executed this 31st day of June, 1999, by GRUMP E. PAPABEAR, first part, to LIL MISSY GOLDILOCKS, whose post office address is 2254 Garden Path Lane, Storytown, Fremont, second party:

WITNESSETH, that the said first party, for and in consideration of the sum of Ten Thousand Dollars ($10,000.00) in hand paid by the said second party, the receipt whereof is hereby acknowledged, does hereby remise, release, and quitclaim unto the said second party forever, all the right, title, interest, claim, and demand which the said first party has in and to the following described lot, piece or parcel of land, situate, lying and being in the County of Longago, State of Fremont, to-wit:

Lots 6 and 7, Block 105, Forest Estates, Fourth Addition, Longago County Public Records, Plat Book U, Page 94.

TO HAVE AND TO HOLD the same together with all and singular the appurtenances whereunto belonging or in anywise appertaining, and all the estate, right, title, interest, lien, equity, and claim, whatsoever of the said first party, either in law or equity, to the only proper use, benefit, and behalf of the said second party forever.

IN WITNESS WHEREOF, the said first party has signed and sealed these presents the day and year first above written.

Signed, sealed, and delivered
in the presence of:

_____   _____
Witness   GRUMP E. PAPABEAR

_____
Witness

STATE OF FREMONT

COUNTY OF LONGAGO

I HEREBY CERTIFY that on this day, before me, an officer duly authorized in the State aforesaid and in the County aforesaid to take acknowledgments, personally appeared GRUMP E. PAPABEAR to me known to be the person described in and who executed the foregoing Quitclaim Deed, and he acknowledged before me that he executed the same.

WITNESS my hand and official seal in the County and State last aforesaid this 31st day of June, 1999.

_____
I. Ema Notary
My Commission Expires:

(SEAL)

FIGURE 3–2 A model quitclaim deed

Property Description. The property description portion of the deed is part of the conveyance clause, providing an accurate and full legal description of the property. (See Figure 3–2, Exhibit 4.)

Warranty Clause. The *warranty clause* is that portion of the deed where the grantor obligates himself or herself to defend the title conveyed against any lawful claims. It is in this clause that the grantor makes a specific representation as to his or her title:

> *AND the grantor hereby covenants with said grantee that he is lawfully seized of said land in fee simple; that he has good right and lawful authority to sell and convey said land; that he hereby fully warrants the title to said land and will defend the same against the lawful claims of all persons whomsoever; and that said land is free of all encumbrances.*

The warranty language varies slightly with the special warranty deed and is not included in the quitclaim deed.

Execution. The execution portion of the deed is the language that exists immediately above the signature lines at the end of the deed. Depending upon the number of grantors and whether the grantor is a corporation, the language will vary. (See Figure 3–2, Exhibit 5.) With one grantor, it should read:

> *IN WITNESS WHEREOF the grantor has caused these presents to be executed in his name, and by his signature hereunto affixed, the day and year first above written.*

Individual states may have mandatory statutory language that should be consulted before the preparation of any deed. The following checklist will assist the preparer in securing information beyond that required by statute:

A. Parties
- Names
- Tax addresses
- Marital status
- Competency
- Age
- Corporate authority

B. Property
- Description
- Survey
- Extent of interest conveyed
- Encumbrances
- Appurtenances
- Restrictive covenants
- Mortgage recitation

C. Conveyance language
- Statutory requirements
- Covenants of title

D. Consideration

E. Dates
- Execution
- Conveyance

F. Spousal interest
- Dower or curtesy
- Homestead

G. Signature of grantor

H. Acknowledgment

I. Miscellaneous
- No erasures
- No blank spaces
- Name and address of preparer
- Delivery by grantor
- Receipt and acceptance by grantee

Every real estate transaction involves a contract for purchase and sale of real property and a deed. It is essential that the preparer of these documents consult state law on specific matters.

§ 3.3 PROMISSORY NOTES AND MORTGAGES

A real estate transaction may involve a large sum of money requiring that the purchaser obtain a loan to complete the sale. To obtain a loan for the purchase of real property, the purchaser must provide some guarantee to the lender that the monies will be repaid as agreed in the contractual agreement between them. Therefore, the modern real estate transaction involves a loan of money evidenced by a written document in the form of a contract, known as a promissory note, and the provision of security for the repayment of that money through a security document called a mortgage. Mortgage transactions are subject to federal and state consumer credit protection laws that should be consulted before any transaction.

Promissory Notes

A **promissory note** is a promise in writing to pay a specified sum at a specified time. In a real estate transaction, the note reflects the relationship of the parties to the loan. The lender is called the **mortgagor**, and the borrower is called the **mortgagee**. The note also provides for a specified interest rate along with a repayment schedule.

A promissory note should include the following:

- an identification of the parties
- the amount of the loan
- a repayment schedule
- default provisions
- security statement
- the signature of the borrower/mortgagor

promissory note: A written promise to pay a specific sum of money by a specified date or on demand.

mortgagor: A person who mortgages his or her property; the borrower.

mortgagee: The person to whom a mortgage is made; the lender.

Parties. After the caption of the note identifying the nature of the document (see Figure 3–3, Exhibit 1), the parties to the agreement are identified. Not only should the contract represent the names of the lender/mortgagee and the borrower/mortgagor, it should also reflect their corporate and marital status. (See Figure 3–3, Exhibit 2.) Further information may be included in this clause to identify the parties, such as their respective addresses and the corporate status of the signer.

Amount of Loan. The promissory note must state the exact amount of the loan that constitutes the mortgage amount. In addition, this portion should also reflect the interest rate on the note as well as whether it is an adjustable rate or fixed rate of interest. (See Figure 3–3, Exhibit 3.)

Repayment Schedule. Once the principal and interest of the obligation has been established, the note should provide details regarding the agreed upon schedule for repaying the loan. The precise terms of the repayment schedule will vary greatly, depending upon the size of the loan and the length of time over which payments are to be made. (See Figure 3–3, Exhibit 4.) It is significant to note that any prepayment will reduce the principal, and not be used as prepayment on the interest.

Default Provisions. The promissory note must address the question of the remedies of the lender upon a breach of the agreement by the borrower through nonpayment. If there is such a default, the balance of the loan becomes due immediately through an *acceleration clause* allowing the lender to proceed to judgment on the entire principal balance.

This clause containing default provisions may also provide for any late charges, costs, or attorney fees that may be incurred as a result of a default. (See Figure 3–3, Exhibit 5.)

Statement of Security. The promissory note is secured by a mortgage on the property that is the subject of the transaction. That fact must be reflected in the note to provide enforceability. The *security* is provided in the form of an assurance that the mortgagee will be furnished with a resource to be used in case of a failure of the mortgagor to pay the indebtedness on the note. The mortgage itself is enforceable only to the extent of the validity of the underlying obligation. (See Figure 3–3, Exhibit 6.)

Signature of Borrower/Mortgagor. The note must bear the signature of the borrower/mortgagor to be binding on him or her. It is a form of a contractual agreement and must be executed with the same formalities as any other contract. Most states do not require that the note be acknowledged by a notary public, but the provision of the notary's signature aids in its enforcement. (See Figure 3–3, Exhibit 7.)

Mortgages

A **mortgage** is a written instrument creating an interest in real property as security for the repayment of a debt. Under the English common law, mortgages were considered a type of conveyance of title. When the mortgage was paid in full, the title was returned to the mortgagor.

mortgage: A pledge of real property to secure a debt.

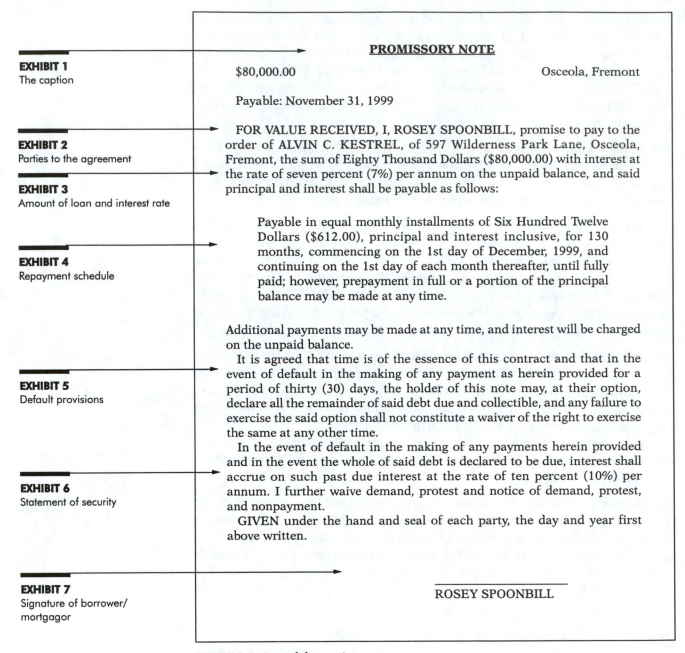

PROMISSORY NOTE

$80,000.00   Osceola, Fremont

Payable: November 31, 1999

FOR VALUE RECEIVED, I, ROSEY SPOONBILL, promise to pay to the order of ALVIN C. KESTREL, of 597 Wilderness Park Lane, Osceola, Fremont, the sum of Eighty Thousand Dollars ($80,000.00) with interest at the rate of seven percent (7%) per annum on the unpaid balance, and said principal and interest shall be payable as follows:

Payable in equal monthly installments of Six Hundred Twelve Dollars ($612.00), principal and interest inclusive, for 130 months, commencing on the 1st day of December, 1999, and continuing on the 1st day of each month thereafter, until fully paid; however, prepayment in full or a portion of the principal balance may be made at any time.

Additional payments may be made at any time, and interest will be charged on the unpaid balance.

It is agreed that time is of the essence of this contract and that in the event of default in the making of any payment as herein provided for a period of thirty (30) days, the holder of this note may, at their option, declare all the remainder of said debt due and collectible, and any failure to exercise the said option shall not constitute a waiver of the right to exercise the same at any other time.

In the event of default in the making of any payments herein provided and in the event the whole of said debt is declared to be due, interest shall accrue on such past due interest at the rate of ten percent (10%) per annum. I further waive demand, protest and notice of demand, protest, and nonpayment.

GIVEN under the hand and seal of each party, the day and year first above written.

ROSEY SPOONBILL

EXHIBIT 1
The caption

EXHIBIT 2
Parties to the agreement

EXHIBIT 3
Amount of loan and interest rate

EXHIBIT 4
Repayment schedule

EXHIBIT 5
Default provisions

EXHIBIT 6
Statement of security

EXHIBIT 7
Signature of borrower/mortgagor

FIGURE 3–3 A model promissory note

conventional mortgage: A mortgage granted by a conventional lender, that is, a bank or a savings and loan institution rather than the FHA or VA.

purchase money mortgage: A mortgage executed by a purchaser of real property to secure his or her obligation to pay the purchase price.

The type of mortgage most commonly used in modern real estate transactions is known as a **conventional mortgage**. It is a security device used by the mortgagor to transfer a lien or defeasible title to the mortgagee or lending institution in return for part of the purchase price of the property. Such a mortgage is referred to as a **purchase money mortgage** when the parties to the transaction are private parties, as opposed to a commercial lending institution being one of the parties. The conventional nature of the mortgage stems from the fact that the mortgagee looks only to the mortgagor and the property for security, and not to a third party such as the government for a guaranty of satisfaction. For instance, if Lena sought to buy a home with a loan from The

Great Backwater Savings and Loan for part of the purchase price, she would execute a promissory note and mortgage to the bank. Lena, as the mortgagor, would owe the principal and interest on the note payable in monthly installments to The Great Backwater Savings and Loan, the mortgagee. The mortgage document itself would give the mortgagee a secured interest in the property for satisfaction should Lena not repay the debt.

Some creativity in mortgage loans has occurred recently with recognition of the fact that a fluctuating economy causes significant changes in interest rates. Rather than offer a **fixed rate mortgage**, where the interest rate on the loan remains the same for the life of the mortgage, some lending institutions offer an **adjustable rate mortgage**, sometimes referred to as an ARM. Adjustable rate mortgages have a variable interest rate that is tied to an economic index resulting in the rate moving up or down on a periodic basis. There is usually a limitation, such as two percent, on the extent to which the rate may vary. These mortgages also contain a provision that allows for conversion to a fixed rate mortgage.

Many borrowers find it necessary to obtain a second loan secured by an interest in their property. Secondary financing with a new mortgagee/lender may be arranged whereby the lender refinances the property by assuming the first mortgage and lending additional money above the existing mortgage balance. This is called a **wraparound mortgage** and is used in situations where there is a low interest rate on older financing with a substantial difference between the amount owed on the original mortgage and the value of the property. The difference between the fair market value of property and the debt is called the owner's **equity.**

Frequently observed in today's mortgage market is the form of loan that is insured or guaranteed by the government. An **FHA mortgage** involves a loan that is insured by the Federal Housing Administration. A **VA mortgage** is one in which the loan is insured by the Veterans Administration. These guaranteed loans consist of a conventional loan situation that involves a third party, the government, as the insurer of the obligation. This encourages lending institutions to consider the extension of a loan to individuals who might fail to qualify for a pure conventional loan based on credit rating.

A mortgage loan requiring periodic payments for a specific length of time with the full principal balance due on maturity is termed a **balloon payment mortgage**. Such mortgages occur where the balance due is more than twice the amount of the regular installment payment. Most states have a balloon mortgage law that specifically sets forth the requirements with which the parties must comply. Failure of compliance usually results in an automatic extension of the maturity date until principal and interest are paid in full.

Preparation of the Mortgage

To create an interest in real property as security for a loan, certain requirements must be satisfied in order for the instrument to be valid. In general, the mortgage must meet the basic requirements of a deed, including the following: (1) the names of the mortgagor and the mortgagee, (2) language sufficient to create a lien or constitute a conveyance, (3) a valid legal description of the property, (4) proper execution, and (5) delivery to the mortgagee. Preprinted forms are available for most typical real estate transactions, and

fixed rate mortgage: A mortgage in which the rate of interest is absolute, that is, not adjusted from time to time.

adjustable rate mortgage: A mortgage in which the rate of interest is not absolute but is adjusted from time to time based upon conditions in the money market; often referred to as an ARM.

wraparound mortgage: Secondary financing with a new mortgagee/lender, whereby the lender refinances the property by assuming the first mortgage and lending additional money above the existing mortgage balance, that is used where there is a low interest rate on older financing with a substantial difference between the amount owed on the original mortgage and the value of the property.

equity: A system for ensuring justice in circumstances where the remedies customarily available under conventional law are inadequate; a system of jurisprudence less formal and more flexible than the common law, available in particular types of cases to better ensure a fair result.

FHA mortgage: A mortgage in which the loan is insured by the Federal Housing Administration, which is an agency of the United States that supports the availability of housing and a sound mortgage market by insuring bank mortgages granted to borrowers who meet its standards.

VA mortgage: A mortgage in which the loan is insured by the Veterans Administration, which is the federal agency that administers federal statutes providing for the welfare of military veterans and their dependents.

balloon payment mortgage: A mortgage whose final payment is considerably higher than any of the previous regular payments, the final payment representing much if not all of the entire principal.

lending institutions and law firms have their own forms that cover the basic provisions and that have been proven to meet the requirements of state law.

The following matters should be addressed in drafting the typical residential mortgage:

A. Identification of the parties
- Names
- Addresses
- Marital status
- Legal competence

B. Indebtedness secured by the mortgage
- Nature
- Loan charges
- Amount
- Interest
- Due date
- Prepayment and late charges

C. Legal description of the property
- Physical description
- Extent of interest mortgaged
- Appurtenances
- Personal property
- Encumbrances

D. Consideration

E. Warranty covenants as in warranty deed

F. Dates
- Date of execution
- Maturity date/right of extension
- Termination of lien

G. Release or discharge
- Final
- Partial

H. Mortgagee's rights
- Apply payments
- Acceleration
- Taxes
- Condemnation

I. Miscellaneous provisions
- Interest rate changes
- Insurance
- Taxes
- Reimbursement of mortgagee's expenses in protecting his interest
- Foreclosure
- Right of possession
- Preservation and maintenance of the property
- Right of inspection
- Condemnation
- Successors and assigns bound
- Notices

- Governing law
- Transfer of property
- Acceleration
- Riders
- Release of dower and curtesy
- Delivery and acceptance

See Figure 3–4 for a sample mortgage.

In the normal course of most real estate transactions, the formal mortgage document is preprinted with the outlined concerns set forth by section. The actual specific terms vary according to the individual transaction. The checklist is provided to help the reader appreciate the amount of information necessary to complete the transaction.

Satisfaction and Discharge

A mortgage is discharged once the debt has been paid. Although the interest in the property created by the mortgage has been discharged, the mortgage continues to appear as a matter of public record, preventing conveyance by the mortgagor. Therefore, it is necessary for the mortgagor to prepare and file a formal document called a **Satisfaction of Mortgage** or **Release of Mortgage**. If there has been a satisfaction of the debt secured by a part of the affected property, the mortgagor is entitled to have a **Partial Release of Mortgage** executed and filed.

The drafting of the Satisfaction of Mortgage document, as shown in Figure 3–5, requires that the following concerns be addressed in a brief manner and simply stated:

- Identification of the mortgagee
- Reference to the underlying indebtedness
- Mortgage
  a. Parties
  b. Date
  c. Recordation
- Legal description of the property
- Language reflecting the satisfaction and discharge
- Date of execution of the document
- Signature and acknowledgment

Local statutes frequently regulate the form and content of the satisfaction and discharge and should be consulted before preparation. Every state requires that the satisfaction be recorded to make it effective against subsequent purchasers, creditors, and encumbrancers.

§ 3.4 TITLE EXAMINATIONS AND INSURANCE

Inherent in any real estate transaction is the need for the seller to have good title to the interest that he or she is conveying in the property. Title consists of all the elements that make up ownership of real property. The

satisfaction of mortgage: The payment of a mortgage in full.

release of mortgage: A satisfaction, or payment in full, of a mortgage.

partial release of mortgage: A satisfaction, or payment, of a debt secured by part of an affected property.

MORTGAGE

This mortgage is made the 29th day of February, 1999, between VIR-GINIA RAIL, of 1122 North Tern Blvd., City of Osceola, County of Jay, State of Fremont, herein referred to as mortgagor, and BLACK VULTURE SAV-INGS AND LOAN COMPANY, of 1400 East Wren Avenue, City of Osceola, County of Jay, State of Fremont, herein referred to as mortgagee.

Mortgagor, by a note dated September 31, 1999, is indebted to mortgagee in the sum of Sixty-five Thousand Dollars ($65,000.00), with interest from date at the rate of nine percent (9%) per annum on the unpaid balance until paid, principal and interest to be paid at the office of mortgagee, or at such other place as the holder may designate in writing, delivered or mailed to mortgagor, in two hundred (200) monthly installments of Five Hundred Sixty Dollars ($560.00), beginning October 1, 1999, and continu-ing on the first day of each month thereafter until the indebtedness is fully paid; except that, if not paid sooner, the final payment thereof shall be due and payable on February 1, 1999. The terms of such note are incorporated herein by reference.

Mortgagor, in consideration of the above-stated obligation, hereby mort-gages to mortgagee all of the following described property in the County of Jay, State of Fremont, known as 1122 North Tern Blvd., described as Lot 84, Block B, Indigo Bunting Preserve, as recorded, together with the appur-tenances and all the estate and rights of the mortgagor in and to such premises.

Mortgagor covenants and agrees as follows:

I.
PAYMENT

Mortgagor shall pay the indebtedness as hereinbefore provided.

II.
WARRANTY

Mortgagor warrants that she is lawfully seized of an indefeasible estate in fee in the premises.

III.
INSURANCE

Mortgagor shall keep the buildings on the premises insured for loss by fire for mortgagee's benefit; mortgagor shall assign and deliver the policies to mortgagee; and mortgagor shall reimburse mortgagee for any insurance premiums paid by mortgagee on mortgagor's default in so insuring the buildings or in so assigning and delivering the policies.

IV.
TAXES AND ASSESSMENTS

Mortgagor shall pay all taxes and assessments. In default thereof, mort-gagee may pay such taxes and assessments and mortgagor shall reimburse mortgagee therefor.

FIGURE 3-4 A model mortgage

V.
REMOVAL

No building on the premises shall be removed or demolished without mortgagee's consent.

VI.
ACCELERATION

The full amount of the principal sum and interest shall become due at the option of mortgagee: After default in the payment of any installment of principal or of interest for thirty (30) days; or after default in the payment of any tax or assessment for thirty (30) days after notice and demand; or after default after notice and demand either in assigning and delivering the policies insuring the buildings against loss by fire or reimbursing mortgagee for premiums paid on such insurance, as provided above; or after failure to furnish a statement of the amount due on the mortgage and of any offsets and/or defenses existing against the mortgaged debt, after such has been requested as provided below.

VII.
RECEIVER

The holder of this mortgage, in any action to foreclose it, shall be entitled to the appointment of a receiver.

VIII.
AMOUNT DUE

Mortgagor shall furnish to mortgagee, within thirty (30) days when requested in person or by mail, a duly acknowledged written statement of the amount due on the mortgage and whether any offsets and/or defenses exist against the mortgaged debt.

IX.
SALE

In case of a foreclosure sale, the premises, or so much thereof as may be affected by this mortgage, may be sold in one parcel.

X.
ASSIGNMENT

Mortgagor hereby assigns to mortgagee the rents, issues, and profits of the premises, as further security for the payment of the obligations secured hereby, and grants to mortgagee the right to enter on the premises to collect the same, to let the premises or any part thereof, and to apply the monies received therefrom, after payment of all necessary charges and expenses, to the obligations secured by this mortgage, on default under any of the covenants, conditions, or agreements contained herein. In the event of any such default, mortgagor shall pay to mortgagee, or to any receiver appointed to collect the rents, issues, and profits of the premises, the fair and reasonable rental value for the use and occupation of the premises or of such part thereof as may be in mortgagor's possession; and on default in

FIGURE 3–4 (continued)

payment of such rental, mortgagor shall vacate and surrender possession of the premises, or that portion thereof occupied by mortgagor, to mortgagee or the receiver appointed to collect the same.

XI.
EXPENSES

If any action or proceeding is commenced, except an action to foreclose this mortgage or to collect the debt secured hereby, in which it is necessary to defend or assert the lien of this mortgage, whether or not the mortgagee is made or becomes a party to any such action or proceeding, all of mortgagee's expenses incurred in any such action or proceeding to prosecute or defend the rights and lien created by this montage, including reasonable counsel fees, shall be paid by mortgagor and, if not paid promptly on request, shall be added to the debts secured hereby and become a lien on the mortgaged premises, and shall be deemed to be fully secured by this mortgage and to be prior and paramount to any right, title, interest, or claim to or on the premises accruing or attaching subsequent to the lien of this mortgage, and shall bear interest at the rate provided for the obligations secured hereby. This covenant shall not govern or affect any action or proceeding to foreclose this mortgage or to recover or collect the debt secured hereby, which action or proceeding shall be governed by the provisions of the law respecting the recovery of costs, disbursements, and allowances in foreclosure actions.

XII.
CONDEMNATION

If the premises or any part thereof shall be condemned and taken under the power of eminent domain, or if any award for any change of grade of streets affecting the premises shall be made, all damages and awards for the property so taken or damaged shall be paid to the holder of this mortgage, up to the amount then unpaid on the indebtedness hereby secured, without regard to whether the balance remaining unpaid on the indebtedness may then be due and payable; and the amount so paid shall be credited against the indebtedness and, if it is insufficient to pay the entire amount thereof, it may, at the option of the holder of this mortgage, be applied to the last maturing installments. The balance of such damages and awards, if any, shall be paid to mortgagor. Mortgagee and subsequent holders of this mortgage are hereby given full power, right, and authority to receive and receipt for all such damages and awards.

XIII.
BANKRUPTCY

If mortgagor or any obligor on the note secured hereby (1) files a voluntary petition in bankruptcy under the Bankruptcy Act of the United States, (2) is adjudicated a bankrupt under that act, (3) is the subject of a petition filed in federal or state court for the appointment of a trustee or receiver in bankruptcy or insolvency, or (4) makes a general assignment for the benefit of creditors, then and on the occurrence of any of these conditions, at the option of mortgagee, the entire balance of the principal sum secured hereby, together with all accrued interest thereon, shall become immediately due and payable.

FIGURE 3–4 (continued)

XIV.
WASTE

Mortgagor shall not commit, suffer, or permit any waste, impairment, or deterioration of the premises or of any improvement thereon and shall maintain the premises and all improvements thereon in good condition and repair. If mortgagor fails or neglects to make any necessary repair or replacement in any improvement for thirty (30) days after notice to do so from mortgagee, mortgagee may effect such repair or replacement and the cost thereof shall be added to the debt secured hereby, shall bear interest at the rate provided in the note secured hereby, and shall be covered by this mortgage and the lien hereof.

XV.
COMPLIANCE

Mortgagor shall comply with all statutes, ordinances, and governmental requirements that affect the premises. If mortgagor neglects or refuses to so comply and such failure or refusal continues for three (3) months, then, at mortgagee's option, the entire balance of the principal sum secured hereby, together with all accrued interest, shall become immediately due and payable.

Wherever the sense of this mortgage so requires, the word "mortgagor" shall be construed as if it read "mortgagors" and the word "mortgagee" shall be construed as if it read "mortgagees." The word "holder" shall include any payee of the indebtedness hereby secured or any transferee thereof whether by operation of law or otherwise. Unless otherwise provided, any notice and demand or request specified in this mortgage may be made in writing and may be served in person or by mail.

In witness whereof, this mortgage has been duly executed by mortgagor the day and year first written above.

_____
VIRGINIA RAIL

(Acknowledgment)

This instrument was prepared by:

FIGURE 3–4 (continued)

purchaser must be assured that the seller owns the interest to be conveyed. That assurance is provided through a diligent search of the public real property records to review the recorded chain of title. Based upon the examination of title, the purchaser may then obtain a form of title guarantee through the issuance of an insurance policy. It is through this process of examination and insurance that the purchaser for value can take the property that will be secure from claims or interests of other parties.

SATISFACTION OF MORTGAGE

The undersigned, NORTHERN PARULA STATE BANK, of 5400 South Atlantic Drive, City of Osceola, County of Jay, State of Fremont, hereby certifies that the mortgage, dated June 31, 1999, executed by BELVA GREBE, as mortgagor, to mortgagee, and recorded in the office of the County of Jay, State of Fremont, in Book 54 of mortgage, Page 112, together with the debt secured by such mortgage, has been fully paid, satisfied, released, and discharged, and that the property secured thereby has been released from the lien of such mortgage.

IN WITNESS WHEREOF, the undersigned has executed this release at the City of Osceola, County of Jay, State of Fremont, on December 7, 1999.

NORTHERN PARULA STATE BANK

BY:_____

HOWARD JUNCO, President

[Acknowledgment]

FIGURE 3–5 A model satisfaction of mortgage

Title Examination

The English common law contained a principle that is still the basic real property law of most states. That principle is that one who has purchased property for value without notice of any defect of title takes the property free and clear of any adverse claims. Notice of any defect in title, which would preclude a clear title, is obtained through a title examination. A **title examination** is the process of searching the public records relating to real property to determine whether any defects in the seller's title may exist. If no defects are revealed in the public records, the purchaser takes good title, and he or she is said to be a **bona fide purchaser.**

Once the title examination has been completed, a summary of the recorded instruments that may affect or encumber the title is prepared. That historical summary of a particular parcel of land is called an **abstract of title**. To fully satisfy the purchaser's requirement of notice, the abstract must reflect a full summary of grants, conveyances, wills, judicial proceedings, releases, encumbrances, and any other matters of record that may affect title. An adequate abstract of title should include a summary of the following:

- Legal description of the property
- Grantors and grantees
- Contents of recorded matters of title
- Deeds
- Assignments

title examination: A search of all documents of record relating to the status or condition of the title to a given piece of real estate (including deeds reflecting past ownership and outstanding mortgages and other liens) in order to verify title.

bona fide purchaser: A person who purchases something in good faith for what it is worth, without knowing that anyone else has any legal interest in it.

abstract of title: A short account of the state of the title to real estate, reflecting all past ownership and any interests or rights, such as a mortgage or other liens, that any person might currently have with respect to the property.

- Releases
- Contracts for sale
- Mortgages
- Liens
- Easements
- Restrictive covenants
- Judicial proceedings
- Taxes
- Zoning ordinances
- Affidavits

It is through the information provided in the abstract of title that the purchaser is placed on notice of any defects in the seller's title. Only if no defects appear can the purchaser become a bona fide purchaser with good title.

To provide the measure of security essential to the modern real estate transaction, an attorney may review the abstract of title and render an opinion as to the legal effect of the matters of record. He or she would then issue what is called an **attorney's opinion letter** summarizing his or her examination of the abstract (see Figure 3–6). Through the process of the preparation of the abstract and the provision of the attorney's opinion letter, the purchaser is assured that he or she will be a bona fide purchaser and receive good title to the property.

Title Insurance

The most complete protection that a purchaser of real property can obtain comes through the purchase of an insurance policy. The policy, known as *title insurance*, serves to protect the purchaser from any loss resulting from defects in the title to real property. Title companies are in the business of providing experts to examine records, prepare abstracts, render opinions, and issue insurance policies that warrant the title as well as indemnifying the purchaser for any loss. It is the responsibility of the issuer of a policy of title insurance to make good any loss resulting from a defect or failure of title.

Each state has within its insurance code a set of regulations governing the issuance of title insurance policies and the companies permitted to issue them. The state in which the property is located decides the regulatory provisions that apply to any particular purchase.

§ 3.5 THE REAL ESTATE CLOSING

The modern real estate closing transaction is a complex matter that involves the assembly of a large body of information, the preparation of multiple documents, the actual execution of the necessary documents, and the recording of the documents as required. From a technical standpoint, a **closing** is the formal portion of the transaction where the consideration is paid, the mortgage is secured, title is exchanged, and the necessary recordings are made. The key element in a successful real estate closing transaction is preparation through information gathering.

attorney's opinion letter: A summary of an attorney's examination of an abstract of title, providing an opinion as to the legal effect of the matters of record.

closing: Completing a transaction, particularly a contract for the sale of real estate.

CROW & CURLEW, P.A.

Attorneys at Law
7200 North Meadowlark Lane
Osceola, Florida 32345
(813) 555-1234

January 16, 1999
Mrs. Magnolia Wren
32 Sora Rail Place
Osceola, Florida 32345

Re: 1000 Redstart Lane, Osceola, Florida

Dear Mrs. Wren:

I have examined title to the property located at the above address in Jay County, Florida, and described as:

Lot Z, Block 73 of BUZZARD TREE SUBDIVISION, as per plat thereof recorded in Plat Book 23, Page 75505, of the Public Records of Jay County, Florida.

From Abstracts of Title 9876 through 9888 of Osprey Title Company, covering the period of time from the earliest public records to and including June 31, 1999, we find the fee simple title to said property to be vested in Harmon Kiskadee.

County and city taxes for 1997 have been paid. The taxes for 1998, although not due and payable until December 1, 1998, became a lien on the property as of January 1, 1999.

Easement for public utilities over the rear of the property is reserved in the restrictions referred to in the Public Records of Jay County, Florida.

If this office can be of further service, please contact me.

Sincerely,

ARNOLD CURLEW, Esq.

FIGURE 3–6 A model title opinion letter

Documents

The closing involves many documents to provide for all contingencies. The title examination, survey, abstract of title, opinion letter, and title insurance policy must be obtained before the closing can be completed. All questions relating to the seller's ability to convey clear title must be resolved before the formal closing transaction.

Many states require a termite inspection before closing. In those states, the inspection must be obtained from a licensed pest control company, and a termite clearance letter must be provided at the closing. If there is evidence of termite damage on the structure, the problem should be resolved to prevent a delay in closing.

Since many real estate transactions involve property with some insurable interest other than the land, it is necessary for both parties to avoid any lapse in insurance coverage. The seller should arrange for the cancellation of his or her coverage on the same date that the purchaser's insurance commences.

The mortgage loan documents must be prepared and ready for execution at the time of the closing. A representative of the mortgage company will provide the promissory note and mortgage documentation for execution.

The seller and the purchaser will each provide their own **closing statement**. The statement consists of a detailed accounting of the transaction showing the purchase price, deductions, taxes, credits, and the net amount due the seller. No particular form is required for the statements, but most companies or law firms have their own prepared forms.

At the time of the closing, the purchaser must obtain the following items if applicable to the particular transaction:

- Deed
- Title insurance
- Owner's affidavit
- Estoppel notices
- Evidence of release of seller's mortgage
- Insurance
- Tax bills with proration
- Utility bills with proration
- Delivery of the premises

The items the seller must obtain at the time of the closing are as follows:

- Check (certified or cashier's)
- Final release of his or her mortgage and note
- Evidence of satisfaction of any broker's commission
- Tax and utility proration

Although often difficult to obtain, receipts should be secured for each document exchanged. A memorandum of the closing setting forth the documents involved will suffice if executed by the seller and the purchaser.

In 1974, Congress passed the Real Estate Settlement Procedures Act. As stated in the first section of the act:

The Congress finds that significant reforms in the real estate settlement process are needed to insure that consumers throughout the Nation are provided with greater and more timely information on the nature and costs of the settlement process and are protected from unnecessarily high settlement charges by certain abusive practices that have developed in some areas of the country. 12 U.S.C.A. § 2601.

The act required the Secretary of Housing and Urban Development to create a uniform closing settlement statement to be used in such transactions. Under no circumstance does the federal regulation of real estate transactions abridge the rights of the individual states from enacting their own regulatory legislation. State laws governing real estate transactions apply to each closing except to the extent that those regulations conflict with the federal act.

closing statement: A document prepared in connection with a real estate closing that details the financial aspects of the transaction.

Recording

It is the act of **recording** that renders the conveyance of the real property effective against any subsequent purchaser. Recording is the act of filing the deed and mortgage with the local county governing body, such as a Register of Deeds, by which an official copy of the document is deposited with an officer designated by law. When such an instrument is recorded in the appropriate public office, it serves to provide constructive notice to all subsequent purchasers and creditors of its contents.

Most states have statutes governing the recording of deeds and mortgages to provide notice to prospective purchasers, creditors, encumbrancers, or any other person who may be interested in the property. Those statutes establish the first deed to be recorded for a parcel of real property as the valid deed. The first to record has a superior right to the property over one who subsequently records. The statutes of each state must be individually reviewed to learn of the recording requirements.

§ 3.6 LEASES

The relationship between parties with respect to real property may be governed by contract. A contract can determine one party's legal right to possession of property and define his or her use of the premises, without disturbing the right of ownership. Such a contractual relationship is called a **lease.**

Within the agreement, the owner/landlord of the property is considered the *lessor*, while the tenant is considered the *lessee*. There is no requirement of any specific language to constitute a lease. The relationship can be created as long as the words are sufficient to express the intention of the parties. The primary purpose of a lease, whether for residential premises or commercial property, is to provide for the payment of rent in exchange for possession of the property for a period, with a return of possession to the lessor at the end of the period.

Specifically, a lease should address the following concerns: (1) identification of the parties, (2) identification of the premises, (3) duration of the lease, (4) amount of rent and manner of payment, (5) conditions and restrictions, and (6) execution.

recording: The act of making a record.

lease: A contract for the possession of real estate in consideration of payment of rent, ordinarily for a term of years or months, but sometimes at will. The person making the conveyance is the landlord or lessor; the person receiving the right of possession is the tenant or lessee.

Parties

The lease begins with an identification of the parties to the agreement, both lessor and lessee, and their marital or corporate status if it is relevant. If a corporation is involved, the officer signing on behalf of the company and his or her title should be identified. (See Figure 3–7, Exhibit 1.)

Premises

An identification of the premises under lease should follow with either an address or a legal description of the property if an entire parcel of land is the subject of the agreement. A mere address will suffice if the property is an

LEASE

THIS LEASE, made this 22nd day of January, A.D. 1999, by and between BERTRUM B. BARNES, herein called the lessor, and PETER J. SAMPSON and ELISA N. SAMPSON, his wife, herein called the lessees; regarding the following described property:

20868 Emmett Street, Foxglove, Freemont 32789

TO HAVE AND TO HOLD the same for the term of one (1) year from the 1st day of February, A.D. 1999, the said lessees paying therefor the annual rent of Six Thousand Dollars ($6,000.00).

And the said lessees covenant with the said lessor to pay the said rent in payments of Five Hundred Dollars ($500.00) each on the 1st day of each and every month for the said term, the first payment to be made on the 1st day of February, A.D. 1999; to make no unlawful, improper, or offensive use of the premises; not to assign this lease or to sublet any part of said premises without the written consent of the lessor; not use said premises for any other purpose than as a dwelling; and to quit and deliver up said premises at the end of said term in as good condition as they are now (ordinary wear and decay and damage by the elements only excepted). And the said lessees hereby covenant and agree that if default shall be made in the payment of the rent as aforesaid, or if the said lessees shall violate any of the covenants of this lease, then said lessees shall become tenants at sufferance.

Witness our hands and seals this 22nd day of January, A.D. 1999.

Signed, Sealed, and Delivered
in the Presence of:

_____
Witness

_____
BERTRUM B. BARNES, Lessor

_____
Witness

_____
PETER J. SAMPSON, Lessee

_____
Witness

_____
ELISA N. SAMPSON, Lessee

STATE OF FREEMONT
COUNTY OF LIME

I HEREBY CERTIFY that on this day, before me, an officer duly authorized in the state aforesaid and in the county aforesaid to take acknowledgments, personally appeared PETER J. SAMPSON, ELISA N. SAMPSON,

EXHIBIT 1
Parties to the agreement

EXHIBIT 2
Identification of the premises

EXHIBIT 3
Duration and rent

FIGURE 3–7 A model lease

and BERTRUM B. BARNES, to me known to be the persons described in and who executed the foregoing instrument, and they acknowledged before me that they executed the same.

WITNESS my hand and official seal in the county and state last aforesaid this 22nd day of January, A.D. 1999.

_____
Notary Public
My Commission Expires:

This instrument prepared by:

FIGURE 3–7 (continued)

apartment or office. If the property is a home or a particular piece of real property, a legal description should follow. (See Figure 3–7, Exhibit 2.)

Duration and Rent

Since a lease conveys only possession of land, and only for a limited defined period, the lease must establish its time frame and the amount of rent to be applied on a periodic basis. (See Figure 3–7, Exhibit 3.)

Conditions

Both residential and commercial leases contain numerous conditions that form an integral part of the agreement. The nature of the conditions will vary greatly, depending on the premises and its intended use. Some of the conditions that may need to be specifically addressed include the following:

- Security deposit
- Maintenance and repair
- Right of access by lessor
- Notice of any intent
- Insurance coverage
- Assignability and sublease
- Renewal and purchase options
- Default
- Cancellation

Execution

Following those clauses expressing the parties' agreement on the various specific conditions, the lease must be formally executed by the parties to make it enforceable. The signature of the lessor and lessee or their agents should appear, along with any witness requirements provided by state law, followed by the acknowledgment of a notary public.

Government Regulation

The Federal Consumer Leasing Act serves to regulate the disclosure level required for consumer leases, 15 United States Code Annotated section 1667 *et seq*. Many states also have enacted legislation regulating leases to protect the lessee. Those statutes must be consulted before any lease is drafted.

SUMMARY

- In any real estate transaction, there is a complex set of considerations that must be addressed before reaching the ultimate goal of the orderly transfer of ownership of real property. That goal is accomplished only after (a) the nature of the seller's interest has been identified; (b) the elements of the contract for sale have been satisfied; (c) the appropriate deed has been prepared; (d) the title work, mortgage, and promissory note have been completed; and (e) the closing documents have been prepared.

- The orderly transfer of title and possession, along with the recording of the documents, protects the purchaser's title against any existing claims. The achievement of the quiet enjoyment of one's title to real property is also dependent upon compliance with all federal and local state laws and regulations.

IN REVIEW

1. What are the basic considerations in preparing a contract for sale of real property?
2. What are the principal areas to be emphasized in the preparation of any deed?
3. What are the two documents most commonly prepared to finance the purchase of real property?
4. What are the primary concerns in the preparation of the closing statement?
5. How does a lease differ from a sale of real property?

PUTTING IT ALL TOGETHER

You are employed by Mr. Norman Conquest, Attorney at Law, representing Mr. Bill S. Pade and his wife, Willa. The Pades have recently retired and are seeking to purchase a house located in the Harmony Homes Retirement Village at 711 Bluehair Blvd. The legal description locates the property as follows: Lot 50, Block N, Prune Lake Estates. The home is being purchased from Mr. Sherwood Forest for the asking price of $72,000, for which the Pades wish to tender a deposit of $2,000. The Pades have already sought a mortgage from The Liens and Loans Savings Bank in the amount of $60,000. They have arranged for the title examination and insurance with Marshland Title Co., who in turn has arranged for the survey with Metes and Bounds, Inc. The pest inspection has also been secured from Spray & Spay Pest Control for $75.00. The closing has been scheduled for June 1, at which time the following amounts will be due:

Prorated county taxes - $390.00

Prorated utilities - $149.00

Prorated interest - $196.54

Loan origination fee to bank - $600.00

Hazard insurance premium - $64.00

Title insurance premium - $412.00

Surveyor - $125.00

Recording fees - deed, $5.00; mortgage, $10.00; state tax stamps, $422.00

The Pades have requested that your office prepare a Contract for Sale and Purchase and the necessary closing settlement statement. The mortgage and loan documents and the title documents have already been arranged.

Exercises

Using your knowledge of real estate documents, prepare:

1. Contract for Sale of the property in Harmony Homes Retirement Village from Forest to the Pades.

2. A Closing Statement reflecting the various charges and costs.

CHAPTER
4
Corporations

A corporation is an artificial being, invisible, intangible, and existing only in contemplation of law. Being the mere creature of law, it possesses only those properties which the charter of its creation confers upon it, either expressly, or as incidental to its very existence.

———

CHIEF JUSTICE JOHN MARSHALL, *TRUSTEES OF DARTMOUTH COLLEGE V. WOODWARD*, 17 U.S. (4 WHEAT.) 518, 636 (1819)

OBJECTIVES

After completing this chapter, you will be able to:

1. Identify the preliminary steps to be taken in the formation of a contract
2. Prepare a preincorporation agreement
3. Prepare a stock subscription agreement
4. Prepare the articles of incorporation
5. Prepare notices and waivers
6. Prepare the corporate bylaws
7. Prepare a stock certificate
8. Prepare a proxy
9. Prepare the corporate minutes
10. Prepare the corporate annual reports

BALLENTINE'S REVIEW

corporation—An artificial person, existing only in the eyes of the law, to whom a state or the federal government has granted a charter to become a legal entity, separate from its shareholders, with a name of its own, under which its shareholders can act and contract and sue and be sued.

partnership—An undertaking of two or more persons to carry on, as coowners, a business or other enterprise for profit; an agreement between or among two or more persons or entities to put their money, labor, and skill into commerce or business and to divide the profit in agreed-upon proportions.

sole proprietorship—Ownership by one person, as opposed to ownership by more than one person or by a corporation or partnership.

The legal document preparation necessary to form corporate business enterprises constitutes a major area of study. A corporation is a form of business ownership and requires the preparation of several critical documents. This chapter introduces the corporate form of ownership and provides a detailed look at its document requirements.

§ 4.1 FORMATION OF THE CORPORATION

The formation of a separate legal entity created under the state laws governing corporations is a relatively simple process prescribed by state law. There are certain preliminary concerns to be addressed between the attorney and the client seeking incorporation. Once those matters have been settled, the preparation of the documents to form the corporation can be accomplished on a step-by-step basis. It is advisable that a checklist be developed as a preliminary step in the preparation of the documents needed to accomplish the formation of a corporation. Figure 4–1 provides an example of a basic checklist to obtain the information necessary to incorporate.

Preincorporation Concerns

Before the instruments for incorporation are prepared, there are certain matters that must be addressed. These concerns are best submitted to an attorney or other individual skilled in such matters for consultation and advice.

Initially, the type of corporate structure must be selected. The determination of the type of corporate structure is based upon the form of stock ownership, the purpose of the corporation, and its financial basis. The documents used in the formation of the corporation are essentially the same for each type of corporate structure.

Second, the choice of the state of incorporation, called its **domicile,** must be selected. The state in which the corporation does its principal business is the logical choice. Yet, many businesses prefer to choose a state where the corporate laws and tax structure are more favorable. It is an individual decision that involves careful research and consultation.

Steps in the Formation of a Corporation

After the type of corporation and the state of domicile have been selected, there are procedural steps to be followed that are common to the laws of most states:

- preparation of a preincorporation agreement
- selection and reservation of the corporate name with the secretary of state
- preparation and filing of the articles of incorporation
- preparation of the stock subscription agreements and issuance of stock certificates
- preparation of the corporate bylaws
- first meeting of stockholders
- first meeting of board of directors

domicile: The relationship that the law creates between a person and a particular locality or country.

TICKLER/CHECKLIST FOR INCORPORATION OF

_____

1. Name:
   Call secretary of state re: name availability   _____
   Reserve corporate name   _____

2. Draft incorporation documents:
   Articles   _____
   Designation of registered agent   _____
   Bylaws   _____
   Minutes and waiver or consent   _____
   Subscriptions   _____
   Stock certificates   _____

3. Prepare miscellaneous forms:
   Application for federal employer identification number   _____
   Application for sales tax   _____
   Application for business license   _____

4. Prepare miscellaneous letters:
   Secretary of state/articles   _____
   City/business licenses   _____
   IRS filing subchapter S, election and power of attorney   _____

5. Prepare minute books   _____

6. Send articles to secretary of state   _____
   Rec'd _____

7. Send city/business licenses   _____
   Rec'd _____

8. Send application for federal employer identification number   _____
   Rec'd _____

9. Send application for sales tax   _____
   Rec'd _____

10. Order corporate seal/corporate kit   _____
    Rec'd _____

11. Schedule organizational meeting of board of directors   _____

12. Hold organizational meeting of board   _____

13. Prepare corporate bank account resolution   _____

14. Prepare the waiver of notice of the annual shareholders'
    and directors' meeting   _____

15. Prepare the annual shareholders' and directors' resolution   _____

FIGURE 4–1 A checklist for incorporation

The laws of each state vary slightly as to the formal requirements for each of these matters. The corporation laws of each state should be reviewed prior to formation.

§ 4.2 THE PREINCORPORATION AGREEMENT

When two or more persons associate themselves for the purpose of forming a corporation, it is advisable that an agreement be prepared containing the basic understanding between those individuals, called **promoters.** The resulting document is called the **preincorporation agreement.** The promoters are those individuals responsible for organizing the corporation, securing the necessary capital, and complying with the state's requirements. A corporation has no existence prior to its creation pursuant to the applicable state statutes, and therefore, there is nothing to bind it to a promotional agreement. The solution is provided by the preincorporation agreement that binds the individual promoters to each other to fulfill their obligation to form the corporation.

The preincorporation agreement should contain the mutual assent of the promoters on the following matters:

- the agreement to incorporate
- the name of the corporation and its place of business
- the purpose and powers of the new corporation
- the capitalization of the corporation
- the stock subscription
- the articles of incorporation
- the officers

The length and detail of the preincorporation agreement will vary, depending upon the number of promoters and the complexity of the venture. Thus, each agreement should be carefully considered and drafted to meet the individual needs of the promoters. Figure 4–2 provides a general form to be used in the preparation of the preincorporation agreement.

§ 4.3 THE CORPORATE NAME

The identity and individuality of a corporation is expressed in its corporate name. The process of name selection may be quite simple in the case of a plumbing supply company, or it may be quite complex if the business is to be a holding company for real estate investments. The name of the corporation will have a value of its own as the corporation prospers and, therefore, is of the utmost importance to most promoters.

Most states have some fundamental rules with regard to the selection of the corporate name that must be adhered to:

- The name must be distinguishable from any name that is in use or reserved by some other business enterprise.

promoters: Persons who organize a business venture or are major participants in organizing the venture.

preincorporation agreement: An agreement that contains the basic understanding between two or more persons who associate themselves for the purpose of forming a corporaiton.

AGREEMENT TO INCORPORATE

Agreement made this 30th day of February, 1999, between WILLIAM GATES, of City of Boulder, County of Citrus, State of Fremont, and HEWLITT PACKARD, of City of Boulder, County of Citrus, State of Fremont, hereinafter sometimes called the "incorporators."

In consideration of the mutual promises herein contained, the incorporators agree to form a corporation under the laws of the State of Fremont, and particularly the General Corporation Law of the state, for the purpose of undertaking and carrying on a business or businesses, as follows:

SECTION ONE
NAME OF CORPORATION

Subject to availability, the name of the corporation shall be CYBER-SPACE, INCORPORATED.

SECTION TWO
PURPOSE AND POWERS

The corporation shall be formed for the purpose of engaging in and maintaining a computer software business and such other lawful businesses as may from time to time be determined by the board of directors. The authorized corporate purposes shall include any lawful business purpose or purposes which a corporation organized under the General Corporation Law may be permitted to undertake.

SECTION THREE
PRINCIPAL OFFICE

The principal office for the transaction of the business of the corporation shall be located in the County of Citrus, State of Fremont.

SECTION FOUR
CAPITALIZATION

The authorized capital of the corporation shall be Ten Thousand Dollars ($10,000.00). The authorized capital stock of the corporation shall be all common stock with a par value of One Dollar ($1.00) per share.

SECTION FIVE
STOCK SUBSCRIPTION

Each of the incorporators subscribes as capital of the corporation the sum set out opposite his name below and agrees to accept in exchange for the amounts so specified the shares of stock following his name:

Name of Subscriber	Subscription	Stock
WILLIAM GATES	$5000.00	5000 shares
HEWLITT PACKARD	$5000.00	5000 shares

FIGURE 4–2 An incorporation agreement

SECTION SIX
INCORPORATION; PERMIT TO ISSUE SHARES;
PAYMENT OF SUBSCRIPTION

The incorporators shall cause the corporation to be formed under the provisions of section 1010 of the Fremont Business Corporation Act, formed within ninety (90) days from the date of this agreement, and thereupon with all reasonable diligence shall cause the corporation to apply for and secure a permit authorizing issuance of stock as hereinabove subscribed.

SECTION SEVEN
SIGNING ARTICLES; FIRST DIRECTORS

The parties to this agreement, or so many of them as may be necessary for the purpose, shall sign the articles of incorporation as incorporators. The persons named below shall be designated in the articles of incorporation as the first directors of the corporation and shall serve as such until their respective successors are duly elected and qualified:

Office	Name of officer
President	WILLIAM GATES
Vice president	HEWLITT PACKARD
Secretary-treasurer	I. B. HEMM

IN WITNESS WHEREOF the undersigned incorporators have executed this agreement at Boulder, Fremont, the day and year first above written.

_____
WILLIAM GATES

_____
HEWLITT PACKARD

FIGURE 4–2 (continued)

- The name must contain the words "company," "corporation," "incorporated," "corp.," "inc.," "co.," or a similar word or abbreviation to denote its corporate status.
- The name must not imply that the business is engaged in some illegal activity or enterprise or violates public policy.
- The name must not imply that the company has any relation to a federal or state agency.

Once the secretary of state has verified the availability of a corporate name, most states allow for the reservation of the name with the secretary of state pending the filing of the corporate documents. In some instances, the state provides a form for the reservation of the corporate name (see Figure 4–3).

The failure to ensure that the corporate name does not resemble that of any existing company may result in costly litigation. Conflicts may be avoided

---

APPLICATION FOR RESERVATION OF CORPORATE NAME

_____

Printed Name of Applicant

_____

Street or Post Office of Applicant

_____

City, State, Zip of Applicant

_____

Telephone Number of Applicant

Pursuant to the provisions of section _____, the undersigned hereby applies for reservation of the following name for a period of 120 days non-renewable. Filing fee for reservation: $35.00

_____

_____

_____

_____
                                    Signature of Applicant

Dated:_____, 19___

FIGURE 4–3 A sample application for reservation of corporate name

by consulting the local county government, the secretary of state, and the United States Patent and Trademark Office for potential similarity to another business name.

All states have a provision for the registration of the name of a foreign corporation. A **foreign corporation** is a corporation doing business in a state other than the state of incorporation. Most states have a set of laws allowing foreign corporations to do business within their borders as long as they have complied with the registration procedures.

§ 4.4 ARTICLES OF INCORPORATION

Corporate existence begins with the filing of articles of incorporation. The **articles of incorporation** is a legal instrument filed with the appropriate state agency, usually the secretary of state, that creates the corporate entity.

foreign corporation: A corporation incorporated under the laws of one state, doing business in another.

articles of incorporation: The charter or basic rules that create a corporation and by which it functions.

The document may be referred to also as the corporate "charter," "articles of association," "certificate of incorporation," or "articles of organization." The controlling state statutes dictate the contents of the instrument and usually include the following:

- the name and place of business of the corporation
- the duration of the corporation
- the purpose for which the corporation was formed
- the total number of shares of stock
- the identity of the incorporators
- the identity of the registered agent
- the date of incorporation

Some states require only a minimum of information, while others demand more detailed information. The Model Business Corporation Act, section 2.02, contains mandatory requirements for the articles of incorporation:

Articles of Incorporation

(a) *The articles of incorporation must set forth:*
  (1) *a corporate name for the corporation that satisfies the requirements of section 4.01;*
  (2) *the number of shares the corporation is authorized to issue;*
  (3) *the street address of the corporation's initial registered office and the name of its initial registered agent at that office; and*
  (4) *the name and address of each incorporator.*

(b) *The articles of incorporation may set forth:*
  (1) *the names and addresses of the individuals who are to serve as the initial directors:*
  (2) *provisions not inconsistent with law regarding:*
    (i) *the purpose or purposes for which the corporation is organized:*
    (ii) *managing the business and regulating the affairs of the corporation;*
    (iii) *defining, limiting, and regulating the powers of the corporation, its board of directors, and shareholders;*
    (iv) *a par value for authorized shares or classes of shares;*
    (v) *the imposition of personal liability on shareholders for the debts of the corporation to a specified extent and upon specified conditions;*
  (3) *any provisions that under this Act is required or permitted to be set forth in the by-laws; and*
  (4) *a provision eliminating or limiting the liability of a director to the corporation or its shareholders for money damages for any action taken, or any failure to take any action, as a director, except liability for (A) the amount of a financial benefit received by a director to which he is not entitled; (B) an intentional infliction of harm on the corporation or the shareholders; (C) a violation of section 8.33; or (D) an intentional violation of criminal law.*

(c) *The articles of incorporation need not set forth any of the corporate powers enumerated in this Act.*

The Title

The title of the articles of incorporation will vary, depending upon how the state laws refer to the document. The title should be centered between the margins and fully capitalized, as shown in Figure 4–4, Exhibit 1.

Name Clause

Following the guidelines set forth by statute for the corporate name, the first article of the instrument should identify the new entity (see Figure 4–4, Exhibit 2).

Purpose Clause

The purpose for which a corporation can be formed is governed by the laws of the state of incorporation. Most states have very broad guidelines to encourage the expansion of commercial enterprise. As long as the purpose is legal and does not violate public policy, it will be allowed. In setting forth the purpose, the preparer of this instrument should make the stated purpose as broad as possible to allow for the future expansion into areas of business perhaps not contemplated at the time of incorporation. (See Figure 4–4, Exhibit 3.)

Registered Agent Clause

Every state requires that a corporation maintain a corporate office with a registered agent within its boundaries. It is not necessary that the corporate office address be the principal place of business of the corporation. The **registered agent** is that individual appointed by the corporation and required by statute for the purpose of receiving service of process. It is the existence of the registered agent, and of the registered office of the corporation, that gives the corporate entity a physical existence. This article of incorporation should read as shown in Figure 4–4, Exhibit 4.

Duration Clause

The corporation act of every state allows its corporations to have perpetual existence, which means that if an owner/shareholder of the corporation dies or becomes disabled, the business will continue. That individual's stock will pass to his or her heirs without any interruption in the operation of the business. This is contrary to what would occur with another form of business ownership where a death would terminate the existence of the business enterprise. The provision in the articles of incorporation should simply read like that shown in Figure 4–4, Exhibit 5.

Board of Directors Clause

The initial board of directors named in the formal articles of incorporation does not necessarily reflect the permanent board to be later elected by the shareholders pursuant to the corporate bylaws. The initial board of directors may be for organizational purposes only and serve through the first meetings

registered agent: That individual appointed by a corporation and required by statute for the purpose of receiving service of process.

EXHIBIT 1
The title

EXHIBIT 2
A sample Article I identifying
the corporate name

EXHIBIT 3
A sample Article II establishing
the purpose of the corporation

EXHIBIT 4
A sample Article III appointing
the registered agent

EXHIBIT 5
A sample Article IV establishing
the duration of the corporation

EXHIBIT 6
A sample Article V indicating
the initial board of directors

EXHIBIT 7
A sample Article VI identifying
the incorporators

**ARTICLES OF INCORPORATION
OF
CYBERSPACE, INCORPORATED**

ARTICLE I.

Name. The name of this corporation is CYBERSPACE, INCORPORATED.

ARTICLE II.

Purposes. The purpose for which this corporation is formed is for any lawful purpose permitted by the laws of the State of Fremont and the United States.

ARTICLE III.

Registered Agent. The name and address of the initial registered agent of the corporation is: Truman T. Font, 567 N. Byte Avenue, City of Cascade, County of Tile, State of Fremont.

ARTICLE IV.

Duration. The period of this corporation's duration is perpetual.

ARTICLE V.

Directors. The number of directors constituting the initial board of directors is three (3), and the names and addresses of the persons who are to serve as directors until the first annual meeting of the shareholders are:

RUDOLPH BORLUND	111 N. Print St. Cascade, FT 56765
WILHELM GATES	222 S. Micro Rd. Cascade, FT 56765
ARNOLD OREM	333 W. Perfect St. Cascade, FT 56765

ARTICLE VI.

Incorporators. The names and addresses of the incorporators are:

RUDOLPH BORLUND	111 N. Print St. Cascade, FT 56765

FIGURE 4–4 A sample articles of incorporation

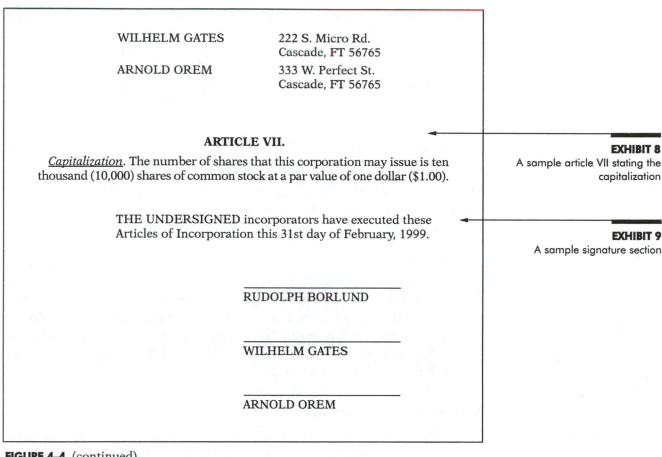

WILHELM GATES   222 S. Micro Rd.
Cascade, FT 56765

ARNOLD OREM   333 W. Perfect St.
Cascade, FT 56765

ARTICLE VII.

Capitalization. The number of shares that this corporation may issue is ten thousand (10,000) shares of common stock at a par value of one dollar ($1.00).

THE UNDERSIGNED incorporators have executed these Articles of Incorporation this 31st day of February, 1999.

_____
RUDOLPH BORLUND

_____
WILHELM GATES

_____
ARNOLD OREM

EXHIBIT 8
A sample article VII stating the capitalization

EXHIBIT 9
A sample signature section

FIGURE 4–4 (continued)

to initiate the enterprise. The preparer of the articles of incorporation should draft the clause to reflect the number of directors constituting the board, along with their names and addresses. In many cases, the initial board of directors, the promoters, and the incorporators will be the same individuals. The directors clause should so state (as shown in Figure 4–4, Exhibit 6).

Incorporators Clause

The individuals who sign the formal articles of incorporation are called the **incorporators.** In many states, the role of the incorporators is nothing more than the formality of signing the articles of incorporation. The real organization of the corporation is performed by the initial board of directors. The formal identification of the incorporators is accomplished with the incorporators clause in the body of the articles and the provision of their signatures for the execution of the instrument. (See Figure 4–4, Exhibit 7.)

Capitalization Clause

Most states require some information in the articles of incorporation regarding the shares of stock to be issued by the corporation. State laws vary

incorporators: Persons who form a corporation.

greatly as to the amount of information required. The term **capitalization** refers to the amount of the types of stock to be issued by the corporation. The stock may have an arbitrary value assigned to it, called the **par value,** which is nothing more than a stated value for accounting purposes on the corporate balance sheet. The clause may state the amount. (See Figure 4–4, Exhibit 8.)

Signatures

The incorporators listed in the articles of incorporation are the individuals whose names must appear as the signers to execute the instrument. The formal requirements vary from state to state, with some states requiring an acknowledgment by a notary public. (See Figure 4–4, Exhibit 9.)

§ 4.5 THE STOCK

Ownership of a corporation and its assets is represented by **stock.** For an individual to have an ownership interest in a corporate business enterprise, he or she must own a portion of the corporate stock, having acquired that ownership through purchase, gift, or devise.

Stock Subscription Agreement

In the formation of a future corporation, the incorporators or promoters may agree to purchase shares of stock in the new venture once it has been formally established. The agreement to purchase a set number of shares of stock of the new corporation at a stated price is called a **stock subscription agreement.** The agreement is a contract to be performed once the corporation has come into existence. Once the corporation is established, the shares of stock will be issued to the parties to the agreement, and those shares will be paid for by those individuals creating the corporate capital structure.

The stock subscription agreement should contain the following basic information:

- the name and address of the parties to the agreement
- the number and type of shares agreed to be purchased
- the price to be paid for the shares of stock
- the date for issuance of stock and payment of price

The corporate laws of many states contain a provision that the agreement to purchase stock pursuant to a stock subscription agreement is irrevocable for a set period of time, such as six months. Figure 4–5 provides an example of a stock subscription agreement.

Stock Certificate

The documentary evidence of an individual's ownership in a corporation is represented by the **certificate of stock.** It represents ownership similar to

capitalization: The total value of the stocks, bonds, and other securities issued by a corporation.

par value: The value of a share of stock or of a bond, according to its face; the named or nominal value of an instrument.

stock: Shares in a corporation or a joint-stock company owned by shareholders; the sum of all the rights and duties of the shareholders.

stock subscription agreement: The agreement of incorporators or promotors to purchase a set number of shares of stock in a new corporation at a stated price.

certificate of stock: An instrument issued by a corporation stating that the person named is the owner of a designated number of shares of its stock.

SUBSCRIPTION AGREEMENT

The undersigned incorporators of the corporation, CYBERSPACE, INC., pursuant to the Preincorporation Agreement signed by them, do severally subscribe for the number of shares of said corporation set opposite our signatures, and agree to purchase same from the corporation at Ten Dollars ($10.00) per share. The obligation of each of the undersigned shall not be dependent upon performance by any of the other signatories.

All subscriptions shall be payable at such time or times as the Board of Directors may determine and shall be paid in cash.

IN WITNESS WHEREOF the subscribers have executed this subscription at the City of Cascade, State of Fremont, this 31st day of November, 1999.

Name and signature of subscriber	Number of shares	Amount

FIGURE 4–5 A sample stock subscription agreement

a document of title, entitling the owner of the stock to all the rights and privileges guaranteed by law and set forth in the corporate bylaws.

The certificate is generally a preprinted form, which may vary from state to state, and contains the following information:

- the name of the corporation
- the name of the owner of the stock
- the number of shares represented and their type
- the certificate number

To be valid, the shares must be formally executed by a corporate officer designated as having such authority by the corporate bylaws, usually the secretary. An example of a typical certificate of stock is shown in Figure 4–6. The reverse side of most certificates of stock contains the language and space for the owner of the shares of stock to endorse a transfer of those shares by sale, gift, or devise.

The corporation must maintain records as to the identity of the shareholders of record, which is done through the maintenance of the **stock transfer ledger.** This record contains the identity of each owner of the shares of the corporation, the date of his or her purchase, and a record of the transfer of any of those shares. (See Figure 4–7.)

§ 4.6 THE ORGANIZATIONAL MEETING

In establishing the corporation, the **organizational meeting** is the final act of the incorporators to complete the process of the formation of the corporation. No one format for the organizational meeting will suffice due to the variance in state laws. In most cases, a single meeting is sufficient. The purpose of that meeting is to:

stock transfer ledger: A corporation's record of the identity of each owner of the shares of the corporation, the date of his or her purchase, and any transfer of those shares.

organizational meeting: The final act of the incorporators to complete the process of establishing a corporation.

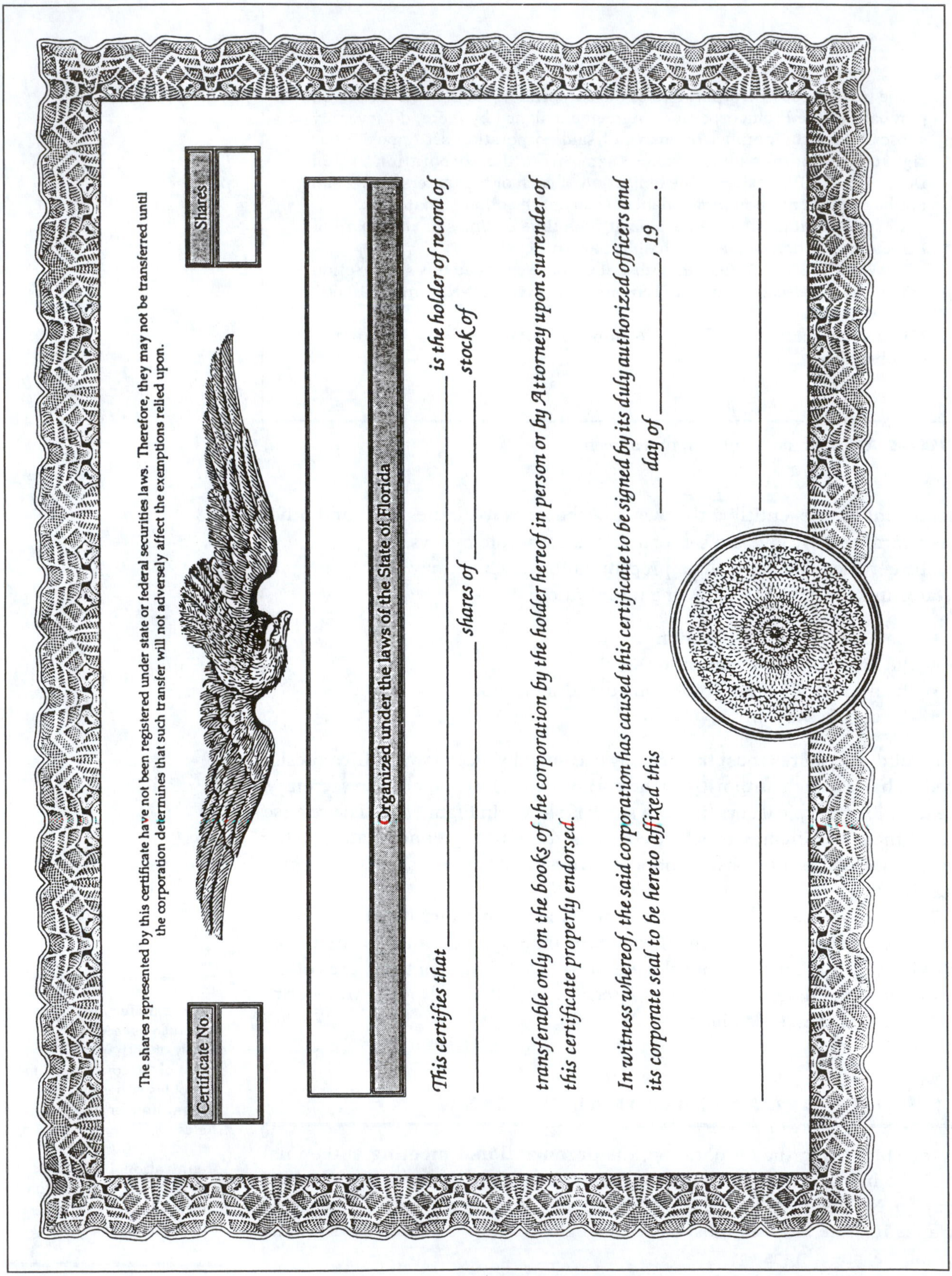

The shares represented by this certificate have not been registered under state or federal securities laws. Therefore, they may not be transferred until the corporation determines that such transfer will not adversely affect the exemptions relied upon.

Shares

Certificate No.

Organized under the laws of the State of Florida

This certifies that _____ is the holder of record of

_____ shares of _____ stock of

transferable only on the books of the corporation by the holder hereof in person or by Attorney upon surrender of this certificate properly endorsed.

In witness whereof, the said corporation has caused this certificate to be signed by its duly authorized officers and its corporate seal to be hereto affixed this _____ day of _____, 19____.

_____

_____

FIGURE 4-6 A typical certificate of stock

Name of Stockholder	Place of Residence	Time Be-came Owner	Certificate Issued		From Whom Shares Were Transferred (If original issue enter as such)	Amt Paid	Date of Transfer of Share	To Whom Shares are Transferred	Certificates Surrendered		No. of Shares Held (Bal.)	Value of Stock Transfer tax stamp affixed
			Cert Nos.	No. Shares					Cert Nos.	No. Shares		

FIGURE 4-7 A sample stock transfer ledger

- accept stock subscription agreements
- elect officers
- adopt the corporate bylaws

Since the meeting is generally held by the same individuals acting as promoters, incorporators, and directors, the meeting may be a mere formality that is satisfied through the unanimous written consent of the incorporators. That consent is recorded in the *minutes* of the corporation maintained by the corporate secretary. The form of the entry in the minutes may appear as shown in Figure 4–8.

Most corporate bylaws require that notice be given to shareholders and directors for both regularly scheduled meetings and any special meetings to be held. The requirement for notice may be waived by a written consent. Therefore, the minutes of the first meeting, should contain a notice of the first meeting to the incorporators along with their waiver of that notice (see Figure 4–9).

§ 4.7 CORPORATE BYLAWS

The corporation laws of most states require that the corporation adopt a set of rules that govern the internal operation of the business. The **bylaws** of a corporation are the rules and regulations that define the corporate structure and provide the rights and obligations of the officers, directors, and shareholders. The bylaws may be adopted by either the incorporators, the board of directors, or the shareholders upon formation of the corporation.

A well-drafted set of corporate bylaws should be specific in defining the basic rules of the business, addressing such areas as:

- the location of the corporate office
- the stockholder meetings
- the rights of stockholders
- the number, duties, and obligations of directors
- the removal of directors
- the meetings of directors
- the number, duties, and obligations of officers
- the capital stock and dividends
- the fiscal year of the corporation
- the corporate seal
- adoption and amendment of bylaws

The specific language of each provision of the bylaws will vary greatly, depending upon the nature of the business and the individual needs of the corporate owners and directors.

Most law firms have preprinted sets of corporate bylaws that have proven to be effective. The corporate laws of some states may dictate the content of the bylaws on matters such as shareholder meetings and should be consulted before preparation of the bylaws for a corporation. Also, there are a number of form books available with sample language appropriate for most corporate enterprises.

bylaws: Regulations adopted by a group or organization.

CONSENT TO ACTION TAKEN IN
LIEU OF ORGANIZATIONAL MEETING
OF
CYBERSPACE, INCORPORATED

The undersigned, being the incorporators of the corporation, consent to and ratify the action taken to organize the corporation as follows:

The Certificate of Incorporation filed on June 14, 1999, with the Secretary of State, State of Fremont, was approved and inserted in the minute book of the corporation.

A director of the corporation was elected by the shareholders to serve for a period of one year or until a successor is appointed or elected and shall qualify as follows: ARNOLD OREM.

Officers were appointed to serve for a period of one year or until their successors are appointed or elected and shall qualify as follows:

President	Arnold Orem
Vice president	Rudolph Borlund
Secretary-treasurer	Wilhelm Gates

Bylaws, prepared by Garth Packard, attorney for the corporation, regulating the conduct of business, affairs of the corporation, and duties of officers and directors were adopted and ordered inserted in the minute book.

The seal, an impression of which appears in the margin of this consent, was adopted as the corporate seal of the corporation.

(Seal)

The specimen stock certificate presented by counsel was adopted as the corporate stock certificate and ordered inserted in the minute book.

Directors were authorized, in their discretion, to issue the capital stock of the corporation to the full amount or number of shares authorized by the Certificate of Incorporation, in such amounts and for such consideration as set forth in any subscription agreements or from time to time determined by the board and as permitted by law.

The treasurer was authorized to open a bank account with FirstCascade City Bank, and a resolution for that purpose on the printed form of said bank was adopted and inserted in the record book.

All drafts, checks, and notes of the corporation, payable on said account, were directed to be made in the name of the corporation and signed by both the president and the treasurer.

The directors were authorized to elect to form this corporation as an "S" corporation under section 1362 of the Internal Revenue Code.

Dated: _____, 19__.

_____

_____

_____

FIGURE 4-8 A sample consent to action in lieu of an organizational meeting

---

NOTICE OF ORGANIZATIONAL MEETING
OF
CYBERSPACE, INC.

To: All Incorporators

The first meeting of incorporators of CYBERSPACE, INCORPORATED will be held at 1:00 p.m. on July 31, 1999, at the corporate offices located at 163 Concord Boulevard, Suite 201, Cascade, Fremont 98765. The purpose of the meeting shall be to elect officers and directors for the corporation, to establish banking procedures, to determine corporate status for income tax purposes, to approve the bylaws of the corporation, and any other business that may come before the members.

If you cannot be present at the meeting, please contact the law firm of Holden, Packard and Glenn, (623) 333-8400.

WAIVER OF NOTICE
OF ORGANIZATIONAL MEETING
OF
CYBERSPACE, INC.
INCORPORATORS

We, the undersigned, being all of the incorporators of CYBERSPACE, INCORPORATED, a corporation organized under the laws of Fremont, do severally waive all statutory requirements as to notice of the time, place, and purpose of the organizational meeting of incorporators and consent that the meeting shall be held at 1:00 p.m., July 31, 1999, at the corporate offices in Cascade, Fremont. We consent to the transaction of any and all business that may be properly addressed at the meeting.

Dated July 15, 1999.

_____

_____

_____

FIGURE 4–9 A sample notice and waiver

§ 4.8 CORPORATE MINUTE BOOK

The corporate record of the actions of the shareholders and directors of a corporation is kept in the **corporate minute book.** The book is generally maintained by the corporate attorney and contains:

corporate minute book: The corporate record of the actions of the shareholders and directors of a corporation.

- the articles of incorporation
- the corporate bylaws
- the minutes of the initial organizational meeting
- the minutes of the annual shareholder meetings

- the minutes of the annual board of director meetings
- the stock transfer ledger

A corporate minute book can be purchased from any reputable office supply facility and will contain samples of the documents along with individual state statutory guidelines and blank stock certificates. The corporate seal can be ordered with the minute book and used to authenticate corporate acts and resolutions.

§ 4.9 CORPORATE ANNUAL REPORT

Most states require each corporation doing business within its borders to file a report for stockholders every year to be furnished to the proper state agency. An **annual report** is a statutory report to be filed with the local secretary of state providing the basic information regarding the corporation and an identification of its officers. A typical report should include:

- the name of the corporation and its state of incorporation (if foreign)
- the date of incorporation
- the address of the corporate office
- the corporate federal identification number
- the name and address of the corporate registered agent
- optional information relating to capital structure and corporate indebtedness

The annual report is a matter of public record for every corporation doing business within a state and is open for public inspection.

annual report: A report issued yearly by a corporation, informing its stockholders, the government, and the public, in some detail, of its operations, particularly its fiscal operations, during the year.

SUMMARY

- The corporate form of business ownership is an association conforming with state statutory requirements establishing a distinct legal entity. That entity exists independent from its individual owners and survives their resignation or death. It can sue and be sued, enter into contracts, and must pay taxes in its own right. The formation of the corporate enterprise is relatively simple from a documentary standpoint requiring adherence to state law.

- The process of the formation of a corporation begins with a decision about the type of corporation to be established, a decision dictated by the size of the enterprise and its purpose. The preincorporation agreement and the stock subscription agreement among the incorporators serve to bind the promoters by contract to the completion of the formation process. The articles of incorporation filed with the state serve to charter the entity, providing it with a legal identity. The organizational meetings serve to organize the corporate government in order to commence operations following the adoption of the bylaws that provide the rules for conducting the business.

- The preparation of the documents necessary to accomplish the formation procedure varies from state to state. Individual statutory requirements must be complied with at each stage of corporate development. Forms and kits are available in most states for such purposes.

IN REVIEW

1. What is a corporation?
2. What are the five basic types of corporations?
3. What are the preliminary preincorporation concerns?
4. What are the seven basic steps in the corporate formation process?
5. What are the acceptable terms used in corporate names to designate the enterprise as a corporation?
6. What are the seven basic elements of articles of incorporation to be considered during preparation?
7. What are the elements of a stock subscription agreement?
8. What is a stock certificate?

PUTTING IT ALL TOGETHER

Your office has been contacted by three individuals to form a corporation in your state. The promoters are Lief Pyle, Arnold Prunes, and Stan Strait, Sr. They want to name their corporation Roaring Twenties, Ltd., and will be in the business of land development. In particular, they will be developing a senior citizen theme park, called the Victorian Village, to provide senior citizens with a unique return to a kinder, gentler time where the old values in entertainment can be appreciated without the commercialization of today. A shopping mall, condominiums, and single family homes are also contemplated.

The three promoters will serve as the incorporators and directors and will be the only three stockholders. They plan to contribute $100,000 each for their stock and wish to authorize 100,000 shares with a par value of $100.00. Pyle will be the designated registered agent.

Exercises

1. Prepare articles of incorporation to be filed with the appropriate state agency for the formation of Roaring Twenties, Ltd.

CHAPTER
5

Partnerships

There is a tide in the affairs of men which, taken at the flood, leads on to Fortune; Omitted, all the voyage of their life is bound in shallows and in Miseries. On such a full sea we are now afloat, and we must take the current When it serves, or lose our ventures.

WILLIAM SHAKESPEARE, *JULIUS CAESAR*

OBJECTIVES

After completing this chapter, you will be able to:

1. Outline the essential provisions of a general partnership agreement
2. Draft a general partnership agreement
3. Outline the essential provisions of a limited partnership agreement
4. Draft a limited partnership agreement
5. Draft a dissolution of partnership agreement

BALLENTINE'S REVIEW

dissolution—A breaking up; the separation of a thing into its component parts.

general partnership—An ordinary partnership, as distinguished from a limited partnership; synonymous with *partnership*.

limited partnership—A partnership in which the liability of one or more of the partners is limited to the amount of money they have invested in the partnership.

§ 5.1 THE NATURE OF A PARTNERSHIP

The foundation of the law of partnership arises from the common law, the law of contracts, and the Uniform Partnership Act. The National Conference of Commissioners on Uniform State Laws of the American Bar Association approved the act in 1914 and recommended its adoption by state legislatures. Most states have now ratified the Uniform Partnership Act in some form to apply to those situations where there is no written contractual agreement between the parties or where the written agreement fails to address some matter of concern.

§ 5.2 THE GENERAL PARTNERSHIP

The law of partnership contemplates two basic forms: the general partnership and the limited partnership. The essential nature of either type of partnership as a form of business ownership is the *contract* between the partners of the business that defines the relationship and determines its type. A partnership may exist without the benefit of a written agreement, but the majority of formal partnership enterprises are based upon the written contract. Thus, the nature of a general partnership can be described as consisting of:

- a mutual agreement in writing
- two or more competent persons
- a lawful business
- a sharing of the profits and losses

§ 5.3 THE GENERAL PARTNERSHIP AGREEMENT

A partnership relationship does not arise by operation of law but is the product of a negotiated agreement among the principals. A written partnership agreement is advisable due to the complex nature of the agreement and the wide variety of its provisions. While most states have enacted the Uniform Partnership Act establishing the rights and duties of the partners, that act serves only to enforce those rights where the agreement is silent or nonexistent. It is best to have the agreement specifically set forth the understanding between the partners.

A well-drafted general partnership agreement specifically sets forth the understanding of the partners on the following matters:

- title
- names and addresses of the partners
- name, purpose, and domicile of the partnership
- duration of the agreement
- contribution of the partners
- allocation of expenses
- ownership of partnership assets
- accounting procedures

- distribution of profits and losses
- liability of the partners to each other
- management, duties, and restrictions
- compensation of the partners
- effect of the death or resignation of a partner
- alternative form of dispute resolution
- termination of the partnership
- execution of the agreement

Title

The title of the general partnership agreement should serve to identify the nature of the agreement in establishing a partnership. As with any contract, the title should be centered on the page between the margins, fully capitalized, and underlined (as shown in Figure 5–1, Exhibit 1).

Names and Addresses of Partners

A complete identification of the parties to the agreement is necessary with any general partnership agreement. The first article of the agreement should contain the name and address of each of the general partners, as shown in Figure 5–1, Exhibit 2.

Name, Purpose, and Domicile of Partnership

The name of the partnership should be set forth fully along with the principal place of business. The name does not need to be made up of the names of all of the partners, or even some of them, but may be entirely fictitious. For instance, if Adams and Brown were to form a partnership for the purpose of industrial design, they could choose to call their business, ADAMS, BROWN & ASSOCIATES. As an alternative, they could elect a fictitious name for the enterprise, for example, INDUSTRIAL DESIGN CONSULTANTS. (See Figure 5–1, Exhibit 3.)

Duration of Agreement

The section of the partnership agreement setting forth the duration of the partnership is dependent on the purpose of the business enterprise and the intention of the partners. If the enterprise is for a limited period or until some result is accomplished, the agreement should reflect the duration contemplated. For instance, if a partnership were formed to design a specific piece of industrial machinery and was not intended to continue beyond completion of the design, the agreement would reflect the duration through the completion of the project. If a partnership is intended to continue as long as the partners do business together, the partnership is considered a **partnership at will.** Such a partnership continues to operate until dissolved according to the agreement or until the death or resignation of one of the partners (see Figure 5–1, Exhibit 4).

partnership at will: A partnership that is intended to continue as long as the partners do business together, i.e., until the partnership is dissolved according to the agreement or until the death or resignation of one of the partners.

KING, QUEEN & SQUIRE
PARTNERSHIP AGREEMENT

ARTICLE I

THIS AGREEMENT made this 30th day of November, 1999, between REX KING of 1044 Hastings, City of Orange, State of Fremont, COURTNEY QUEEN, 1215 Bayeaux St., City of Orange, State of Fremont, and MARSHALL SQUIRE, 1100 Norman Dr., City of Orange, State of Fremont, herein after referred to as Partners.

ARTICLE II

The Partnership shall be carried under the name of KING, QUEEN & SQUIRE, with its principal place of business at 10 Court St., City of Orange, State of Fremont. The partnership may engage in any and all activities as may be necessary, incidental, or convenient to carry out the business of providing paralegal services.

ARTICLE III

The Partnership shall commence upon the signing of this Agreement and continue until terminated as provided in the Agreement.

ARTICLE IV

The capital of the Partnership shall be contributed in cash by the Partners as follows:

REX KING	$10,000	11/31/99
COURTNEY QUEEN	$10,000	11/31/99
MARSHALL SQUIRE	$10,000	11/31/99

In the event the cash funds of the Partnership are insufficient to meet its operating expenses, the Partners shall make additional capital contributions in the same proportions in which they share in the net profits of the Partnership.

ARTICLE V

The expenses of the Partnership, including rent, repairs, alterations, taxes, insurance, wages, and others, are payable from the general account of the partnership to be maintained at CAMELOT NATIONAL BANK & TRUST COMPANY. If the funds of the general account shall be deficient, then the expenses shall be paid from the capital contributions of the Partners, and if those shall be deficient, then the Partners shall be liable on a pro rata basis in proportion to their original contributions.

ARTICLE VI

The assets of the Partnership, both real and personal, set forth as Schedule A attached hereto and made a part of this Agreement, shall be deemed to be Partnership property, and ownership of those assets shall be in the Partnership name. The assets of the Partnership may be altered through addition or deletion at the discretion of the Partners. Upon dissolution of the Partnership, any net assets after satisfaction of indebtedness will be distributed to the Partners on a pro rata basis in proportion to their original contributions.

FIGURE 5–1 A general partnership agreement

ARTICLE VII ◄

The Partnership books shall be maintained at the principal office of the Partnership, and each Partner at all times shall have access to those books. The books shall be kept on a fiscal year basis, commencing January 1st and ending December 31st, and shall be closed and balanced at the end of each fiscal year, with an audit as of the closing date. The general accounting shall be made with proper entries of all sales, purchases, receipts, payments, transactions, and property of the Partnership.

ARTICLE VIII ◄

The net profits and losses of the Partnership shall be divided by the Partners in proportion to their capital investment. The profits and losses of the Partnership shall be determined in the manner in which the Partnership reports the income and expenses for federal income tax purposes.

ARTICLE IX ◄

Each Partner shall be indemnified by the Partnership for all obligations incurred by that Partner in the normal course of the business of the Partnership. Each partner shall indemnify the Partnership on a pro rata basis in proportion to their original contribution.

ARTICLE X ◄

Each Partner shall have an equal voice in the management of the Partnership business. Each Partner shall devote his full time to the Partnership business with such exceptions as may be agreed upon by a majority vote of the Partners. No partner without the consent of the others shall:

a. borrow or lend money or make, deliver, or accept any commercial paper on behalf of the Partnership.
b. execute any mortgage, security agreement, bond, or lease, or purchase or contract to purchase, or sell or contract to sell, any property for or of the Partnership other than the type of property bought and sold in the regular course of its business.
c. assign, mortgage, grant a security interest in, transfer, or pledge any debt to the Partnership or release any such debt due, except on payment in full.
d. compromise any claim due to the Partnership or submit to arbitration of dispute or controversy involving the Partnership.

ARTICLE XI ◄

A separate income account shall be maintained for each Partner to which profits and losses shall be charged or credited. Each Partner shall be at liberty to draw out of his or her account in anticipation of expected profits any sums that may be mutually agreed upon. The draw for each Partner shall be deducted from the sum that Partner is entitled to under Article VIII of this Agreement. No Partner shall receive any salary for services rendered to the Partnership unless agreed upon by a majority of the Partners.

EXHIBIT 8
A sample Article VII setting forth the accounting procedures

EXHIBIT 9
A sample Article VIII setting forth the distribution of profits and losses

EXHIBIT 10
A sample Article IX setting forth the liability of the partners to each other

EXHIBIT 11
A sample Article X describing the management duties of the partners

EXHIBIT 12
A sample Article XI showing the compensation of the partners

FIGURE 5–1 (continued)

EXHIBIT 13
A sample Article XII describing the effect of the death or resignation of a partner

EXHIBIT 14
A sample Article XIII setting forth the arbitration clause

EXHIBIT 15
A sample Article XIV providing for termination

EXHIBIT 16
A sample execution of the general partnership agreement

> **ARTICLE XII**

Any Partner shall have the right to withdraw or retire from the Partnership at any time by written notice of intention to withdraw served upon the Partnership at its principal place of business. The remaining Partners shall have the right to either purchase that Partner's interest or terminate the Partnership business. In the event of the death of a Partner, the remaining Partners shall have the right to either purchase that Partner's interest or terminate the Partnership business. If the remaining Partners elect to purchase the interest of a withdrawing, retiring, or deceased Partner, that interest may be purchased at the full value to which that Partner shall be entitled at the time of distribution of Partnership assets after termination of the Partnership business pursuant to Article XIV. The Partnership business may continue at the option of the surviving Partners on notice given to all interested persons.

> **ARTICLE XIII**

Any dispute that may arise between the Partners regarding their rights, duties, responsibilities, and liabilities pursuant to this Agreement shall be submitted to an independent arbitrator from the American Arbitration Association, and the decision of that independent arbitrator shall be final as to the interpretation of this Agreement and its resolution.

> **ARTICLE XIV**

The Partnership may be dissolved at any time by agreement of the Partners, in which event the Partners shall proceed with reasonable promptness to liquidate the business of the Partnership. The Partnership name shall be sold with the other assets of the business. The assets of the Partnership business shall be used and distributed in the following order: (a) to pay all Partnership liabilities; (b) to equalize the income accounts of the Partners; (c) to discharge the balance of the capital accounts of the Partners.

IN WITNESS WHEREOF, the parties to this Agreement, referred to in it as Partners, have executed this Agreement at 10 Court St., City of Orange, State of Fremont, this 30th day of November, 1999.

Witnesses:

_____

_____   _____
                                              REX KING

_____

_____   _____
                                              COURTNEY QUEEN

_____

_____   _____
                                              MARSHALL SQUIRE

FIGURE 5–1 (continued)

Contribution of Partners

This section of the partnership agreement reflects the amount of money and property, either real or personal, that each of the partners originally contributed to the business. The agreement should reflect the dollar amount of any contribution of cash and the date of the contribution. If property was contributed, the agreement should reflect the date of the contribution along with the nature of the property and its value on the date of contribution. The agreement should also provide for additional contributions of capital in the future as necessary. Provision should be made to reflect the circumstances and recording of any such transaction. (See Figure 5–1, Exhibit 5.)

Allocation of Expenses

The agreement should provide for the payment of the normal operating expenses of the business from the general account of the partnership. A separate account may be kept for wages if desired for accounting purposes. The name of the banking institution may be included in this section along with the designated signers of checks. If there is to be an allocation of liability for expenses between the partners on the basis of their contributions, this section should reflect that allocation, as shown in Figure 5–1, Exhibit 6.

Ownership of Partnership Assets

The assets of the partnership, both real and personal, should be identified in the agreement, with the provision that those assets will be supplemented and replaced in the normal course of business expansion. The ownership of those assets should be in the partnership name as a tenancy in partnership, with each owner receiving his or her proportionate share of the value upon dissolution. (See Figure 5–1, Exhibit 7.)

Accounting Procedures

The agreement should set forth the understanding between the partners regarding the books and records of the business, the fiscal year, the accounting procedures, the right of inspection, and the location of the books of account. (See Figure 5–1, Exhibit 8.)

Distribution of Profits and Losses

A critical section of the general partnership agreement concerns the manner in which profits and losses of the enterprise are to be distributed. This section may schedule distribution and reserves for operations and reflect the percentage distributive share of each partner (see Figure 5–1, Exhibit 9).

Liability of Partners to Each Other

A well-drafted general partnership agreement should address the conditions of liability among the partners and the liability of the partnership to others. Included within this section should be the understanding as to the indemnification of one partner by the partnership for any obligation incurred by him or her in the ordinary course of business. (See Figure 5–1, Exhibit 10.)

Management, Duties, and Restrictions

The partnership agreement must specify the understanding of the partners regarding the management responsibilities, duties, and restrictions on control of each individual partner. The duties and powers of the partners are a matter of negotiation, and to a great extent, are determined by the nature of the enterprise. A partnership to develop a tract of land for an industrial park will not involve the same management duties as a dental clinic for the aged. Greater detail in the enumeration of duties will avoid misunderstanding as the enterprise grows. (See Figure 5–1, Exhibit 11.)

Compensation of Partners

The section devoted to the agreement of the partners as to their compensation should contain the partner's understanding of their salaries, draws, vacations, and other benefits. If the partners are to have a drawing account in anticipation of profit, this section should establish that account for purposes of periodic pro rata distribution based upon their original contributions (see Figure 5–1, Exhibit 12).

Death or Resignation of a Partner

The death or voluntary withdrawal of a partner creates the necessity of the purchase of his or her partnership interest by the remaining partners, along with some provision for the continuation of the business. Similarly, if the partners contemplate the addition of a new partner, the agreement needs to be modified accordingly. The agreement should set forth the understanding of the partners as to the conditions of purchase and the reorganization of the partnership. (See Figure 5–1, Exhibit 13.)

Resolution of Disputes

The general partnership agreement should provide for the means of the resolution of disputes between the partners. The best method of dispute resolution is arbitration. *Arbitration* is an alternative dispute resolution process involving an informal procedure without resorting to a court of law. The arbitration process will resolve a conflict without the wasting of the partnership assets through costly litigation (see Figure 5–1, Exhibit 14).

Termination of Partnership

Provision for the voluntary termination of the partnership should be set forth in the general partnership agreement. Any matter contemplated by the partners requiring termination, the procedures, and the distribution of assets may be established by the agreement. (See Figure 5–1, Exhibit 15.)

Execution of Agreement

The general partnership agreement must be signed and dated by all partners to be valid. The formal requirements for execution may vary slightly from state to state, but the basic requirements of contract law apply to the execution of the agreement. (See Figure 5–1, Exhibit 16.)

Miscellaneous Provisions

A well-drafted general partnership agreement must be reflective of the nature of the partnership business. The provisions necessary for a real estate investment group will vary from those essential to commercial architects. The elements outlined above are suggested for most situations and will meet most partnership needs. Some additional provisions to be considered are:

- notice
- modification or amendment of the agreement
- construction of the agreement
- costs and attorney fees
- voting
- limitations on partnership indebtedness
- life insurance on the partners' lives

No single agreement will suffice for all situations, and individual state laws must be consulted prior to the preparation of any general partnership agreement.

§ 5.4 THE LIMITED PARTNERSHIP

The limited partnership is the other major type of partnership. It offers certain advantages over a general partnership, yet also has certain disadvantages and, therefore, limited application. In most states, the limited partnership is governed by state statutes adopted from the Uniform Limited Partnership Act proposed by the American Bar Association.

Characteristics

A **limited partnership** is a form of partnership requiring at least one general partner and one limited partner. A limited partner is one who has contributed capital and shares in the profits but has no role in the management of the business. Characteristic of the limited partner is the fact that he or she faces no liability beyond his or her original contribution. A limited partnership can be distinguished by the following characteristics:

- an agreement with one or more general partners and one or more limited partners
- a contribution of capital only
- a share in the profits
- no role in the day-to-day management of the business
- liability limited to the original contribution

limited partnership: A partnership in which the liability of one or more of the partners is limited to the amount of money they have invested in the partnership.

Limited partners are not subject to the terms and conditions of the general partnership agreement. Their rights and obligations are determined by the limited partnership agreement and the laws of the state of the principal place of business of the enterprise.

Limited Partnership Agreement

The limited partnership agreement contains many of the same elements and considerations as those found in the general partnership agreement. The limited partnership agreement differs from the general partnership agreement in regard to the following matters:

- the classes of partners
- the contributions of the different classes of partners
- the liabilities of the different classes of partners
- the distribution of profits and losses to the different classes of partners
- the duties of the different classes of partners
- the limited partner's rights
- the transfer of a limited partner's interest

The limited partnership agreement is a contractual arrangement governed by the statute of the state of domicile of the enterprise. Therefore, it is incumbent upon the preparer of the agreement to be familiar with the individual state statutes regarding limited partnerships.

Classes of Partners

The limited partnership, under most circumstances, has two classes of partners: the general partners and the limited partners. The first section of the agreement should specify the identity and classification of the various partners (see Figure 5–2, Exhibit 1).

Contributions of Partners

This section of the limited partnership agreement should set forth the cash and property contributions of all classes of partners. For instance, if the general partner is to contribute land to be developed and the limited partner is to contribute the cash for the development of the property, the agreement should recite the respective contributions made at the time of the agreement as well as future additional contributions. (See Figure 5–2, Exhibit 2).

Liabilities of the Limited Partner

As already shown, the general partner is personally liable for all obligations of the partnership. The limited partner's liability is restricted to the amount of his or her investment at the time of the default. The limited partnership agreement should specify the nature of the limits of the liability of the limited partner (as shown in Figure 5–2, Exhibit 3).

ARTICLE I

THIS AGREEMENT made this 30th day of September, 1999, between ARNOLD NICKLAUS, INC., of 18 Long Drive, City of Orange, State of Fremont, hereinafter known as General Partner, and PALMER B. HOGAN, of 21 Putts, City of Orange, State of Fremont, hereinafter referred to as Limited Partner.

EXHIBIT 1
A sample Article I reflecting the identity of the partners

ARTICLE II

The amount and description of property, and the agreed value, contributed by the General Partner and the Limited Partner is:

ARNOLD NICKLAUS, INC. 480-acre plot of land known as Lot 11, Plat 20, Player Subdivision; Six Hundred Fifty Thousand Dollars ($650,000.00)

PALMER B. HOGAN Two Hundred Fifty Thousand Dollars ($250,000.00) with an additional contribution of Two Hundred Fifty Thousand Dollars ($250,000.00) within six (6) months from the execution of the Agreement.

EXHIBIT 2
A sample Article II identifying the contributions of the partners

ARTICLE III

The Limited Partner shall only be liable for losses suffered by the Limited Partnership in an amount equal to the Limited Partner's contribution to the Partnership. All losses from the operation of the Limited Partnership in excess of the Limited Partner's contribution shall be borne by the General Partner.

EXHIBIT 3
A sample Article III setting forth the liability of the limited partner

ARTICLE IV

The share of profit or other compensation by way of income, or loss, that the Limited Partner shall receive by reason of his contribution is: Forty percent (40%) per annum of the net profit or loss from the operation of the business.

EXHIBIT 4
A sample Article IV setting forth the distribution of profits and losses to the limited partner

ARTICLE V

The Limited Partner shall have no active role in the management or conduct of the business of the Partnership, and shall have no power to bind the Partnership by way of any contract or agreement. The General Partner shall devote his best efforts to the business of the Partnership for the joint interest and advantage of the Partnership.

EXHIBIT 5
A sample Article V setting forth the rights and duties of the partners

ARTICLE VI

The Limited Partner shall have the right to assign, sell, devise, give, or transfer his interest, in whole or in part, and shall have the right to confer upon his assignee, buyer, devisee, donee, or transferee the rights of a Limited Partner pursuant to this Agreement as provided by the statutes of this state.

EXHIBIT 6
A sample Article VI setting forth the transferability of the interest of the limited partner

FIGURE 5–2 A limited partnership agreement

Distribution of Profits and Losses

The section of the limited partnership agreement setting forth the manner and amount of the distribution of profits and losses can be very complex. In its simplest form, the section should establish the percentage of distribution to the limited partner from the net income of the operation. Losses are to be attributed to the limited partner on the same proportional basis as profits. (See Figure 5–2, Exhibit 4.)

Rights and Duties of Partners

Each class of partner in a limited partnership has certain rights and duties as outlined above. The general partner has the responsibility for the daily management of the enterprise free from the interference of the limited partner. The limited partner in turn is owed a fiduciary duty by the general partner. The specifics of the rights and duties may be set forth with great detail or may be referred to in general terms (see Figure 5–2, Exhibit 5).

Transfer of Limited Partner's Interest

In the limited partnership relationship, the interest of the limited partner is freely transferable, unlike the interest of the general partner. If there are to be any restrictions on the transfer of the interest of the limited partner, they should be specified in this section. (See Figure 5–2, Exhibit 6.)

The limited partnership is a creation of the statutes of the state of domicile of the enterprise. Therefore, care must be taken to comply with the requisite statutory provisions regarding execution of the agreement. As a form of business ownership, the limited partnership provides a better investment vehicle than a general partnership. Its propriety is a matter of counsel and negotiation.

§ 5.5 THE JOINT VENTURE

Similar to a partnership as a form of business relationship is the joint venture. A joint venture is a temporary contractual association of two or more individuals or businesses that agree to share in the responsibilities, profits, and losses of a common enterprise. The joint venture is different from a partnership because it does not involve a continuing relationship among the parties. It is characterized by the following:

- a contractual relationship between two or more persons
- a one-time joint undertaking
- a contribution of assets by all parties
- a right to manage and direct policy by all parties
- a sharing of the profits and losses
- personal liability of the parties
- limited duration
- taxed personally to the individual parties

A joint venture typically is a new business that exists only for the length of time required to complete the project. For example, suppose that a new industrial park is being developed in the community. In addition to the buildings, the developer, Corporate Asylum, Inc., has decided that the park also needs some extensive landscaping. To accomplish the landscaping, Corporate Asylum has contacted Flora & Fauna, Ltd., to provide the plants and trees. It has also contacted Earth Reorganization Specialists, Inc., to provide the earth moving and grading necessary to the beautification of the site. It will be necessary for Flora & Fauna to work together to meet state environmental requirements as well as design the project. The contractual vehicle that would best suit the three parties, Corporate Asylum, Flora & Fauna, and Earth Reorganization Specialists, for the limited project would be a joint venture between Flora & Fauna and Earth Reorganization to contract with Corporate Asylum for its needs.

The joint venture is subject to the same principles and limitations as a general partnership in the preparation of the agreement. The elements of the agreement are the same, and consideration is given to each concern, but for a limited purpose and duration.

§ 5.6 DISSOLUTION OF A PARTNERSHIP

The dissolution of a partnership is distinguished from the termination or winding up of the partnership as contemplated by the partnership agreement. The term **dissolution** refers to a change in the relationship of the partners as a result of one or more partners leaving the partnership. The Uniform Partnership Act, adopted by most states, provides the rules for the orderly dissolution of a partnership. The partnership ceases to exist upon dissolution, but it is still incumbent upon the partners to proceed to terminate the business, satisfy obligations, and distribute the assets. Dissolution is the first step in an orderly process of the termination of a partnership relationship.

The orderly dissolution process is best accomplished through the execution of a **dissolution agreement,** which is the formal contractual agreement between the partners to wind up the partnership business and terminate its existence. A simple dissolution agreement will contain the following elements:

- identification of the parties
- statement of termination
- agreement to liquidate
- execution

See Figure 5–3 for a sample dissolution agreement.

A partnership may face a termination other than the orderly voluntary dissolution by agreement. In such a case, the provisions of the general partnership agreement regarding arbitration apply. The dissolution agreement serves the purpose of providing an orderly termination of business without the expense and delay of litigation.

dissolution: The change in the relation of partners caused by any partner's ceasing to be associated in the carrying on of the business.

dissolution agreement: A formal contractual agreement between the partners to wind up the partnership business and terminate its existence.

DISSOLUTION AGREEMENT

THIS AGREEMENT made this 30th day of April, 1999, by and between REX KING, COURTNEY QUEEN, AND MARSHALL SQUIRE, of the City of Orange, State of Fremont,

WHEREAS, the parties to this Agreement have conducted a Partnership under the firm name of KING, QUEEN & SQUIRE, and

WHEREAS, the parties are desirous of withdrawing from the Partnership and both the parties have agreed that the Partnership shall be dissolved and terminated, and

WHEREAS, the parties have agreed that the assets of the Partnership shall be promptly liquidated and the Partnership terminated and closed,

NOW, THEREFORE, it is mutually agreed that the Partnership existing between the parties to this Agreement shall be liquidated and dissolved at as early a date as can be practically accomplished without loss to the parties in interest and that the net assets realized, after paying all debts and expenses of liquidating the assets and caring for the property of the Partnership, shall be divided equally between the parties.

IN WITNESS WHEREOF, the parties have executed this Agreement.

_____
REX KING

_____
COURTNEY QUEEN

_____
MARSHALL SQUIRE

FIGURE 5–3 A sample dissolution agreement

SUMMARY

- A partnership is based upon an agreement between two or more persons to engage in some lawful business enterprise. The partners must agree to share their talent and pool their resources in exchange for a proportional division of the profits and the losses. The essence of the partnership is the agreement.

- The partnership agreement is a complex document that arises from an understanding between the prospective partners on the fundamental nature of the undertaking. The formation of the agreement begins with the resolution of each of the major areas of concern. The issues to be resolved extend from the simple matter of the partnership name to the details of the division of profits and losses. The partnership agreement is a contract and, as such, is subject to all the rules of preparation discussed in Chapter 2.

- The Uniform Partnership Act has been passed in most states and is the law governing those partnerships that have no written agreement, or where the written instrument is silent as to some material element of the business relationship. The laws of the state of domicile of the partnership must be consulted before preparation of any agreement.

IN REVIEW

1. What are the two basic forms of partnership?
2. What are the primary matters of concern in the preparation of a partnership agreement?
3. What are the primary elements of concern in the preparation of a limited partnership agreement?
4. What are the matters to be considered in the preparation of a dissolution of partnership agreement?

PUTTING IT ALL TOGETHER

Since oil was first discovered in the nineteenth century, oil wells have been negligently reduced into glorious infernos, requiring the services of specialists to cool the conflagration. The most notorious group of fire-fighting roustabouts of this century was Red O'Dare and his Hellfighters, Inc. Red has reduced holocausts from Alaska to Zanzibar and has achieved hero status among the cognoscenti.

Two of Red's most pugnacious "hellfighters," Hope Sodom and Grace Gomorah, have decided to leave the fiery hearth of his tutelage and form their own enterprise. Sodom and Gomorah have a significant reputation on their own and feel that with a capital contribution of $250,000 each, they can start their own business as partners. They plan to share equally the profits, losses, and management of the concern from their headquarters at 88 Perdition Dr., Orange, FR.

Exercises

1. Prepare a general partnership agreement for Sodom & Gomorah for their execution.

CHAPTER
6

Wills

On the Plains of Hesitation bleach the bones of countless millions who, at the Dawn of Victory, sat down to wait, and waiting— died!

—

GEORGE W. CECIL (1923)

OBJECTIVES

After completing this chapter, you will be able to:

1. Apply the basic guidelines for the preparation and execution of a will

2. Outline the basic format for drafting a will

3. Identify the requirements for the typing of wills

4. Prepare a codicil to a will

BALLENTINE'S REVIEW

intestate—Pertaining to a person, or to the property of a person, who dies without leaving a valid will.

probate—The judicial act whereby a will is adjudicated to be valid; a term that describes the functions of the probate court, including the probate of wills and the supervision of the accounts and actions of administrators and executors of decedents' estates.

testator—A person who dies leaving a valid will.

will—An instrument by which a person makes a disposition of his or her property, to take effect after his or her death.

Estate planning is the creation of a method for the orderly handling, disposition, and administration of an estate when the owner dies. Development of an estate plan that satisfies the intent of the owner of an estate requires the use of a will and, in many cases, a trust. This chapter focuses on the basic requirements of wills for estate planning purposes and provides instruction in the creation of the necessary documents. The role of trusts in estate planning is considered in Chapter 7.

§ 6.1 WILLS IN GENERAL

A **will** is an instrument that declares the intended distribution of one's property at death. It is meant to accurately reflect the intent of the maker of the will, called the **testator,** in a written document. The purpose of a will is to provide for the orderly distribution of the property of the testator that makes up his or her estate.

An owner of property who has created a valid will providing for the distribution of his or her estate is said to have died **testate.** An owner of property who does not provide for its orderly distribution on death or fails to create a valid will is said to have died **intestate.** If an individual dies intestate, his or her property is distributed through the **laws of intestate succession.** Every state has a body of statutes determining the manner of the distribution of the deceased's property when there is no valid will concerning that particular property. The terms used to describe that body of law may be the *laws of intestate succession* or the **laws of descent and distribution.** Whichever term is used, the intention of the legislature is the same, namely, to provide for the orderly distribution of property upon death without a will.

Difficulty may arise with a distribution of property by intestate succession in that the deceased may not have intended for his or her property to be distributed in the manner provided by such statutes. Individuals entitled to receive a portion of the estate as provided by state laws of intestacy are known as **heirs at law.** There are individuals considered heirs solely because of legislative designation. Heirs at law may experience considerable delay because of the failure of the owner of property to provide for its orderly distribution.

§ 6.2 REQUIREMENTS OF A WILL

The statutory requirements for the preparation and execution of a will may vary from state to state. All states, however, share certain elements needed for the creation of a valid will. Those requirements are established by state statute in each state's probate code or its equivalent. Since a will is a legally enforceable declaration of property distribution, the procedure to create a legally enforceable document must be followed. The probate code for the state of Texas provides:

Every person who has attained the age of eighteen years, or who is or has been lawfully married, or who is a member of the armed forces of the

---

estate planning: The creation of a method for the orderly handling, disposition, and administration of an estate when the owner dies.

will: An instrument by which a person (the testator) makes a disposition of his or her property, to take effect after his or her death.

testator: A person who dies leaving a valid will.

testate: Pertaining to a person, or to the property of a person, who dies leaving a valid will.

intestate: Pertaining to a person, or to the property of a person, who dies without leaving a valid will.

laws of intestate succession: The laws through which an individual's property is distributed when an individual dies intestate, *i.e.,* without leaving a valid will.

laws of descent and distribution: The laws determining the manner of distribution of a deceased's property when there is no valid will concerning that particular property.

heirs at law: Persons who are entitled to inherit real or personal property of a decedent who dies intestate; persons receiving property by descent.

United States or of the auxiliaries thereof or of the maritime service at the time the will is made, being of sound mind, shall have the right and power to make a last will and testament, under the rules and limitations prescribed by law. Texas Statutes Annotated §57.

Each state's probate code should be consulted for specific compliance.

Writing

Most states require that wills be in writing as evidence of an expression of the testator's intent. The written document may be typed or in the testator's own handwriting. Either form will be allowed if the writing is legible and otherwise meets the statutory guidelines for the creation of a will.

Legal Capacity

The validity of a written will is dependent upon the **capacity** of the testator to create the document. Capacity in the law refers to that level of mental competence necessary to understand the nature of one's acts. A lack of competence can be based upon either age or sanity. Nearly all states require that the testator reach the age of majority, which is eighteen in most states. A testator with sufficient soundness of mind to understand the nature and extent of the property he or she owns is considered competent. The testator can then formulate an intention as to its distribution. It is important to note that the capacity need exist only at the time of the creation of the will, and need not exist at the time of death.

Signatures

The testator's signature must appear at the end of the will. If the testator is unable to execute his or her own signature, then another individual may sign his or hers along with an indication as to the procedure. This must be done in the presence of the witnesses and reflected in the acknowledgment of the procedure. The signing of the will by the testator must occur in the presence of the witnesses, a fact to be *attested* by those witnesses. Attestation is merely the act of witnessing the signing of a written instrument. Witnesses attesting to the signature of the testator must sign the will in the presence of each other.

Most states require that at least two witnesses attest to the testator's signature. While the original of the will must be executed by the testator and the witnesses, it is not a formal requirement that each copy be executed.

The proper execution of the copies of a will acts to protect against the loss of the original and reduce the possibility of a fraudulent claim. Every page of the will should be signed or initialed by the testator and dated, but it is not necessary that the witnesses attest to each page. This is done to avoid a later claim that some material portion of the will content may have been altered.

capacity: A person's ability to understand the nature and effect of the act in which he or she is engaged.

Witnesses

While formal statutory requirements for witnesses generally provide only that they be of the age of majority and of sound mind, the probate codes of most states require merely that a witness have the same qualifications as those required of a testator.

Most states do not prohibit recipients of a gift under the terms of the will from acting as witnesses. The wisdom of such a dual role is affected by the likelihood of a subsequent challenge to the will for fraud or undue influence.

A witness should be informed that he or she may be required to testify about the validity of the will to decide its authenticity at probate. It is not required that a witness be made aware of the contents of the will or have an opportunity to read the document.

Language

No particular language or phrasing is required by statute to achieve the testator's intent. If the intention of the testator is conveyed in a clear manner, the will may be enforced. Every effort, then, should be made to ensure that the language used be simple and unambiguous.

Self-Proving Wills

Before a will can be admitted to probate, its authenticity must be established. The legal term for the establishment of the authenticity of a will is to **prove** the will. The process involved to prove the authenticity of a will can be involved and expensive, requiring the testimony of witnesses. To avoid that eventuality, some states make provision for a will to be **self-proving,** that is, it establishes its own authenticity. To accomplish this self-authentication, an acknowledgment by a notary public or other such official authorized by statute to administer oaths attached to the will proper serves to validate the signatures and prove the will. Once a will has been self-proved, no further authentication procedures in court are necessary.

Will Storage

A question arises frequently about the best location for the storage of the original and copies of the will. Although state statutes are silent on this issue, there are certain practices adopted by most practitioners that serve well the testator's interests. Most testators insist on maintaining a copy of their will for reference. They often choose to store the copy in a safety deposit vault. This form of storage, however, may delay the probate of the will should access to the vault be delayed due to banking procedures and local state laws.

Most banking institutions that are named in wills to act in a fiduciary capacity require that a copy of the will be deposited with them. A bank's fiduciary capacity is the duty to act in good faith with respect to the property of another. Most states make provision for the filing of a copy of a will with the appropriate probate court for safekeeping until probate is required.

It is a common practice for most law firms to maintain a copy of any client's will in their vault for safekeeping. In that way, the presentation of the will may be facilitated when the need for probate arises.

prove: To establish a fact by the required degree of evidence.

self-proving: A document that establishes its own authenticity through the acknowledgment by a notary public or other such official authorized by statute to administer oaths attached to the document proper.

Living Wills

Some state laws allow competent individuals to provide for the contingency wherein they may become incompetent, either physically or mentally, in the future and to express a desire that they not be kept alive by artificial means at such time. State statutes creating health directives for natural deaths are attempts to spare family members the making of such a decision under trying circumstances. They also serve to protect any treating physician or health care facility from potential liability. Each state has a public interest to protect with such legislation. It is necessary to consult each state's statutes for statutory restrictions. Some states even provide for the specific language to be used.

§ 6.3 FORMAT FOR DRAFTING A WILL

While there is no specific requirement that any standardized form or language be used in the drafting of a will, the primary focus is to draft a document that best carries out the intent of the testator. There are certain guidelines that help provide a clear expression of the testator's intentions. The preparer of the will can ensure that the document conforms to the intent of the testator with careful attention to:

- the general revocatory clause
- the provision for debts and expenses
- the provision for taxes
- the clauses containing specific gifts of property
- the residuary clause
- the appointment of the personal representative
- the testimonium clause
- the testator's signature
- the witnesses' signatures
- the self-proving language

Introductory Clause

The opening paragraph of a will should state the name of the testator along with his or her domicile. It should also indicate the nature of the document and affirm that it is the testator's last will and testament. In addition, the introduction should declare that the testator is of a sound and disposing mind and thus competent to execute such a document. The execution of a will generally revokes any prior wills or codicils, yet it is customary to state that it is the testator's intent to do so in what is termed the **general revocatory clause.** This clause shows that it is the testator's intention that this document supersede any previously published will or codicil. An introductory clause should read as shown in Figure 6–1, Exhibit 1. A clause such as this will serve to identify the testator, establish his or her competence, and validate the instrument as his or her last will and testament.

general revocatory clause: A clause in a will that shows that it is the testator's intent that the document supersede any previously published will or codicil.

EXHIBIT 1
A sample introductory clause

EXHIBIT 2
Sample instructions for payment
of last debts and expenses

EXHIBIT 3
Sample instructions for payment
of taxes

EXHIBIT 4
Sample bequest intention
language

EXHIBIT 5
A sample residuary clause

EXHIBIT 6
A sample clause appointing a
personal representative

EXHIBIT 7
A sample testimonium clause

I, ALVIN B. ALERT, a resident of the County of Osceola, State of Florida, being of sound and disposing mind, memory, and understanding, do hereby make, publish, and declare this to be my Last Will and Testament, hereby revoking all wills and codicils at any time heretofore made by me.

I direct that all my legally enforceable debts, funeral expenses, expenses of my last illness, and administrative expenses be paid by my Personal Representative from the assets of my estate as soon as practicable after my death.

I direct that all inheritance, transfer, succession, and other death taxes, which may be payable with respect to any property includable as a part of my gross estate, shall be paid from my residuary estate, without any apportionment thereof.

I give, devise, and bequeath all of my property of whatever kind and wherever located, as follows:

(1) to my wife, ALICE B. ALERT;

(2) if my wife, ALICE B. ALERT, predeceases me, to such of my children as survive me, in equal shares, provided, however, should a child of mine predecease me, survived by a child or children who survive me, such grandchild or grandchildren of mine shall take the share the parent would have taken had such parent survived me;

(3) if my wife, ALICE B. ALERT, and all of my children predecease me, to such grandchildren as survive me, in equal shares.

All the rest, residue, and remainder of my estate, of every nature and kind, which I may own at the time of my death, real, personal, and mixed, tangible and intangible, of whatsoever nature and wheresoever situated, I give, devise, and bequeath to my alma mater, MERIT U.

I appoint FAITH SCRUPLES as Personal Representative of the Will, with full power and authority to sell, transfer, and convey any and all property, real or personal, which I may own at the time of my death, at such time and place and upon such terms and conditions as my Personal Representative may determine, without necessity of obtaining a court order. If FAITH SCRUPLES does not survive me, if she fails to qualify, or, if having qualified, she should die, resign, or become incapacitated, then in that event I nominate and appoint FIRST FIDELITY AND TRUST COMPANY as successor Personal Representative of this Will, with all the powers and duties afforded my Personal Representative herein.

IN WITNESS WHEREOF, I have hereunto freely subscribed my name and affixed my seal at the City of Orange, State of Florida, this 29th day of February, 1999, in the presence of the subscribing witnesses whom I have requested to attest hereto.

FIGURE 6–1 A sample of the language used in a last will and testament

IN WITNESS WHEREOF, I have hereunto subscribed my name and affixed my seal at the City of _____, State of _____, this _____ day of _____, 19_____, in the presence of the subscribing witnesses who I have requested to attest witness hereto.

_____
Testator/Testatrix

EXHIBIT 8
Sample testator's signature format

This instrument was, on the date hereof, signed, published, and declared by ALVIN B. ALERT to be his Last Will, and we, at the same time, at his request, in his presence and in the presence of each other, have hereunto signed our names and addresses as attesting witnesses.

EXHIBIT 9
Sample witnesses' signature format

_____   of   (address)
Witness

_____   of   (address)
Witness

EXHIBIT 10
Sample self-proving language

We, the testator and witnesses, respectively, whose names are signed to the attached or foregoing instrument, having been sworn, declared to the undersigned officer that the testator, in the presence of witnesses, signed the instrument as his last will, that he signed, and that each of the witnesses, in the presence of the testator and in the presence of each other, signed the will as a witness.

FIGURE 6–1 (continued)

Payment of Debts and Expenses

The testator will have certain debts that have accrued at the time of his or her death. It is customary to instruct the personal representative of the estate to pay those debts out of the funds of the estate. Included in those debts existing at the time of death may be some expenses related to the last illness and expenses associated with the funeral arrangements. Instructions for the payment of those expenses and any others that may be reasonably anticipated should be addressed in the initial article.

In conjunction with the question of funeral expenses, many testators include directions for the funeral and burial arrangements. It is not uncommon to have a dispute arise between surviving relatives about the testator's preferences. There also may arise the question of anatomical gifts to be made by the testator at the time of death. These considerations should be formally addressed in the will, and instructions regarding these issues should be given to the personal representative in case disclosure of the will's contents is delayed (see Figure 6–1, Exhibit 2).

A matter closely related to the estate's debts at the time of death is the question of the costs of and payments for the administration of the estate. The personal representative should receive specific instructions from the testator regarding the payment of these expenses from the funds of the estate.

Payment of Taxes

With an estate of substantial value, consideration must be given to the question of the payment of federal estate taxes and state inheritance taxes. If the size of the decedent's gross estate for federal tax purposes creates exposure to tax liability, it is advisable to include directions to the personal representative regarding the payment of taxes from estate funds and assets. If there is any question that such liability may exist, these provisions should be made. The clause may read as shown in Figure 6–1, Exhibit 3. The personal representative must have specific direction from the document if it is the intention of the testator that payment be made from a particular asset.

Devises and Bequests

It is at this point in the preparation of a will that an expression of the testator's intent should be made regarding any specific testamentary gifts, called **devises** or **bequests.** The major concern of most testators is directed to the question of the ultimate distribution of his or her assets. Every individual testator has reasons for his or her bequests, and the will should clearly set forth the testator's intentions without ambiguity (see Figure 6–1, Exhibit 4).

Although the testator's reasons behind his or her devises need not be set forth, it may be valuable should litigation develop in a will contest.

Residuary Clause

It can be anticipated that property will be acquired by the testator after the drafting of the will through acquisition or appreciation in the value of existing assets. It is the duty of the testator to anticipate such an eventuality and provide for the specific distribution of that property. The remainder of the testator's estate that is not subject to a specific devise must also be made the subject of direction. These **residuary** assets generally form the bulk of the decedent's estate and provide the source for the funds to pay debts, expenses, costs, and taxes. Instructions for the distribution of the remainder of the testator's estate should be directed to the personal representative at this juncture. The residuary clause may read as shown in Figure 6–1, Exhibit 5.

If there are insufficient assets in the estate to cover those payments requiring cash, then provision must be made for the sale of the fixed assets of the estate and the order of such liquidation, or **abatement.** Abatement is the process by which the order of liquidation is decided and typically follows this order: (a) residual assets; (b) general devises of cash left to named individuals; (c) specific devises. The actual drafting of this clause requires care to protect the creditors of the estate and the specific devisees as well.

Personal Representative

The personal representative of the estate is responsible for collecting and preserving the assets of the estate at the testator's death, paying the debts, and

devises: Gifts of real property by will, although the term is often loosely used to mean testamentary gifts of either real property or personal property.

bequests: Technically, gifts of personal property by will, *i.e.*, legacies, although the term is often loosely used in connection with testamentary gifts of real estate as well.

residuary: Pertaining to the residue; pertaining to that which is left over.

abatement: The process by which fixed assets of an estate are liquidated in order to cover payments requiring cash for which the estate has insufficient liquid assets.

distributing the property pursuant to the testator's wishes. The actual powers and responsibilities of the personal representative, also called an **executor** (male) or **executrix** (female), are enumerated by statute.

In anticipation of the contingency whereby the chosen personal representative may be unable to act in such a capacity, a successor representative should also be named to avoid any delay or confusion. A clause appointing the personal representative may read as shown in Figure 6–1, Exhibit 6.

As a matter of law in most states, the powers conferred by statute also protect the personal representative from any personal liability while acting in an authorized capacity.

Testimonium Clause

It is customary to conclude the body of the will with a declaration that the testator is signing the will as his or her last will and testament freely and is requesting that the witnesses do so similarly. This reflects the voluntariness of the will and avoids any subsequent claim of fraud or duress. The **testimonium clause,** as it is known, may also include a reference to the total number of pages of the will and refer to the date and place of the signing. A typical testimonium clause reads as shown in Figure 6–1, Exhibit 7.

Testator's Signature

The signature of the testator must appear on the will to make it valid. The signing of the will by the testator must be done in the presence of the witnesses. Any signature will be invalid if the testator is not of the age of majority or not of sound mind or if the signing is not performed before the witnesses. The presentation of the testator's signature should appear as shown in Figure 6–1, Exhibit 8.

Witnesses' Signatures

The witnesses to the testator's signature indicate that they have so witnessed the signing in an **attestation clause.** The actual number of witnesses is controlled by statute, but usually consists of two or three. The witnesses must place their signatures along with their addresses on the will in the presence of each other. Language to be employed may read as shown in Figure 6–1, Exhibit 9.

Additional language may also include an attestation to the effect that there was no undue influence or duress.

Self-Proving Wills

Many states have provided by statute for the proving of a will through the provision of an acknowledgment by a notary public or other officer authorized by the state to administer oaths. Such a procedure establishes the authenticity of the will through an affidavit form to ensure the validity of the signatures of the testator and the witnesses. The procedure for self-proving a will is governed by statutes that call for language such as that shown in Figure 6–1, Exhibit 10.

executor: A person designated by a testator to carry out the directions and requests in the testator's will and to dispose of his or her property according to the provisions of his or her will.

executrix: A term used to describe a female executor.

testimonium clause: A clause at the end of a deed, which recites that the parties have "set their hands and seals" to the deed on the date specified.

attestation clause: A clause, usually at the end of a document such as a deed or a will, that provides evidence of attestation.

§ 6.4 TYPING THE WILL

To ensure the effectiveness of the will following a consideration of its contents, there are certain guidelines beyond the statutory requirements that should be followed to avoid any challenge to the validity of the will.

Paper

Printed forms should not be considered in the preparation of a will. Such forms will not precisely fit the needs of the individual testator and will serve only to facilitate a challenge to the document.

The will is traditionally typed on 8 ½ x 14 inch legal-sized paper, although it may be on 8 ½ x 11 inch paper for convenience. This is typically a matter of attorney preference and aesthetics rather than any formal requirement.

Erasures

It is very important that the will be free from anything that would suggest that any changes were made after the testator had signed. The will cannot contain any marks that might create the impression that something was erased, changed, or altered. Therefore, it is of considerable benefit to use only one typeface for the physical production of the will.

Language

While no specific language is required in the expression of the intention of the testator, it should be recognized that the decedent's wishes will be best served if there is no chance of misunderstanding or misinterpretation. Therefore, if the drafter uses clear, concise, and simple language to draft the individual clauses, the opportunity for challenge may be minimized.

Testator's Acknowledgment

The original will must be signed by the testator and the witnesses. To reduce the possibility of any challenge to the validity of the will, it is advisable to have the copies signed by the testator and the witnesses as well. This goal is further facilitated with the placing of the testator's signature or initials on each individual page of the document, thus eliminating any question about the authenticity of each page. Care should be taken to ensure that the signature or attestation clause does not appear on a separate page from the remainder of the will. Some portion of the text of the previous page should be carried forward to the final page that contains the signature of the testator.

codicil: An addition or supplement to a will, which adds to or modifies the will without replacing or revoking it.

§ 6.5 MODIFICATION OF A WILL

Modification of an existing valid last will and testament is effected through a **codicil.** The codicil is a separate instrument that serves to alter or modify the original will without appearing to be the entire will of the testator.

It serves to "republish" the original will through reference to it and also provides for any alterations or additions to the original.

Most states require that a codicil be executed in the same manner as the will proper in that it needs to be in writing and signed by the testator and witnessed. Any individual state requirements for the execution of the original will must also be followed.

- The last will and testament is one of the most important documents that is prepared for an individual. It can best be described as the final written expression of the intended distribution of one's assets at death. The validity of the will lies in its execution, the integrity of the will in its expression of intention. The preparation of the will is extremely important, as is its execution. It is the task of the preparer of the document to ensure that the will not only reflects the desires of its maker, but also is executed in a form to withstand challenge. A failure in its execution will cost the estate unnecessary sums of money in court costs and attorney fees.

- The Probate Code of each state provides the formal requirements for the creation of a document that will have standing before a court. The content of the will is not covered by statute and must remain the province of the testator and his or her counsel. No single format will serve to meet the needs of each testator. The content of each estate will differ, as well as the desires of the owner of each estate. Keep in mind the need to provide for the certain burden that debts, administration expenses, and taxes will impose. The effect on the size and direction of any devise must be measured in light of the possible diminution of the estate.

IN REVIEW

1. What information should the introductory clause of a will contain?
2. How should the preparer of a will provide for the payment of debts, administration costs, and taxes?
3. How should a specific gift of property by will be made?
4. What language would be preferred to create a residuary clause?
5. What language provides for the appointment and duties of the personal representative of the estate?
6. What document is used to modify a will?

PUTTING IT ALL TOGETHER

Assume that you are employed by the prestigious law firm of an expert estate planner, Ms. Bea Quest. A potential testator, Mr. Philip Anthrope, has approached your office for the preparation of his will.

Anthrope has told you that he is divorced and without current obligation to the mother of his only child, Charity. He has been estranged from his thirty-year-old daughter for a number of years and has decided to leave her the grand sum of one dollar, leaving the balance of his estate to his pet kestrel, named Nike.

Anthrope's estate consists of 10,000 shares of Walt Disney Company stock and 40 acres of salt marsh of which 10% is inhabitable due to its proximity to a local water treatment facility. His liquid assets consist of a money market account in the amount of $25,000 with Hugh, Wendt & Broke, Investment Counselors.

It is Anthrope's intention to leave the residue of his estate to his alma mater, The Galileo School of Flight Safety. His spinster sister, Bambi, is to be his personal representative. If Miss Anthrope should fail to qualify as personal representative, then his brokerage firm will serve. It will be necessary to appoint Miss Anthrope as the guardian for the life of Nike.

Exercises

1. Prepare the necessary last will and testament to achieve the intent of Mr. Philip Anthrope.

CHAPTER
7

Trusts

*This time, like all times, is a very good one, if
we but know what to do with it.*

—

RALPH WALDO EMERSON (1864)

OBJECTIVES

After completing this chapter, you will be able to:

1. Outline the elements of a trust
2. Distinguish between the various trust instruments
3. Prepare a trust instrument

BALLENTINE'S REVIEW

"S" corporation—A corporation electing to be taxed under subchapter S of the Internal Revenue Code. Its income is taxed to the shareholders rather than at the corporate level.

stock—Shares in a corporation or a joint-stock company owned by shareholders; the sum of all the rights and duties of the shareholders.

trust—A fiduciary relationship involving a trustee who holds trust property for the benefit or use of a beneficiary. A trust is generally established through a trust instrument by a person who wishes the beneficiary to receive the benefit of the property but not outright ownership.

The orderly disposition and administration of property on death is the goal of an estate plan. As seen in Chapter 6, a will is the basic estate planning tool to accomplish the orderly distribution of property at death. The other basic estate planning tool is the trust, which can be used to distribute property during the owner's lifetime or at his or her death. This chapter focuses on the trust instrument as a basic document for estate planning purposes.

§ 7.1 THE NATURE OF A TRUST

The fundamental nature of a trust consists of the creation of a separate legal entity to hold property for the benefit of another. This legal entity is called a **trust.** The arrangement places legal title to property in the hands of one person who owes a fiduciary duty to administer that property for the benefit of another. A **fiduciary duty** is the duty to act on another's behalf in good faith and trust. It is a legal obligation that one person owes, requiring prudence, care, and diligence. A trust represents the combination of a legal entity, in the form of a contractual property relationship, and an estate planning tool in one legal instrument.

A trust is illustrated by the following example. Artemus Longreach decided that he wanted his daughter, Alene, to have the benefit and use of the family estate, Cypress Farms, until she turned twenty-five, at which time she was to receive title to the property. It was also his decision to have his long-time and trusted friend, Oswold Cosmold, administer the property on his daughter's behalf until she became old enough to handle the duties herself. The creation of a trust of the property, Cypress Farms, for the use and benefit of his daughter, Alene, until she reached age twenty-five, would fully satisfy his intentions. Oswold Cosmold would be appointed as trustee with the attendant fiduciary responsibilities. The trust would terminate upon Alene Longreach attaining age twenty-five, at which time title to the property would pass to her. During the period of the trust, title to Cypress Farms would be held in the name of the trust—The Alene Longreach Trust.

In the law, a trust may take many forms, including trusts that are created solely by operation of law to correct some inequity. This chapter addresses only those trusts created by an individual expressly for the purposes of estate planning. A trust of this type is called a **private express trust** and requires a written instrument expressing the individual's intentions for the distribution of his or her property.

§ 7.2 THE ELEMENTS OF A TRUST

To create a private express trust, the following four basic elements are required:

- a settlor
- a trustee

trust: A fiduciary relationship involving a trustee who holds trust property for the benefit or use of a beneficiary.

fiduciary duty: The duty to act loyally and honestly with respect to the interests of another.

private express trust: A trust created by an individual expressly for the purposes of estate planning.

- a beneficiary
- property

A valid private express trust fails in its creation if any of the four elements are missing. There must be property to be transferred to a trustee for administration for the benefit of one who can enforce the relationship, created intentionally by the owner of the property.

The Settlor

The **settlor** is the term applied to that individual who is the owner of property that he or she wants to place in a trust. Other terms used in various jurisdictions to describe the settlor are: *creator*, *grantor*, and *trustor*. Regardless of the term used, the individual creating the trust must meet certain requirements:

- competency
- owner of the property
- power to dispose of the property
- intention to create a trust

If the settlor satisfies these requirements, he or she may proceed to create a trust as long as it meets the statutory requirements of the state of domicile of the trust. Each state has its own body of law with respect to trusts, and those laws must be consulted before the trust is created.

The Trustee

In the trust relationship, the settlor is usually the one who appoints the trustee through the trust instrument. The **trustee** is the person who holds legal title to property for the benefit of another person, the beneficiary. The trustee is considered to be the fiduciary of the trust and its administrator. The trustee may be either a natural person or a legal "person" in the form of a corporate entity, as long as it has the power to hold title to property.

The trustee owes a fiduciary duty to the beneficiary of the trust, consisting generally of the duty to act in the beneficiary's best interest. He or she must use ordinary care, skill, diligence, and prudence in the fulfillment of his or her duties. Among other things, those duties consist of:

- maintaining accurate records
- preserving the trust property
- collecting receivables
- acting solely in the best interests of the beneficiary

In addition to his or her active fiduciary duty, it is also incumbent upon the trustee to avoid any conflict of interest between the trustee and the beneficiary. The trustee may not profit from the trust to the detriment of the beneficiary, and he or she may be liable for any breach of his or her fiduciary duty.

settlor: The creator of a trust; the person who conveys or transfers property to another (the trustee) to hold in trust for a third person (the beneficiary).

trustee: The person who holds the legal title to trust property for the benefit of the beneficiary of the trust, with such powers and subject to such duties as are imposed by the terms of the trust and the law.

The Beneficiary

The **beneficiary** of a trust is the individual recipient of the trust benefits or property. The trust must have a beneficiary to be valid. It is the beneficiary who has the power to enforce the terms of the trust. While the trustee holds the legal title to the trust property, the beneficiary holds the **equitable title,** or the beneficial title, which is the right to profit or benefit from the property. The beneficiary's equitable title entitles him or her to the rights and benefits of the trust property during the period of the trust. In some jurisdictions, the beneficiary is referred to as the *cestui que trust* or the *cestui que use*, meaning that he or she is the one for whom property is held.

The beneficiary need not be a particular person named at the time of the creation of the trust as long as he or she is capable of being identified, as in the case of an unborn child. If the beneficiary is not capable of holding title to the property, as in the case of a minor or incompetent, a guardian must be appointed for the beneficiary. In most states, the beneficiary may be a cotrustee but may not be the sole trustee because there would no longer be anyone to enforce the terms of the trust against the trustee.

The Property

The **trust property** is the property interest owned by the settlor and transferred to the trustee for the benefit of the beneficiary. Any transferable interest may be the subject of a trust. Depending upon the jurisdiction, the trust property may be referred to as *body, corpus, principal, res*, or *subject matter*. The property may be a transferable interest in real property or personal property, or it may be a combination of the two. It may not consist of an interest that is not transferable. Since the validity of the trust depends upon its enforceability, there must be an interest to be enforced.

§ 7.3 THE TRUST INSTRUMENT

The trust instrument takes the form of a contract between the settlor and the trustee. It describes the principal and provides for the disposition of that principal to the beneficiary. The instrument must clearly express the intentions of the settlor that the trust property is held by the trustee over time and the income is applied to a designated beneficiary.

A private express trust instrument may take one of four basic forms:

- an irrevocable living trust
- a revocable living trust
- a testamentary trust
- a pour-over trust

It is the intent of the settlor that decides the type of trust. If the property is to be placed in trust during the settlor's lifetime, a *living trust* is created. If the settlor does not intend to make that living trust subject to his or her right to revoke it, the trust is an *irrevocable living trust*. If the settlor wants the trust to be subject to his or her right to revoke it, a *revocable living trust* is used. If the

beneficiary: A person for whom property is held in trust.

equitable title: Title recognized as ownership in equity, even though it is not legal title or marketable title; title sufficient to give the party to whom it belongs the right to have the legal title transferred to him or her.

trust property: Property that is the subject of a trust. It is also referred to as the *trust res*, the *res of the trust*, or the *corpus of the trust*.

settlor intends to place the property in trust only upon his or her death, the form of the trust is either a *testamentary trust* or a *pour-over trust*.

The Irrevocable Living Trust

A **living trust** is a trust created during the settlor's lifetime that becomes operative before his or her death. A living trust is sometimes referred to as an *inter vivos trust*. For estate planning purposes, it may be advisable for the settlor to create a living trust that cannot be revoked once it has been established. An **irrevocable living trust** is a trust created and executed during the settlor's lifetime that cannot be revoked by him or her at any time.

The trust document can be a very complex instrument, depending on the nature of the property, the duties of the trustee, and the character of the beneficiary. A well-drafted irrevocable living trust should contain sections that provide for the following:

- an identification of the parties
- an identification of the trust property
- the distribution of income and principal
- the rights, powers, and duties of the trustee
- an irrevocability clause
- the provision for a successor trustee
- the applicable state law
- the execution

Although the individual needs of the settlor will dictate the complexity of the agreement, as with any legal instrument, there must be compliance with the applicable state law

The Parties. The trust instrument begins with an identification of the parties to the agreement in a form similar to that of a standard contract. The title of the trust should be followed by language establishing the date of the agreement and the identity of the settlor and trustee (as shown in Figure 7–1, Exhibit 1).

The Trust Property. The property clause transfers title to the trust property to the trustee and authorizes the trustee to collect the trust assets and perfect title to the property. The trust property, or *corpus*, must be identified with as much detail as possible. If the property is extensive, an attached "exhibit" may be used to list the items that constitute the principal. Real property should be identified by its legal description. The settlor should contemplate the addition of property to the principal during the life of the trust and should declare that contingency in the agreement (see Figure 7–1, Exhibit 2).

The Distribution of Income and Principal. An important section of the trust instrument is to describe in detail the manner in which income and principal are to be distributed. The directions must be clear and unambiguous to avoid confusion and ensure compliance with the intentions of the settlor. (See Figure 7–1, Exhibit 3.)

The Rights, Powers, and Duties of the Trustee. An essential section of the trust instrument is the section setting forth the rights, powers, and duties of the trustee. Those powers are based in general upon the trustee's fiduciary

living trust: A trust that is effective during the lifetime of the creator of the trust. Also known as an *inter vivos trust*.

irrevocable living trust: A trust created and executed during the settlor's lifetime that cannot be revoked by him or her at any time.

EXHIBIT 1
A sample title and opening paragraph of a trust

EXHIBIT 2
A sample Article I identifying the trust property

EXHIBIT 3
A sample Article II describing the distribution of income and principal

EXHIBIT 4
A sample Article III describing the powers of the trustee

THE ALENE LONGREACH TRUST

THIS AGREEMENT is made this 30th day of June, 1999, between ARTE-MUS LONGREACH, 111 Foxhunt Lane, City of Orange, State of Fremont, hereinafter referred to as Settlor, and OSWOLD COSMOLD, 222 Scribe Court, City of Orange, State of Fremont, hereinafter referred to as Trustee.

ARTICLE I

Settlor hereby transfers, and Trustee hereby agrees to receive, certain assets described in Exhibit "A" attached hereto and incorporated by reference, constituting the initial principal of this trust, thereby establishing this trust. Settlor declares that it is his purpose in establishing this trust to provide a means for the conservation and management of income-producing assets and other properties and to provide for the comfort, maintenance, and support of the Beneficiary. Trustee is authorized to receive additional property added to the trust principal from any person acceptable to the Trustee.

ARTICLE II

Settlor hereby authorizes Trustee to manage the trust principal and collect income therefrom. Trustee shall pay all taxes and assessments incident to the management thereof and shall apply and dispose of the net income from the trust principal as follows:

During the life of Beneficiary, ALENE LONGREACH, Trustee shall pay to or for the benefit of Beneficiary any amounts of the net income he deems advisable for the care, maintenance, and general welfare of Beneficiary after consideration of the standard of living to which she is accustomed at the time of the creation of this trust.

When Beneficiary, ALENE LONGREACH, reaches her twenty-fifth (25th) birthday, she shall be empowered to appoint or withdraw up to one-half of the then remaining trust property of her trust as of said date. When she reaches her thirtieth (30th) birthday, she shall be empowered to withdraw the remaining trust property of her trust. If she predeceases the date of distribution of her trust, Trustee shall, as soon as practicable following her death, pay all debts, funeral expenses, expenses of last illness, administration expenses, and estate taxes, and shall distribute the remaining trust property to Beneficiary's surviving heirs, whereupon this trust shall terminate.

ARTICLE III

Trustee and his successor shall be governed by the provisions of the laws of the State of Fremont not in conflict with this instrument and shall have additional responsibilities granted and imposed by statute. In addition, without limiting any common law or statutory authority, and without the need to apply to any court, Trustee shall have the following powers and responsibilities:

FIGURE 7–1 A sample irrevocable living trust

To acquire, retain, improve, manage, protect, invest, reinvest, exchange, lease, sell or option to sell, borrow, mortgage, pledge, transfer, and convey trust property, real property, tangible personal property, and intangible personal property, without regard to any law, court ruling, or rule or regulation governing fiduciaries in the manner that Trustee shall deem advisable.

To pay all expenses of management and administration of the trust estate, all or any part of which may, in Trustee's discretion, be charged either to income or principal.

To perform any and all acts, institute proceedings, and exercise all other rights and powers that an absolute owner of the property would otherwise have the right to do, subject to the Trustee's fiduciary responsibility.

Any enumeration of rights, powers, and duties of Trustee in this Agreement shall not limit the general or implied powers of Trustee.

ARTICLE IV

Settlor hereby declares that the trust created by this Agreement shall be irrevocable and not subject to alteration, amendment, revocation, or termination by Settlor.

EXHIBIT 5
A sample Article IV stating the irrevocability of the trust

ARTICLE V

Settlor hereby appoints the **SABAL BANK AND TRUST COMPANY** as successor Trustee in the event that Trustee shall die, resign, become incapacitated, or for any reason fail to act as trustee. The successor Trustee shall have all the powers, rights, and duties of the trustee named herein.

EXHIBIT 6
A sample Article V providing for a successor trustee

ARTICLE VI

This Agreement has been established pursuant to the laws of the State of Fremont, and Settlor is a resident of the State of Fremont at the time of its execution. Any interpretation of this Agreement, and any question concerning its validity, and all questions relating to its performance shall be adjudged pursuant to the laws of the State of Fremont.

EXHIBIT 7
A sample Article VI establishing the applicable state law

IN WITNESS WHEREOF, Settlor and Trustee have executed this Agreement at the City of Orange, State of Fremont, on this 30th day of June, 1999.

EXHIBIT 8
A sample execution of the trust instrument

WITNESS	ARTEMUS LONGREACH

WITNESS	OSWOLD COSMOLD

(acknowledgment of notary public)

FIGURE 7–1 (continued)

duty to the beneficiary, along with those specific powers and rights authorized by the trust agreement. Individual state statutes provide certain guidelines governing the authority of the trustee as well and should be consulted before the preparation of the instrument. The section detailing the trustee's authority should contain any limitations that the settlor may wish to impose on the trustee. (See Figure 7–1, Exhibit 4.)

The Irrevocability Clause. The trust instrument creating an irrevocable living trust must contain clear and unambiguous language expressing the intent of the settlor that the trust is to be irrevocable. The purpose of this section is to state clearly that the property is to be held for the benefit of another without any reservation of authority by the settlor (see Figure 7–1, Exhibit 5).

The Provision for a Successor Trustee. The trust agreement must include a provision establishing the procedure for the appointment of a successor trustee should the named trustee fail for any reason. The instrument must recognize the fact that the trustee may die, become incompetent, refuse the position, or otherwise become ineligible to act on behalf of the trust, thus creating the necessity for a successor. (See Figure 7–1, Exhibit 6.)

The Applicable State Law. In most jurisdictions, the law of the state of the domicile of the trust property governs the provisions of the trust agreement. If there is property in multiple states, the state of domicile of the settlor is the law of choice as long as the laws of the states involved have received compliance. (See Figure 7–1, Exhibit 7.)

The Execution. The laws of the state of domicile of the settlor control the formalities of the execution of the trust instrument. As a general procedure, it is advisable to provide for the signatures of the settlor, trustee, witnesses, and an acknowledgment of a notary public (see Figure 7–1, Exhibit 8).

Miscellaneous Provisions. In addition to the various requirements of individual state statutes governing trust agreements, the specific intentions of each settlor will vary, depending upon the nature of the property and the beneficiary. Some optional provisions to provide for a complete agreement may include such areas as:

- definition of terms
- spendthrift provisions
- rule against perpetuities provision
- accounting procedures
- compensation of trustee
- bond of trustee
- transactions with third parties

The length and complexity of the agreement is determined by the individual requirements of the creator of the trust. As always, care should be taken to avoid any ambiguity in providing for the settlor's wishes.

The Revocable Living Trust

A trust created by a settlor during his or her lifetime that reserves the right of revocation of the trust is called a **revocable living trust,** or a *revocable inter*

revocable living trust: A trust created by a settlor during his or her lifetime that reserves the right of revocation of the trust, i.e., the settlor can change, alter, or amend the terms of the agreement during his or her lifetime.

vivos trust. The right of revocation retained by the settlor can take the form of any power to change, alter, or amend the terms of the trust agreement during his or her lifetime. Upon the death of the settlor, the right of revocation is terminated, and the terms of the trust become irrevocable at that time.

Estate planners find the revocable living trust to be a useful planning tool due to its flexibility, and for that reason, it has been termed a *will substitute*. It has certain advantages over a will in that it avoids the expense and delay of probate administration and allows the settlor the power to manage his or her property during his or her lifetime.

The trust instrument used to create a revocable living trust is similar in most respects to the document used to create the irrevocable living trust. The exception comes with the clause referring to the revocable nature of the trust. In such trusts, the settlor usually serves as a cotrustee with another individual. He or she not only exercises the powers of a trustee but also retains the sole right to revoke the trust at any time. The language used to establish the revocable nature of the trust should be clear and unambiguous (see Figure 7–2).

The revocable living trust does not result in tax savings, but it does allow the settlor to maintain control over his or her property until death.

The Testamentary Trust

A trust created by a will and executed with the statutory formalities required by state law is called a **testamentary trust.** Since a will does not become effective until the testator's death, such a conveyance in trust does not become effective until the death of the testator.

Upon the testator's death, the trust becomes effective and operates as a typical trust situation with the property held by the designated trustee for the benefit of a named beneficiary. As with any will, there must be probate administration, which includes the proving of the will prior to its contents taking effect. The validity of the trust arrangement is dependent on the validity of the will itself.

testamentary trust: A trust created by will.

ARTICLE IV

Settlor reserves the power and right by written direction signed by him, and effective on delivery to Trustees, to revoke this instrument and the trust created by it and to receive back from Trustees all the trust property. Upon receipt of such written notice, Trustees shall surrender all trusts properties belonging to the trust estate as described in such notice.

FIGURE 7–2 A sample clause creating a revocable living trust

SUMMARY

- A trust is a basic estate planning tool allowing the creator to distribute his or her property for the benefit of his or her heirs, or any other person or organization, without the delay and expense of probate administration. While the trust property is held by the beneficiary, the property is managed for the benefit of the beneficiary on the basis of the trustee's fiduciary duty. Once the terms of the trust have been satisfied, the beneficiary receives legal title in his or her own name.

- The preparation of the trust instrument requires a careful investigation into the intentions of the creator of the trust to determine the exact distribution. The instrument is an expression in written form of the settlor's intentions, setting forth the specific powers of the trustee and the nature of the beneficiary's equitable interest. The document must declare the primary elements of a trust and set forth its revocability without ambiguity.

IN REVIEW

1. What is the definition of a trust?
2. What are the four elements required to form a valid trust?
3. What is the primary duty of a trustee?
4. What is the nature of the title to the trust corpus held by the beneficiary?
5. What is the distinction between a revocable living trust and an irrevocable living trust?
6. What is the advantage of a revocable living trust?
7. What is the reason for a successor trustee?
8. What state law applies to a trust?
9. What formalities are required in the execution of a trust?
10. What is a testamentary trust?

PUTTING IT ALL TOGETHER

The Industrial Revolution of the nineteenth century brought with it not only the giants of American industry but also the unsung heroes of primitive technology. One such notable was one Ebenezer Coates, full-time horse thief and part-time tinker. Prior to his own hanging, Ebenezer Coates perfected a device for hanging women's outer garments so that their shape was retained. The device was a thin wire formed into a loop in the shape of an isosceles triangle with a hook at the top. With the law about to terminate his gainful employment, Ebenezer had the foresight to patent his device with the United States Patent Office, calling it Coates Hanger. While old Ebenezer was never able to enjoy the economic prosperity resulting from his device, his family was able to take Coates Hanger to the American people where it found immediate acceptance with that buttress of the United States economy, the housewife. It was not long before Coates Hanger became not only a household word, as has occurred with *Kleenex* and *Xerox*, but also the source of a considerable fortune for Ebenezer's heirs.

Today, the Coates family has built upon the entrepreneurial tradition of their infamous heir. Having withstood the obvious threats presented by both plastic and polyester, the family is now on the verge of introducing the world's first digital coat hanger with resident RAM to store personal information relative to the owner's dress size and hygiene. The Coates family fortune is now controlled by Ebenezer Coates IV, affectionately known to the family as "Top."

It is Top's intention to place the entire family fortune in a trust to be administered by his loyal attorney, Larsen S. Hart. Top does not want to relinquish control until his death and does not think that his twin children, Rupert and Gretchen, will be competent to handle their own affairs until they have attained the age of thirty-five.

Top's estate consists of (a) the family home, Upside Downs; (b) one hundred percent of the stock in Coates Hangers, Incorporated; and (c) a substantial stock portfolio with the brokerage firm of Catch & Lynch (because of old Ebenezer—he just could not resist).

Exercises

1. Prepare a testamentary trust, placing Top Coates' entire estate in trust for his children at his death, with Larsen S. Hart as trustee and the firm of Catch & Lynch as successor trustees.

CHAPTER
8

Bankruptcy

But the restructuring of debtor-creditor relations, which is at the core of the federal bankruptcy power, must be distinguished from adjudication of state-created rights . . .

———

NORTHERN PIPELINE CONSTRUCTION CO. V. MARATHON
458 U.S. 50 (1982)

OBJECTIVES

After completing this chapter, you will be able to:

1. Prepare a checklist for an individual bankruptcy
2. Prepare a bankruptcy petition and schedules

BALLENTINE'S REVIEW

bankruptcy—The circumstances of a person who is unable to pay his or her debts as they come due; the system under which a debtor may come into court or be brought into court by his or her creditors, either seeking to have his or her assets administered and sold for the benefit of his or her creditors and to be discharged from his or her debts, or to have his or her debts reorganized.

creditor—A person to whom a debt is owed by a debtor.

debt—An unconditional and legally enforceable obligation for the payment of money; that which is owing under any form of promise, including obligations arising under contract (EXAMPLES: mortgage; installment sale contract) and obligations imposed by law without contract (EXAMPLES: judgment; unliquidated damages).

debtor—A person who owes another person money; a person who owes another person anything.

§ 8.1 THE DEBT

A well-ordered legal environment is based upon the protection of the rights of creditors from the dishonest acts of debtors. The rights of creditors find their origin in the English common law, and are guaranteed in the United States Constitution with its prohibition against any impairment of the obligation of contracts. The law of creditors' rights is based upon the concept that the creditor can claim property of the debtor as payment of the debt.

The Nature of Debt

A **debt** is a fixed obligation owed by one person to another. The obligation most frequently arises out of a matter of contract but also can originate as a result of some legal action that has been reduced to a judgment.

There are three basic elements that constitute a debt. The debt must be:

- *Certain:* The debt must not consist of a contingency but must be certain and presently definable.
- *Liquidated:* The debt must be for a sum certain and not for some sum to be determined at a later date.
- *Enforceable:* The normal process of law must be available for enforcement of the debt.

When all three elements exist, a debt in the legal sense exists, whether based upon a judgment or a contract.

The Debtor-Creditor Relationship

The relationship between a debtor and a creditor arises as a result of the terms of a contract or, in some instances, by operation of law. A *debtor* is one who owes money to another. The one to whom the money is owed is called the *creditor*. If the relationship has arisen as a result of a contractual relationship, the debtor is the party to the contract who has obligated himself or herself to pay money in exchange for receipt of something of value.

The debtor-creditor relationship also may occur as a result of the operation of law. The creditor may achieve the status of a **judgment creditor** by obtaining a money judgment against the debtor upon which the creditor can then force collection. A judgment creditor is called an *execution creditor* in some jurisdictions.

§ 8.2 THE NATURE OF BANKRUPTCY

The realities of our modern commercial environment provide protection for an individual from creditors and for the orderly settlement of his or her obligations. The *bankruptcy* system has evolved to protect both debtor and creditor, equitably balancing their respective interests.

debt: An unconditional and legally enforceable obligation for the payment of money; that which is owing under any form of promise, including obligations arising under contract, e.g., mortgage or installment sale contract, and obligations imposed by law without contract, e.g., judgment or unliquidated damages.

judgment creditor: A creditor who has secured a judgment against his or her debtor that has not been satisfied.

§ 8.3 TYPES OF BANKRUPTCY

The decision to file a proceeding in bankruptcy is one that must be made with the advice of counsel and should not be taken lightly by any individual. Often there are alternate solutions available to the debtor and the creditor short of bankruptcy. These must be carefully explored to decide which of the alternatives, if any, would be in the individual's best interest.

The Voluntary or Involuntary Petition

A proceeding in bankruptcy begins with the filing of a legal pleading in the form of a **petition.** If the filing of the petition is initiated by the debtor under one of the provisions of the Bankruptcy Code, the petition is said to be a **voluntary petition.** If the petition is filed by a creditor that is forcing the debtor into the proceeding, the petition is said to be an **involuntary petition.**

The filing of a petition in bankruptcy has a broad effect. It serves to place the creditors on notice that the debtor is seeking relief under the protection of the court and is attempting to obtain a discharge. The petition also serves as an **automatic stay** of proceedings that may be pending in another court. Upon the filing of a petition in bankruptcy, all actions in other courts are automatically held in abeyance until the matter has been resolved in the bankruptcy court. Any collection efforts against the debtor are barred as of the moment of filing. An additional effect of the filing of a petition is the creation of the estate in bankruptcy at that time. Those assets that are not exempt become the property of the court.

The Bankruptcy Code provides for three basic types of petitions to initiate a proceeding. The three major types of bankruptcy are:

- the Chapter 7 liquidation
- the Chapter 11 reorganization
- the Chapter 13 plan

The Chapter 7 Petition

A petition filed for the liquidation and distribution of the debtor's estate is filed under Chapter 7 of the Bankruptcy Code. This procedure is available to any debtor, whether it is an individual, partnership, or corporation. Under Chapter 7, the trustee collects all nonexempt assets of the debtor, sells or liquidates them, and makes a distribution of the proceeds to the creditors.

Once the liquidation has been accomplished, the debtor may receive a formal *discharge*. Following the issuance of the discharge, the debt is no longer a charge against the debtor or his or her remaining assets, and the debtor is free to resume his or her business and acquire property without interference from prior creditors.

The Chapter 11 Reorganization

Chapter 11 of the Bankruptcy Code involves the use of the concept of a *debtor in possession*. A **debtor in possession** is the legal term used by the

petition: A formal request in writing, addressed to a person or body in a position of authority, signed by a number of persons or by one person; the name given in some jurisdictions to a complaint or other pleading that alleges a cause of action.

voluntary petition: A bankruptcy petition that is initiated by the debtor under one of the provisions of the Bankruptcy Code.

involuntary petition: A bankruptcy petition that is filed by a creditor to force the debtor into a bankruptcy proceeding.

automatic stay: A halt to any proceedings that may be pending in another court, which is effected by the filing of a petition in bankruptcy.

debtor in possession: A debtor who continues to operate his or her business while undergoing a business reorganization under the jurisdiction of the Bankruptcy Court.

code to refer to the retention of the property by the debtor during the pendency of the bankruptcy proceeding. The debtor serves as a fiduciary for the creditors until the conclusion of the matter.

The **reorganization** concept of Chapter 11 refers to the preparation of a plan for restructuring the debt of a business to meet with the approval of the court. Chapter 11 allows the debtor to remain in business and to preserve his or her ongoing operations while the debt is resolved. It also provides relief from the demands of the creditors. If no plan can be developed that is satisfactory to the court, the assets may be liquidated under a Chapter 11 liquidation plan.

The Chapter 13 Adjustment of Debts of an Individual

Similar to the reorganization plan of Chapter 11 for businesses, the wage earner's petition under Chapter 13 allows the individual with regular income to develop a plan of payment of creditors out of his or her income after the filing of the petition. A Chapter 13 petition is a voluntary petition only and may not be initiated by a creditor. Also, Chapter 13 relief is not available to partnerships or corporations. Creditors are paid by the trustee from earned income, allowing the debtor to remain in possession of his or her assets while continuing at regular employment.

§ 8.4 THE BANKRUPTCY PROCEDURE

The bankruptcy case begins with the filing of a petition, either voluntary or involuntary, under one of the three chapters discussed previously. The filing of the petition gives the Bankruptcy Court jurisdiction over the assets of the debtor for liquidation or reorganization and creates an automatic stay of proceedings in any other matter affecting the assets of the debtor.

Following the filing of the petition, the court notifies the creditors of the filing. Those wishing to participate in the distribution or reorganization plan must file their proof of claim. The creditor's claim is submitted to the Bankruptcy Court in the form of a pleading called a "proof of claim." A **proof of claim** is a legal document submitted under oath that sets forth the amount owed and the details forming the basis for the claim. The proof of claim is submitted on the form shown in Figure 8–1.

The proof of claim form can be found in the "Official and Procedural Bankruptcy Forms" that are part of the Federal Rules of Bankruptcy (see section 8.5). The form must be filed within ninety days of the **first meeting of creditors,** which is the initial hearing scheduled by the court to allow the creditors an opportunity to obtain information concerning the debtor. As with any standardized form, the proof of claim form must be tailored to meet the individual creditor's particular situation. The principal amount of the claim, interest, security, and expiration of the debt are factors that vary with each claim.

The **trustee in bankruptcy** is an impartial person elected by the creditors to administer the debtor's estate. If a trustee is not elected by the creditors, one is chosen by the court. The trustee automatically becomes the owner of

reorganization: Chapter 11 of the Bankruptcy Code allows a debtor to restructure the debt of a business in order to remain in business and preserve ongoing operations while the debt is resolved.

proof of claim: In bankruptcy, a statement in writing, signed by a creditor, setting forth the amount owed and the basis of the claim.

first meeting of creditors: The first meeting of creditors of a bankrupt, required for the purpose of allowing the claims of creditors, questioning the bankrupt under oath, and electing a trustee in bankruptcy.

trustee in bankruptcy: A person appointed by a bankruptcy court to collect any amounts owed the debtor, well the debtor's property, and distribute the proceeds among the creditors.

FORM B10 (6-90)

FORM 10. PROOF OF CLAIM

United States Bankruptcy Court _____ District of _____	PROOF OF CLAIM
In re (Name of Debtor)	Case Number

NOTE: This form should not be used to make a claim for an administrative expense arising after the commencement of the case. A "request" of payment of an administrative expense may be filed pursuant to 11 U.S.C. §503.

Name of Creditor (*The person or entity to whom the debtor owes money or property*)

☐ Check box if you are aware that anyone else has filed a proof of claim relating to your claim. Attach copy of statement giving particulars.

Name and Addresses Where Notices Should be Sent

☐ Check box if you have never received any notices from the bankruptcy court in this case.

☐ Check box if the address differs from the address on the envelope sent to you by the court.

Telephone No.

THIS SPACE IS FOR COURT USE ONLY

ACCOUNT OR OTHER NUMBER BY WHICH CREDITOR IDENTIFIES DEBTOR:

Check here if this claim ☐ replaces ☐ amends a previously filed claim, dated_____

1. BASIS FOR CLAIM
☐ Goods sold
☐ Services performed
☐ Money loaned
☐ Personal injury/wrongful death
☐ Taxes
☐ Other (Describe briefly)

☐ Retiree benefits as defined in 11 U.S.C. §1114(a)
☐ Wages, salaries, and compensations (Fill out below)
Your social security number_____
Unpaid compensations for services performed from (date)
_____ to _____ (date)

2. DATE DEBT WAS INCURRED | **3. IF COURT JUDGMENT, DATE OBTAINED**

4. CLASSIFICATION OF CLAIM. Under the Bankruptcy Code all claims are classified as one or more of the following: (1) Unsecured Nonpriority, (2) Unsecured Priority, (3) Secured. It is possible for part of a claim to be in one category and part in another.
CHECK THE APPROPRIATE BOX OR BOXES that best describe your claim and STATE THE AMOUNT OF THE CLAIM.

☐ SECURED CLAIM $_____
Attach evidence of perfection of security interest
Brief Description of Collateral:
☐ Real Estate ☐ Motor Vehicle ☐ Other (Describe briefly)

☐ UNSECURED PRIORITY CLAIM $_____
Specify the priority of the claim.
☐ Wages, salaries, or commissions (up to $2000), earned not more than 90 days before filing of the bankruptcy petition or cessation of the debtor's business, whichever is earlier - 11 U.S.C. §507(a)(3)
☐ Contributions to an employee benefit plan - 11 U.S.C. §507(a)(4)
☐ Up to $900 of deposits toward purchase, lease, or rental of property or services for personal, family, or household use - 11 U.S.C. §507(a)(6)
☐ Taxes or penalties of governmental units - 11 U.S.C. §507(a)(7)
☐ Other - 11 U.S.C. §§507 (a)(2), (a)(5) - (Describe briefly)

Amount of arrearage and other charges included in secured claim above, if any $_____
☐ UNSECURED NONPRIORITY CLAIM $_____
A claim is unsecured if there is no collateral or lien on property of the debtor securing the claim or to the extent that the value of such property is less than the amount of the claim.

5. TOTAL AMOUNT OF CLAIM AT TIME CASE FILED: $_____ (Unsecured) $_____ (Secured) $_____ (Priority) $_____ (Total)
☐ Check this box if claim includes prepetition charges in addition to the principal amount of the claim. Attach itemized statement of all additional charges.

6. CREDITS AND SETOFFS: The amount of all payments on this claim has been credited and deducted for the purpose of making this proof of claim. In filing this claim, claimant has deducted all amounts that claimant owes to debtor.

7. SUPPORTING DOCUMENTS: Attach copies of supporting documents, such as promissory notes, purchase orders, invoices, itemized statements of running accounts, contracts, court judgments, or evidence of security interests. If the documents are not available, explain. If the documents are voluminous, attach a summary.

8. TIME-STAMPED COPY: To receive an acknowledgment of the filing of your claim, enclose a stamped, self-addressed envelope and copy of this proof of claim.

THIS SPACE IS FOR COURT USE ONLY

Date	Sign and print the name and title, if any, of the creditor or other person authorized to file this claim (attach copy of power of attorney, if any).

Penalty for presenting fraudulent claim: Fine of up to $500,000 or imprisonment for up to 5 years, or both. 18 U.S.C. §§152 and 3571.

FIGURE 8–1 The proof of claim form from the Official Forms

the debtor's property that is not considered exempt. A significant power of the trustee is the power to void certain transfers made by the debtor before the filing of the debtor's petition. A **voidable transfer** is one that is made within one year of the filing of the petition with the intent to defraud creditors. The trustee also may void any transfers that have been made by the debtor within ninety days of the filing of the petition to a creditor who receives more than he or she would have received if listed in the petition. Such a transfer is considered to be a **preferential transfer.** Preferential transfers represent the preference by the debtor of one creditor over another, for example, repayment of a loan made by a parent who later is in need.

§ 8.5 THE PREPARATION OF DOCUMENTS

The Bankruptcy Code provides the statutory authority for proceedings in Bankruptcy Court. The United States Supreme Court and the administrator of the United States courts have declared the rules for the implementation of the code in the "Rules of Practice and Procedure in Bankruptcy," frequently referred to as the Federal Rules of Bankruptcy. These rules determine the information required on the various forms as well as the format of the documents. The rules contain the "Official and Procedural Bankruptcy Forms" that provide the content and appearance of the forms.

A Checklist

The checklist is an indispensable tool for the maintenance of a litigation file and the preparation of any legal document. The type of checklist used depends upon the type of case and the complexity of the issues.

Checklists for bankruptcy can be developed in two basic forms:

- a litigation checklist that records the actions to be performed on the case
- a file summary that records the information concerning the client

The litigation checklist is designed to contain an easy reference for the location of information relating to the case. It also serves as a reminder that actions must be taken and of filing deadlines. Each case is unique, and the list must be carefully reviewed for each case. A sample general checklist for the filing of a Chapter 7 petition in bankruptcy is provided in Figure 8–2.

The file summary checklist varies greatly from office to office, depending on the preference of the attorneys. Its function is to provide a quick and easy method to obtain and locate information about a client without having to review multiple sources. The file summary checklist for a bankruptcy petition should include the following:

- debtor's name and address
- social security and/or tax identification number
- prior bankruptcy
- property with a secured interest
- other real property

voidable transfer: A transfer that is made by a debtor, within one year of the filing of a petition for bankruptcy, with the intention and for the purpose of defrauding creditors.

preferential transfer: Under the Bankruptcy Code, a transfer of property by an insolvent debtor to one or more creditors to the exclusion of others, enabling such creditors to obtain a greater percentage of their debt than other creditors of the same class.

```
      Client: _____        File No. _____

      _____   Open file
      _____   Retention letter
      _____   Client summary
      _____   Obtain documents
      _____   Prepare petition
      _____   Prepare schedules
      _____   Prepare statement of financial affairs
      _____   File petition
      _____       _____   Date
      _____       _____   Case no.
      _____   First meeting of creditors
      _____   Trustee: Name and address

      _____   Hearings on motions
      _____   Discharge
```

FIGURE 8–2 A sample litigation checklist

- personal property
- secured debts
- unsecured debts
- priority claims
- exempt property
- current income sources

No single checklist will cover every case. The development of individualized lists is required for certain types of cases. Experience will add to the information contained in each checklist.

The Bankruptcy Forms

The Official Forms contained in the Federal Rules of Bankruptcy provide for the content and appearance of each form to be filed in court. Each local federal court has its own set of rules that should be consulted before the submission of any document.

The Caption. Form 16A of the Official Forms provides the appearance of the caption for any matter filed in the Bankruptcy Court. The caption should include the title of the case and the debtor's name, social security number, and federal tax identification number, if any. The form is to be used on the petition, the notice of the meeting of creditors, and the order of discharge. (See Figure 8–3.)

The Petition. The initiation of a proceeding in bankruptcy occurs with the filing of the petition that is set forth in Official Form 1. The form is self-

---

UNITED STATES BANKRUPTCY COURT
IN THE NORTHERN DISTRICT OF FREMONT

In re WILLIAM DODGE, a/k/a/

WILL DODGE,

                       Debtor   Case No. 123456

                                            Chapter 7

Social Security No. 123-45-6789

_____/

VOLUNTARY PETITION

FIGURE 8–3 A sample caption

explanatory regarding what information is required. The information may be taken from the client information checklist. The purpose of the petition is to inform the court and the creditors of the nature of the allegations. The petition can be either voluntary, pursuant to the dictates of Form 1 (see Figure 8–4), or involuntary, pursuant to Form 5 (see Figure 8–5).

The choice of the proper bankruptcy court for the filing of the petition refers to venue. **Venue** is the term for the geographical location of the proper court in which to file a matter. In bankruptcy, venue is proper if it is in the district in which the debtor resides or has a place of business or in which the debtor's principal assets are located.

Statement of Financial Affairs. Within fifteen days of the filing of a petition in bankruptcy, the debtor must file a "statement of financial affairs" and a "schedule of assets and liabilities." These documents are commonly referred to as the "statements and schedules."

The statement of financial affairs is a questionnaire designed to provide the court with sufficient information to decide if a discharge should be granted. Official Form 7 is the statement of financial affairs for an individual debtor, providing the debtor's sworn answers to the following areas of inquiry:

- Name and residence
- Occupation and income
- Tax returns and refunds
- Financial accounts, certificates of deposit, and safe deposit boxes
- Books and records
- Property held for another person
- Property held by another

venue: The county or judicial district in which a case is to be tried; in bankruptcy, it is the district in which the debtor resides or has a place of business or in which the debtor's principal assets are located.

United States Bankruptcy Court	VOLUNTARY PETITION
District of	

IN RE (Name of debtor-If individual, enter Last, First, Middle)	NAME OF JOINT DEBTOR (Spouse) (Last, First, Middle)

ALL OTHER NAMES used by the debtor in the last 6 years (including married, maiden and trade names)	ALL OTHER NAMES used by the joint debtor in the last 6 years (include married, maiden and trade names)

SOC. SEC./TAX I.D. NO. (If more than one, state all)	SOC. SEC./TAX I.D. NO. (If more than one, state all)

STREET ADDRESS OF DEBTOR (No. and street, city, state, zip)	STREET ADDRESS OF JOINT DEBTOR (No. and street, city, state, zip)
COUNTY OF RESIDENCE OR PRINCIPAL PLACE OF BUSINESS	COUNTY OF RESIDENCE OR PRINCIPAL PLACE OF BUSINESS

MAILING ADDRESS OF DEBTOR (If different from street address)	MAILING ADDRESS OF JOINT DEBTOR (If different from street address)

LOCATION OF PRINCIPAL ASSETS OF BUSINESS DEBTOR (If different from addresses listed above)	VENUE (Check one box)
	☐ Debtor has been domiciled or has had a residence, principal place of business or principal assets in this District for 180 days immediately preceding the date of this petition or for a longer part of such 180 days than in any other District.
	☐ There is a bankruptcy case concerning debtor's affiliate, general partner or partnership pending in this District

INFORMATION REGARDING DEBTOR (Check applicable boxes)

TYPE OF DEBTOR (Check one box)		CHAPTER OR SECTION OF BANKRUPTCY CODE UNDER WHICH THE PETITION IS FILED (Check one box)		
☐ Individual	☐ Corporation Publicly Held			
☐ Joint (H&W)	☐ Corporation Not Publicly Held	☐ Chapter 7	☐ Chapter 11	☐ Chapter 13
☐ Partnership	☐ Municipality	☐ Chapter 9	☐ Chapter 12	☐ §304-Case Ancillary to Foreign Proceeding
☐ Other _____		SMALL BUSINESS (Chapter 11 only)		

NATURE OF DEBT (Check one box)

☐ Non-Business Consumer   ☐ Business - Complete A&B below

☐ Debtor is a small business as defined in 11 U.S.C. §101.

A. TYPE OF BUSINESS (Check one box)

☐ Debtor is and elects to be considered a small business under 11 U.S.C. §1121(e). (optional)

☐ Farming	☐ Transportation	☐ Commodity Broker
☐ Professional	☐ Manufacturing/Mining	☐ Construction
☐ Retail/Wholesale	☐ Stockbroker	☐ Real Estate
☐ Railroad	☐ Other Business	

FILING FEE (Check one box)

☐ Filing fee attached

☐ Filing fee to be paid in installments. (Applicable to individuals only) Must attach signed application for the court's consideration certifying that the debtor is unable to pay fee except in installments. Rule 1006(b); see page K100-07.

B. BRIEFLY DESCRIBE NATURE OF BUSINESS

NAME AND ADDRESS OF LAW FIRM OR ATTORNEY

Telephone No.

STATISTICAL ADMINISTRATIVE INFORMATION (28 U.S.C. §604) (Estimates only) (Check applicable boxes)	NAME(S) OF ATTORNEY(S) DESIGNATED TO REPRESENT THE DEBTOR (Print or Type)
☐ Debtor estimates that funds will be available for distribution to unsecured creditors. ☐ Debtor estimates that after any exempt property is excluded and administrative expenses paid, there will be no funds available for distribution to unsecured creditors.	☐ Debtor is not represented by an attorney. Telephone no. of debtor not represented by an attorney: ( )

ESTIMATED NUMBER OF CREDITORS
☐ 1-15   ☐ 16-49   ☐ 50-99   ☐ 100-199   ☐ 200-999   ☐ 1000-over

ESTIMATED ASSETS (in thousands of dollars)
☐ Under 50   ☐ 50-99   ☐ 100-499   ☐ 500-999   ☐ 1000-9999   ☐ 10,000-99,000   ☐ 100,000-over

ESTIMATED LIABILITIES (in thousands of dollars)
☐ Under 50   ☐ 50-99   ☐ 100-499   ☐ 500-999   ☐ 1000-9999   ☐ 10,000-99,000   ☐ 100,000-over

ESTIMATED NUMBER OF EMPLOYEES - CH 11 & 12 ONLY
☐ 0   ☐ 1-19   ☐ 20-99   ☐ 100-999   ☐ 1000-over

ESTIMATED NO. OF EQUITY HOLDERS - CH 11 & 12 ONLY
☐ 0   ☐ 1-19   ☐ 20-99   ☐ 100-999   ☐ 1000-over

THIS SPACE FOR COURT USE ONLY

E•Z LEGAL FORMS®   K100-4

FIGURE 8–4 Voluntary petition for bankruptcy

Name of Debtor _____

Case No. _____

FILING OF PLAN

For Chapter 9, 11, 12 and 13 cases only. Check appropriate box.

I A copy of debtor's proposed plan dated _____ Is attached.

☐ Debtor intends to file a plan within the time allowed by statute, rule, or order of the court.

PRIOR BANKRUPTCY CASE FILED WITHIN LAST 6 YEARS (If more than one, attach additional sheet)		
Location Where Filed	Case Number	Date Filed

PENDING BANKRUPTCY CASE FILED BY ANY SPOUSE, PARTNER, OR AFFILIATE OF THIS DEBTOR (If more than one, attach additional sheet)		
Name of Debtor	Case Number	Date
Relationship	District	Judge

REQUEST FOR RELIEF

Debtor requests relief in accordance with the chapter of Title 11, United States Code, specified in this petition.

SIGNATURES

ATTORNEY

X_____   _____
Signature   Date

INDIVIDUAL/JOINT DEBTOR(S)	CORPORATE OR PARTNERSHIP DEBTOR
I declare under penalty of perjury that the information provided in this petition is true and correct.	I declare under penalty of perjury that the information provided in this petition is true and correct, and that the filing of the petition on behalf of the debtor has been authorized.
X_____ Signature of Debtor	X_____ Signature of Authorized Individual
_____ Date	_____ Print or Type Name of Authorized Individual
X_____ Signature of Joint Debtor	_____ Title of Individual Authorized by Debtor to File this Petition
_____ Date	_____ Date

EXHIBIT "A" (To be completed if debtor is a corporation requesting relief under Chapter 11.)

☐ Exhibit "A" is attached and made a part of this petition.

TO BE COMPLETED BY INDIVIDUAL CHAPTER 7 DEBTOR WITH PRIMARILY CONSUMER DEBTS (SEE P.L. 98-353 § 322)

I am aware that I may proceed under chapter 7, 11, 12, or 13 of Title 11, United States Code. I understand the relief available under each such chapter, and choose to proceed under Chapter 7 of such title.

If I am represented by an attorney, exhibit "B" has been completed.

X_____   _____
Signature of Debtor   Date

X_____   _____
Signature of Joint Debtor   Date

EXHIBIT "B" (To be completed by attorney for individual Chapter 7 debtor(s) with primarily consumer debts.)

I, the attorney for the debtor(s) named in the foregoing petition, declare that I have informed the debtor(s) that (he, she, or they) may proceed under Chapter 7, 11, 12, or 13 of Title 11, United States Code, and have explained the relief available under each such chapter.

X_____   _____
Signature of Attorney   Date

CERTIFICATION AND SIGNATURE OF NON-ATTORNEY BANKRUPTCY PETITION PREPARER (See 11 U.S.C. § 110)

I certify that I am a bankruptcy petition preparer as defined in 11 U.S.C. § 110, that I have prepared this document for compensation, and that I have provided the debtor with a copy of this document.

Printed or Typed Name of Bankruptcy Petition Preparer

_____

Social Security Number

Names and Social Security Numbers of all other individuals who prepared or assisted in preparing this document:

Address _____   Tel. No. _____

X_____
Signature of Bankruptcy Petition Preparer

If more than one person prepared this document, attach additional signed sheets conforming to the appropriate Official Form for each person.

A bankruptcy petition preparer's failure to comply with the provisions of Title 11 and the Federal Rules of Bankruptcy Procedure may result in fines or imprisonment or both. 11 U.S.C. § 110; 18 U.S.C. § 156.

E•Z LEGAL FORMS®   K100-5

FIGURE 8–4 (continued)

UNITED STATES BANKRUPTCY COURT
_____ DISTRICT OF _____

In re _____

                             Debtor   Case No. _____

                                                     Chapter _____

Exhibit "A" to Voluntary Petition

1. Debtor's employer identification number is _____.

2. If any of debtor's securities are registered under section 12 of the Securities and Exchange Act of 1934, the SEC file number is _____.

3. The following financial data is the latest available information and refers to debtor's condition on _____.

		Approximate number of holders
a. Total assets	$_____	
b. Total liabilities	$_____	
Fixed, liquidated secured debt	$_____	_____
Contingent secured debt	$_____	_____
Disputed secured claims	$_____	_____
Unliquidated secured debt	$_____	_____

		Approximate number of holders
Fixed, liquidated unsecured debt	$_____	_____
Contingent unsecured debt	$_____	_____
Disputed unsecured claims	$_____	_____
Unliquidated unsecured debt	$_____	_____
Number of shares of preferred stock	_____	_____
Number of shares of common stock	_____	_____

Comments, if any: _____
_____
_____
_____

4. Brief description of debtor's business: _____
_____
_____

(Continued on next sheet)

FIGURE 8–4 (continued)

5. List the name of any person who directly or indirectly owns, controls, or holds, with power to vote, 20% or more of the voting securities of debtor:_____
_____
_____
_____

6. List the names of all corporations of which 20% or more of the outstanding voting securities are directly or indirectly owned, controlled, or held, with power to vote, by debtor:_____
_____
_____
_____

DECLARATION UNDER PENALTY OF PERJURY
ON BEHALF OF A CORPORATION OR PARTNERSHIP

I [the president *or* other officer *or* an authorized agent of the corporation] [*or* a member *or* an authorized agent of the partnership] named as the debtor in this case, declare under penalty of perjury that I have read the foregoing Exhibit "A" and that it is true and correct to the best of my information and belief.

Date _____

Signature _____

_____
(Print Name and Title)

FIGURE 8–4 (continued)

FORM B5 (6-90)

FORM 5. INVOLUNTARY PETITION

United States Bankruptcy Court	INVOLUNTARY
_____ District of _____	PETITION

IN RE (Name of debtor - If individual, enter: Last, First, Middle)

ALL OTHER NAMES used by debtor in the last 6 years (Include married, maiden and trade names)

SOC. SEC./TAX I.D. NO. (If more than one, state all)

STREET ADDRESS OF DEBTOR (No. and street, city, state and zip code)

MAILING ADDRESS OF DEBTOR (If different from street address)

COUNTY OR RESIDENCE OR PRINCIPAL PLACE OF BUSINESS

LOCATION OF PRINCIPAL ASSETS OF BUSINESS DEBTOR (If different from previously listed addresses)

CHAPTER OF BANKRUPTCY CODE UNDER WHICH PETITION IS FILED

☐ Chapter 7   ☐ Chapter 11

INFORMATION REGARDING DEBTOR (Check applicable boxes)

Petitioners believe

☐ Debts are primarily consumer debts

☐ Debts are primarily business debts (Complete sections A and B)

TYPE OF DEBTOR

☐ Individual   ☐ Corporation Publicly Held

☐ Partnership   ☐ Corporation Not Publicly Held

☐ Other _____

A. TYPE OF BUSINESS (Check one)

☐ Professional   ☐ Transportation   ☐ Commodity Broker

☐ Retail/Wholesale   ☐ Manufacturing/Mining   ☐ Construction

☐ Railroad   ☐ Stockbroker   ☐ Real Estate

☐ Other _____

B. BRIEFLY DESCRIBE NATURE OF BUSINESS

VENUE

☐ Debtor has been domiciled or has had a residence, principal place of business, or principal assets in the District for 180 days immediately preceding the date of this petition or for a longer part of such 180 days than in any other District.

☐ A bankruptcy case concerning debtor's affiliate, general partner or partnership is pending in this District.

PENDING BANKRUPTCY CASE FILED BY OR AGAINST ANY PARTNER OR AFFILIATE OF THIS DEBTOR (Report information for any additional cases on attached sheets.)

Name of Debtor	Case Number	Date
Relationship	District	Judge

ALLEGATIONS
(Check applicable boxes)

COURT USE ONLY

1. ☐ Petitioner(s) are eligible to file this petition pursuant to 11 U.S.C. §303(b).

2. ☐ The debtor is a person against whom an order for relief may be entered under title 11 of the United States Code.

3.a. ☐ The debtor is generally not paying such debtor's debts as they become due, unless such debts are the subject of a bona fide dispute;

or

b. ☐ Within 120 days preceding the filing of this petition, a custodian, other than a trustee, receiver, or agent appointed or authorized to take charge of less than substantially all of the property of the debtor for the purpose of enforcing a lien against such property, was appointed or took possession.

FIGURE 8–5 Involuntary petition for bankruptcy

- Prior bankruptcy
- Receiverships, general assignments, and other modes of liquidation
- Suits, executions, and attachments
- Payment of loans, installment purchases, and other debts
- Setoffs
- Transfers of property
- Repossessions and returns
- Losses
- Payments and transfers to attorneys

The document is executed by the debtor with a statement that the answers to the questions are true to the best of his or her knowledge under penalty of perjury. Figure 8–6 contains Official Form 8, the statement of financial affairs for a debtor engaged in business.

The Schedules. Official Form 6 contains the **schedules,** which, read as a composite, form a general financial statement of the debtor. Assets are separated as to specific type, and liabilities are listed according to their priority. The debtor's exemptions are also listed to complete the picture.

Schedule A provides a list of the real property of the debtor. All real property is listed, even though some of the property may be exempt by statute. Leases are not included in this schedule but are represented in Schedule G, which itemizes contracts and leases. (See Figure 8–7.)

Schedule B provides a list of the personal property of the debtor. The form contains thirty-three separate items describing the various types of personal property that the debtor may possess constituting his or her estate. The column designated "NONE" must be marked with an "X" if the debtor does not possess such property. If additional space is required, exhibits may be attached to the schedule as long as they are reflected in the total. (See Figure 8–8.)

Schedule C itemizes the property that the debtor claims as exempt. It is important to note here that each exempt item should be identified *and* the corresponding statutory provisions allowing the exemption should be cited. There will be a divergence between the value of the exemption allowed by statute and the market value of the asset as shown in the form. (See Figure 8–9.)

Schedule D provides a list of creditors that hold a secured interest in any property of the debtor. The creditors should be listed in alphabetical order, followed by an identification of the nature of the collateral. The schedule will reflect the debtor's equity in the property. (See Figure 8–10.)

Schedule E lists those creditors that have a priority claim that is not secured by any property interest. The priority of claims is set forth in section 507 of the Bankruptcy Code. The amounts reflected as the indebtedness should be as close an approximation of the amount owed as possible. Inaccuracies will not affect the dischargeability of the debt. (See Figure 8–11.)

Schedule F provides an itemization of the unsecured creditors that do not have any priority claim. The creditors should be listed alphabetically with an approximation of the amount owed. Failure to list a creditor means that there will be no discharge of that debt. (See Figure 8–12.)

Schedule G presents the debtor's obligations on any contracts or leases. It also serves to cover any contracts under which the debtor may be owed monies, constituting an asset. (See Figure 8–13.)

schedules: Pages attached to a document listing additional details relating to the matter contained in the main document.

STATEMENT OF FINANCIAL AFFAIRS OF DEBTOR
ENGAGED IN BUSINESS

1. *Nature, location, and name of business.*

   a. Under what name and where do you carry on your business?

   b. In what business are you engaged?

   c. When did you commence your business?

   d. Where else, and under what other names, have you carried on business within the six years immediately preceding the filing of the original petition herein?

2. *Books and records.*

   a. By whom, or under whose supervision, have your books of account and records been kept during the six years immediately preceding the filing of the original petition herein?

   b. By whom have your books of account and records been audited during the six years immediately preceding the filing of the original petition herein?

   c. In whose possession are your books of account and records?

   d. If any of these books or records are not available, explain.

   e. Have any books of account or records relating to your affairs been destroyed, lost, or otherwise disposed of within the two years immediately preceding the filing of the original petition herein?

3. *Financial statements.* Have you issued any written financial statements within the two years immediately preceding the filing of the original petition herein?

4. *Inventories.*

   a. When was the last inventory of your property taken?

   b. By whom, or under whose supervision, was this inventory taken?

   c. What was the amount, in dollars, of the inventory?

   d. When was the next prior inventory of your property taken?

   e. By whom, or under whose supervision, was this inventory taken?

   f. What was the amount, in dollars, of the inventory?

   g. In whose possession are the records of the two inventories above referred to?

5. *Income other than from operation of business.* What amount of income, other than from operation of your business, have you received during each of the two years immediately preceding the filing of the original petition herein?

FIGURE 8–6 Statement of Financial Affairs

6. *Tax returns and refunds.*

   a. In whose possession are copies of your federal, state, and municipal income tax returns for the three years immediately preceding the filing of the original petition herein?

   b. What tax refunds (income or other) have you received during the two years immediately preceding the filing of the original petition herein?

   c. To what tax refunds (income or other), if any, are you, or may you be, entitled?

7. *Financial accounts, certificates of deposit, and safe deposit boxes.*

   a. What accounts or certificates of deposit or shares in banks, savings and loan, thrift, building and loan, and homestead associations, credit unions, brokerage houses, pension funds, and the like have you maintained, alone or together with any other person, and in your own or any other name, within the two years immediately preceding the filing of the original petition herein?

   b. What safe deposit box or boxes or other depository or depositories have you kept or used for your securities, cash, or other valuables within the two years immediately preceding the filing of the original petition herein?

8. *Property held for another.* What property do you hold for any other person?

9. *Property held by another person.* Is any other person holding anything of value in which you have an interest?

10. *Prior bankruptcy procedures.* What cases under the Bankruptcy Act or title 11, United States Code, have previously been brought by or against you?

11. *Receiverships, general assignments, and other modes of liquidation.*

    a. Was any of your property, at the time of the filing of the original petition herein, in the hands of a receiver, trustee, or other liquidating agent?

    b. Have you made any assignment of your property for the benefit of your creditors, or any general settlement with your creditors, within the two years immediately preceding the filing of the original petition herein?

12. *Suits, executions, and attachments.*

    a. Were you a party to any suit pending at the time of the filing of the original petition herein?

    b. Were you a party to any suit terminated within the year immediately preceding the filing of the original petition herein?

FIGURE 8–6 (continued)

    c. Has any of your property been attached, garnished, or seized under any legal or equitable process within the year immediately preceding the filing of the original petition herein?

13. a. *Payments of loans, installment purchases, and other debts.* What payments in whole or in part have you made during the year immediately preceding the filing of the original petition herein on any of the following: (1) loans; (2) installment purchases of goods and services; (3) other debts?

    b. *Setoffs.* What debts have you owed to any creditor, including any bank, which were setoff by that creditor against a debt or deposit owing by the creditor to you during the year immediately preceding the filing of the original petition herein?

14. *Transfers of property.*

    a. Have you made any gifts, other than ordinary and usual presents to family members and charitable donations, during the year immediately preceding the filing of the original petition herein?

    b. Have you made any other transfer, absolute or for the purpose of security, or any other disposition that was not in the ordinary course of business during the year immediately preceding the filing of the original petition herein?

15. *Accounts and other receivables.* Have you assigned, either absolutely or as security, any of your accounts or other receivables during the year immediately preceding the filing of the original petition herein?

16. *Repossession and returns.* Has any property been returned to, or repossessed by, the seller, lessor, or a secured party during the year immediately preceding the filing of the original petition herein?

17. *Business leases.* If you are a tenant of business property, what is the name and address of your landlord, the amount of your rental, the date to which rent had been paid at the time of the filing of the original petition herein, and the amount of security held by the landlord?

18. *Losses.*

    a. Have you suffered any losses from fire, theft, or gambling during the year immediately preceding the filing of the original petition herein?

    b. Was the loss covered in whole or in part by insurance?

19. *Withdrawals.*

    a. If you are an individual proprietor of your business, what personal withdrawals of any kind have you made from the business during the year immediately preceding the filing of the original petition herein?

FIGURE 8–6 (continued)

b. If the debtor is a partnership or corporation, what withdrawals, in any form (including compensation, bonuses, or loans), have been made or received by any member of the partnership, or by any officer, director, insider, managing executive, or shareholder of the corporation, during the year immediately preceding the filing of the original petition herein?

20. *Payments or transfers to attorneys and other persons.*

a. Have you consulted an attorney during the year immediately preceding the filing of the original petition herein?

b. Have you, during the year immediately preceding or since the filing of the original petition herein, paid any money or transferred any property to the attorney, to any other person on the attorney's behalf, or to any other person rendering services to you in connection with this case?

c. Have you, either during the year immediately preceding or since the filing of the original petition herein, agreed to pay any money or transfer any property to any attorney-at-law, to any other person on the attorney's behalf, or to any other person rendering services to you in connection with this case?

21. *Members of partnership: officers, directors, managers, and principal stockholders of corporation.*

a. What is the name and address of each member of the partnership, or the name, title, and address of each officer, director, insider, and managing executive, and of each stockholder holding 20% or more of the issued and outstanding stock of the corporation?

b. During the year immediately preceding the filing of the original petition herein, has any member withdrawn from the partnership, or any officer, director, insider, or managing executive of the corporation terminated his or her relationship, or any stockholder holding 20% or more of the issued stock disposed of more than 50% of those stockholder's holdings?

c. Has any person acquired or disposed of 20% or more of the stock of the corporation during the year immediately preceding the filing of the petition?

    I, _____, declare under penalty of perjury that I have read the answers contained in the foregoing statement of affairs and that they are true and correct to the best of my knowledge, information, and belief.

    Executed on _____.

                        Signature _____

FIGURE 8–6 (continued)

In re_____,   Case No._____
                          Debtor   (If known)

SCHEDULE A - REAL PROPERTY

Except as directed below, list all real property in which the debtor has any legal, equitable, or future interest, including all property owned as a co-tenant, community property, or in which the debtor has a life estate. Include any property in which the debtor holds rights and powers exercisable for the debtor's own benefit. If the debtor is married, state whether husband, wife, or both own the property by placing an "H," "W," "J," or "C" in the column labeled "Husband, Wife, Joint, Or Community." If the debtor holds no interest in real property, write "None" under "Description and Location of Property."

Do not include interests in executory contracts and unexpired leases on this schedule. List them in Schedule G - Executory Contracts and Unexpired Leases.

If an entity claims to have a lien or hold a secured interest in any property, state the amount of the secured claim. See Schedule D. If no entity claims to hold a secured interest in the property, write "None" in the column labeled "Amount of Secured Claim."

If the debtor is an individual or if a joint petition is filed, state the amount of any exemption claimed in the property only in Schedule C - Property Claimed as Exempt.

DESCRIPTION AND LOCATION OF PROPERTY	NATURE OF DEBTOR'S INTEREST IN PROPERTY	HUSBAND, WIFE, JOINT OR COMMUNITY	CURRENT MARKET VALUE OF DEBTOR'S INTEREST IN PROPERTY, WITHOUT DEDUCTING ANY SECURED CLAIM OR EXEMPTION	AMOUNT OF SECURED CLAIM
		Total ->	$	

(Report also on Summary of Schedules.)

E-Z LEGAL FORMS®   K100-10

FIGURE 8–7 Schedule A—Real Property

In re_____,   Case No._____
                    Debtor   (If known)

SCHEDULE B - PERSONAL PROPERTY

Except as directed below, list all personal property of the debtor of whatever kind. If the debtor has no property in one or more of the categories, place an "X" in the appropriate position in the column labeled "None." If additional space is needed in any category, attach a separate sheet properly identified with the case name, and the number of the category. If the debtor is married, state whether husband, wife, or both own the property by placing an "H," "W," "J," or "C" in the column labeled "Husband, Wife, Joint, or Community." If the debtor is an individual or a joint petition is filed, state the amount of any exemptions claimed only in Schedule C - Property Claimed as Exempt.

Do not list interests in executory contracts and unexpired leases on this schedule. List them in Schedule G - Executory Contracts and Unexpired Leases.

If the property is being held for the debtor by someone else, state that person's name and address under "Description and Location of Property."

TYPE OF PROPERTY	NONE	DESCRIPTION AND LOCATION OF PROPERTY	HUSBAND, WIFE, JOINT OR COMMUNITY	CURRENT MARKET VALUE OF DEBTOR'S INTEREST IN PROPERTY, WITH- OUT DEDUCTING ANY SECURED CLAIM OR EXEMPTION
1. Cash on hand.				
2. Checking, savings or other financial accounts, certificates of deposit, or shares in banks, savings and loan, thrift, building and loan, and homestead associations, or credit unions, brokerage houses, or cooperatives.				
3. Security deposits with public utilities, telephone companies, landlords, and others.				
4. Household goods and furnishings, including audio, video, and computer equipment.				
5. Books; pictures and other art objects; antiques; stamp, coin, record, tape, compact disc, and other collections or collectibles.				
6. Wearing apparel.				
7. Furs and jewelry.				
8. Firearms and sports, photographic, and other hobby equipment.				
9. Interests in insurance policies. Name insurance company of each policy and itemize surrender or refund value of each.				
10. Annuities. Itemize and name each issuer.				

E-Z LEGAL FORMS®   K100-11A

FIGURE 8–8 Schedule B—Personal Property

In re_____,   Case No._____
                    Debtor   (If known)

SCHEDULE B - PERSONAL PROPERTY
(Continuation Sheet)

TYPE OF PROPERTY	NONE	DESCRIPTION AND LOCATION OF PROPERTY	HUSBAND, WIFE, JOINT OR COMMUNITY	CURRENT MARKET VALUE OF DEBTOR'S INTEREST IN PROPERTY, WITHOUT DEDUCTING ANY SECURED CLAIM OR EXEMPTION
11. Interests in IRA, ERISA, Keogh, or other pension or profit sharing Plans. Itemize.				
12. Stock and interests in incorporated and unincorporated businesses. Itemize.				
13. Interests in partnerships or joint ventures. Itemize.				
14. Government and corporate bonds and other negotiable and nonnegotiable instruments.				
15. Accounts Receivable.				
16. Alimony, maintenance, support, and property settlements to which the debtor is or may be entitled. Give particulars.				
17. Other liquidated debts owing debtor including tax refunds. Give particulars.				
18. Equitable or future interests, life estates, and rights or powers exercisable for the benefit of the debtor other than those listed in Schedule of Real Property.				
19. Contingent and non-contingent interests in estate of a decedent, death benefit plan, life insurance policy, or trust.				
20. Other contingent and unliquidated claims of every nature, including tax refunds, counterclaims of the debtor, and rights to setoff claims. Give estimated value of each.				
21. Patents, copyrights, and other intellectual property. Give particulars.				
22. Licenses, franchises, and other general intangibles. Give particulars.				

E-Z LEGAL FORMS®   K100-11B

FIGURE 8–8 (continued)

In re_____ , Case No._____
　　　　　　Debtor　　　　　　　　　　　　　　　　　　　　　　　　　　(If known)

SCHEDULE B - PERSONAL PROPERTY
(Continuation Sheet)

TYPE OF PROPERTY	NONE	DESCRIPTION AND LOCATION OF PROPERTY	HUSBAND, WIFE, JOINT OR COMMUNITY	CURRENT MARKET VALUE OF DEBTOR'S INTEREST IN PROPERTY, WITH-OUT DEDUCTING ANY SECURED CLAIM OR EXEMPTION
23. Automobiles, trucks, trailers, and other vehicles and accessories.				
24. Boats, motors, and accessories.				
25. Aircraft and accessories.				
26. Office equipment, furnishings, and supplies.				
27. Machinery, fixtures, equipment, and supplies used in business.				
28. Inventory.				
29. Animals.				
30. Crops - growing or harvested. Give particulars.				
31. Farming equipment and implements.				
32. Farm supplies, chemicals, and feed.				
33. Other personal property of any kind not already listed. Itemize.				
		_____ continuation sheets attached　　Total　->		$

(Include amounts from any continuation sheets attached. Report total also on Summary of Schedules.)

FIGURE 8–8 (continued)

In re_____, Case No._____

Debtor   (If known)

SCHEDULE C - PROPERTY CLAIMED AS EXEMPT

Debtor elects the exemptions to which debtor is entitled under:

(Check one box)

☐ 11 U.S.C. § 522(b)(1): Exemptions provided in 11 U.S.C. § 522(d). **Note: These exemptions are available only in certain states.**

☐ 11 U.S.C. § 522(b)(2): Exemptions available under applicable nonbankruptcy federal laws, state or local law where the debtor's domicile has been located for the 180 days immediately preceding the filing of the petition, or for a longer portion of the 180-day period than in any other place, and the debtor's interest as a tenant by the entirety or joint tenant to the extent the interest is exempt from process under applicable nonbankruptcy law.

DESCRIPTION OF PROPERTY	SPECIFY LAW PROVIDING EACH EXEMPTION	VALUE OF CLAIMED EXEMPTION	CURRENT MARKET VALUE OF PROPERTY WITHOUT DEDUCTING EXEMPTION

E-Z LEGAL FORMS®   K100-12

FIGURE 8–9 Schedule C—Property Claimed as Exempt

In re_____,   Case No._____
                    Debtor   (If known)

SCHEDULE D - CREDITORS HOLDING SECURED CLAIMS

State the name, mailing address, including zip code, and account number, if any, of all entities holding claims secured by property of the debtor as of the date of filing of the petition. List creditors holding all types of secured interests such as judgment liens, garnishments, statutory liens, mortgages, deeds of trust, and other security interests. List creditors in alphabetical order to the extent practicable. If all secured creditors will not fit on this page, use the continuation sheet provided.

If any entity other than a spouse in a joint case may be jointly liable on a claim, place an "X" in the column labeled "Codebtor," include the entity on the appropriate schedule of creditors, and complete Schedule H - Codebtors. If a joint petition is filed, state whether husband, wife, both of them, or the marital community may be liable on each claim by placing an "H," "W," "J," or "C" in the column labeled "Husband, Wife, Joint, or Community."

If the claim is contingent, place an "X" in the column labeled "Contingent." If the claim is unliquidated, place an "X" in the column labeled "Unliquidated." If the claim is disputed, place an "X" in the column labeled "Disputed." (You may need to place an "X" in more than one of these three columns.)

Report the total of all claims listed on this schedule in the box labeled "Total" on the last sheet of the completed schedule. Report this total also on the Summary of Schedules.

☐ Check this box if debtor has no creditors holding secured claims to report on this Schedule D.

CREDITOR'S NAME AND MAILING ADDRESS INCLUDING ZIP CODE	CODEBTOR	HUSBAND,WIFE,JOINT OR COMMUNITY	DATE CLAIM WAS INCURRED, NATURE OF LIEN, AND DESCRIPTION AND MARKET VALUE OF PROPERTY SUBJECT TO LIEN	CONTINGENT	UNLIQUIDATED	DISPUTED	AMOUNT OF CLAIM WITHOUT DEDUCTING VALUE OF COLLATERAL	UNSECURED PORTION, IF ANY
ACCOUNT NO.								
			VALUE $					
ACCOUNT NO.								
			VALUE $					
ACCOUNT NO.								
			VALUE $					
ACCOUNT NO.								
			VALUE $					

Subtotal -> (Total of this page) $_____
Total -> (Use only on last page) $_____

_____ continuation sheets attached

(Report total also on Summary of Schedules)

E-Z LEGAL FORMS®   K100-13A

Figure 8–10 Schedule D—Creditors Holding Secured Claims

In re_____, Case No._____
      Debtor   (If known)

SCHEDULE D - CREDITORS HOLDING SECURED CLAIMS
(Continuation Sheet)

CREDITOR'S NAME AND MAILING ADDRESS INCLUDING ZIP CODE	CODEBTOR	HUSBAND,WIFE,JOINT OR COMMUNITY	DATE CLAIM WAS INCURRED, NATURE OF LIEN, AND DESCRIPTION AND MARKET VALUE OF PROPERTY SUBJECT TO LIEN	CONTINGENT	UNLIQUIDATED	DISPUTED	AMOUNT OF CLAIM WITHOUT DEDUCTING VALUE OF COLLATERAL	UNSECURED PORTION, IF ANY
ACCOUNT NO.			VALUE $					
ACCOUNT NO.			VALUE $					
ACCOUNT NO.			VALUE $					
ACCOUNT NO.			VALUE $					
ACCOUNT NO.			VALUE $					

Sheet no. ____ of ____ continuation sheets attached to Schedule of Creditors Holding Secured Claims

Subtotal -> $ (Total of this page)
Total -> $ (Use only on last page)

(Report total also on Summary of Schedules)

E-Z LEGAL FORMS®   K100-13B

FIGURE 8–10 (continued)

In re: _____,   Case No._____
              Debtor(s)   (if known)

SCHEDULE E - CREDITORS HOLDING UNSECURED PRIORITY CLAIMS

☐ Check this box if debtor has no creditors holding unsecured claims to report on this Schedule E.

TYPE OF PRIORITY CLAIMS (Check the appropriate box(es) below if claims in that category are listed on the attached sheets)

☐ **Extensions of credit in an involuntary case** Claims arising in the ordinary course of the debtor's business or financial affairs after the commencement of the case but before the earlier of the appointment of a trustee or the order for relief. 11 U.S.C. §507 (a)(2).

☐ **Wages, salaries, and commissions** Wages, salaries, and commissions, including vacation, severance, and sick leave pay owing to employees, and commissions owing to qualifying independent sales representatives up to $4,000* per person, earned within 90 days immediately preceding the filing of the original petition or the cessation of business, whichever occurred first, to the extent provided in 11 U.S.C. §507 (a)(3).

☐ **Contributions to employee benefit plans** Money owed to employee benefit plans for services rendered within 180 days immediately preceding the filing of the original petition or the cessation of business, whichever occurred first, to the extent provided in 11 U.S.C. §507 (a)(4).

☐ **Certain farmers and fishermen** Claims of certain farmers and fishermen, up to $4,000* per farmer or fisherman, against the debtor, as provided in 11 U.S.C. § 507 (a)(5).

☐ **Deposits by individuals** Claims of individuals up to $1,800* for deposits for the purchase, lease, or rental of property or services for personal, family, or household use that were not delivered or provided. 11 U.S.C. §507 (a)(6).

☐ **Alimony, Maintenance, or Support** Claims of a spouse, former spouse, or child of the debtor for alimony, maintenance, or support, to the extent provided in 11 U.S.C. §507 (a)(7).

☐ **Taxes and Certain Other Debts Owed to Governmental Units** Taxes, customs duties, and penalties owing to federal, state, and local governmental units as set forth in 11 U.S.C. §507 (a)(8).

☐ **Commitments to Maintain the Capital of an Insured Depository Institution** Claims based on commitments to the FDIC, RTC, Director of the Office of Thrift Supervision, Comptroller of the Currency, or Board of Governors of the Federal Reserve System, or their predecessors or successors, to maintain the capital of an insured depository institution. 11 U.S.C. §507 (a)(9).

❋ Amounts are subject to adjustment on April 1, 1998, and every three years thereafter with respect to cases commenced on or after the date of adjustment.

CREDITOR'S NAME AND MAILING ADDRESS INCLUDING ZIP CODE	CODEBTOR	HWJC	DATE CLAIM WAS INCURRED AND CONSIDERATION FOR CLAIM	CUD*	TOTAL AMOUNT OF CLAIM	AMOUNT ENTITLED TO PRIORITY
A/C#						
A/C#						
A/C#						
A/C#						
A/C#						

_____ Continuation sheets attached.   Subtotal -> (Total of this page) $ _____

Total -> (use only on last page of the completed Schedule E) $ _____

*If contingent, enter C; if unliquidated, enter U; if disputed, enter D.   (Report total also on Summary of Schedules)

E•Z LEGAL FORMS®   K100-14A

FIGURE 8–11 Schedule E—Creditors Holding Unsecured Priority Claims

In re_____ ,   Case No._____
                          Debtor   (If known)

SCHEDULE E - CREDITORS HOLDING UNSECURED PRIORITY CLAIMS
(Continuation sheet)

TYPE OF PRIORITY

CREDITOR'S NAME AND MAILING ADDRESS INCLUDING ZIP CODE	CODEBTOR	HUSBAND,WIFE,JOINT OR COMMUNITY	DATE CLAIM WAS INCURRED AND CONSIDERATION	CONTINGENT	UNLIQUIDATED	DISPUTED	TOTAL AMOUNT OF CLAIM	AMOUNT ENTITLED TO PRIORITY
ACCOUNT NO.								
ACCOUNT NO.								
ACCOUNT NO.								
ACCOUNT NO.								
ACCOUNT NO.								

Sheet no._____of_____sheets attached to Schedule of Creditors Holding Unsecured Priority Claims

Subtotal -> $____
(Total of this page)
Total -> $____
(Use only on last page of the completed Schedule E.)

(Report total also on Summary of Schedules)

E-Z LEGAL FORMS®   K100-14B

FIGURE 8-11 (continued)

In re_____,   Case No._____
                        Debtor   (If Known)

SCHEDULE F - CREDITORS HOLDING UNSECURED NONPRIORITY CLAIMS

State the name, mailing address, including zip code, and account number, if any, of all entities holding unsecured claims without priority against the debtor or the property of the debtor, as of the date of filing of the petition. Do not include claims listed in Schedules D and E. If all creditors will not fit on this page, use the continuation sheet provided.

If any entity other than a spouse in a joint case may be jointly liable on a claim, place an"X" in the column labeled "Codebtor," include the entity on the appropriate schedule of creditors, and complete Schedule H - Codebtors. If a joint petition is filed, state whether husband, wife, both of them, or the marital community may be liable on each claim by placing an "H," "W," "J," or "C" in the column labeled "Husband, Wife, Joint, or Community."

If the claim is contingent, place an "X" in the column labeled "Contingent." If the claim is unliquidated, place an"X" in the column labeled "Unliquidated." If the claim is disputed, place an "X" in the column labeled "Disputed." (You may need to place an"X" in more than one of these three columns.)

Report total of all claims listed on this schedule in the box labeled "Total" on the last sheet of the completed schedule. Report this total also on the Summary of Schedules.

☐ Check this box if debtor has no creditors holding unsecured nonpriority claims to report on this Schedule F.

CREDITOR'S NAME AND MAILING ADDRESS INCLUDING ZIP CODE	CODEBTOR	HUSBAND,WIFE,JOINT OR COMMUNITY	DATE CLAIM WAS INCURRED AND CONSIDERATION FOR CLAIM. IF CLAIM IS SUBJECT TO SETOFF, SO STATE	CONTINGENT	UNLIQUIDATED	DISPUTED	AMOUNT OF CLAIM
ACCOUNT NO.							
ACCOUNT NO.							
ACCOUNT NO.							
ACCOUNT NO.							

_____ Continuation sheets attached

Subtotal - > (Total of this page) $ _____

Total - > (Use only on last page of the completed Schedule F) $ _____

(Report total also on Summary of Schedules)

K100-15A

FIGURE 8–12 Schedule F—Creditors Holding Unsecured Nonpriority Claims

In re _____ , Case No. _____
(Debtor)   (If known)

SCHEDULE F - CREDITORS HOLDING UNSECURED NONPRIORITY CLAIMS
(Continuation Sheet)

CREDITOR'S NAME AND MAILING ADDRESS INCLUDING ZIP CODE	CODEBTOR	HUSBAND,WIFE,JOINT OR COMMUNITY	DATE CLAIM WAS INCURRED AND CONSIDERATION FOR CLAIM. IF CLAIM IS SUBJECT TO SETOFF, SO STATE	CONTINGENT	UNLIQUIDATED	DISPUTED	AMOUNT OF CLAIM
ACCOUNT NO.							
ACCOUNT NO.							
ACCOUNT NO.							
ACCOUNT NO.							
ACCOUNT NO.							

Sheet no. _____ of _____ sheets attached to Schedule of
Creditors Holding Unsecured Nonpriority Claims

Subtotal - > $ _____
(Total of this page)

Total - > $ _____
(Use only on last page of the completed Schedule F)

(Report total also on Summary of Schedule)

E-Z LEGAL FORMS®   K100-15B

FIGURE 8-12 (continued)

In re_____,   Case No._____

                       Debtor   (If known)

SCHEDULE G. EXECUTORY CONTRACTS AND UNEXPIRED LEASES

    Describe all executory contracts of any nature and all unexpired leases of real or personal property. Include any timeshare interests.

    State nature of debtor's interest in contract, i.e., "Purchaser," "Agent," etc. State whether debtor is the lessor or lessee of a lease.

    Provide the names and complete mailing addresses of all other parties to each lease or contract described.

    NOTE: A party listed on this schedule will not receive notice of the filing of this case unless the party is also scheduled in the appropriate schedule of creditors.

☐   Check this box if debtor has no executory contracts or unexpired leases.

NAME AND MAILING ADDRESS, INCLUDING ZIP CODE, OF OTHER PARTIES TO LEASE OR CONTRACT.	DESCRIPTION OF CONTRACT OR LEASE AND NATURE OF DEBTOR'S INTEREST. STATE WHETHER LEASE IS FOR NONRESIDENTIAL REAL PROPERTY. STATE CONTRACT NUMBER OF ANY GOVERNMENT CONTRACT.

E-Z LEGAL FORMS®   K100-16

FIGURE 8–13 Schedule G—Executory Contracts and Unexpired Leases

Schedule H itemizes any situations in which the debtor is a co-obligor on any debt or obligation. (See Figure 8–14.)

Schedule I provides information about the debtor's current monthly income and his or her dependency status. The schedule also contains information regarding the debtor's spouse's income, providing a clear picture of the family financial status. (See Figure 8–15.)

Schedule J completes the debtor's financial picture with the listing of his or her monthly expenditures. (See Figure 8–16.)

The schedules also include a document called a "summary of schedules," which is a one-page form containing a list of the various schedules submitted. The summary includes totals of the debtor's assets and liabilities. (See Figure 8–17.)

A "declaration concerning debtor's schedules" concludes the schedules with a statement under threat of perjury that the information contained in the documents is true to the best of the debtor's knowledge, information, and belief. (See Figure 8–18.)

The Order Confirming Plan. Proceedings under Chapter 11 of the Bankruptcy Code are the most complex and costly of the bankruptcy proceedings. It is the goal of the debtor to obtain court approval of a plan for reorganization. The reorganization plan must classify the claims of the creditors and provide for their payment.

Following a court hearing to confirm the plan's feasibility, the court issues an "order confirming plan." The order reflects that copies of the complex plan are filed and attached to the order. The effect of the issuance of the order is to provide the debtor with the equivalent of a discharge of the debts subject to the plan.

The Discharge. The ultimate goal of a Chapter 7 liquidation proceeding is the issuance of a "discharge of debtor." The discharge is the court's order relieving the debtor of any obligation for the proven debts that are the subject of the matter. The effect is to vacate any existing judgment against the debtor and to prevent future collection attempts by any creditor on debts subject to the discharge. (See Figure 8–19.)

In re_____.   Case No._____
                        Debtor   (If known)

SCHEDULE H - CODEBTORS

Provide the information requested concerning any person or entity, other than a spouse in a joint case, that is also liable on any debts listed by debtor in the schedules of creditors. Include all guarantors and co-signers. In community property states, a married debtor not filing a joint case should report the name and address of the nondebtor spouse on this schedule. Include all names used by the nondebtor spouse during the six years immediately preceding the commencement of this case.

☐ Check this box if debtor has no codebtors.

NAME AND ADDRESS OF CODEBTOR	NAME AND ADDRESS OF CREDITOR

E-Z LEGAL FORMS®   K100-17

FIGURE 8–14 Schedule H—Codebtors

In re_____,   Case No._____
                   Debtor   (If known)

SCHEDULE I - CURRENT INCOME OF INDIVIDUAL DEBTOR(S)

The column labeled "Spouse" must be completed in all cases filed by joint debtors and by a married debtor in a chapter 12 or 13 case whether or not a joint petition is filed, unless the spouses are separated and a joint petition is not filed.

Debtor's Marital Status:	DEPENDENTS OF DEBTOR AND SPOUSE		
	NAMES	AGE	RELATIONSHIP

Employment:	DEBTOR	SPOUSE
Occupation		
Name of Employer		
How long employed		
Address of Employer		

Income: (Estimate of average monthly income)	DEBTOR	SPOUSE
Current monthly gross wages, salary, and commissions (prorate if not paid monthly.)	$_____	$_____
Estimated monthly overtime	$_____	$_____
SUBTOTAL	$_____	$_____
LESS PAYROLL DEDUCTIONS		
a. Payroll taxes and social security	$_____	$_____
b. Insurance	$_____	$_____
c. Union dues	$_____	$_____
d. Other (Specify:_____)	$_____	$_____
SUBTOTAL OF PAYROLL DEDUCTIONS	$_____	$_____
TOTAL NET MONTHLY TAKE HOME PAY	$_____	$_____
Regular income from operation of business or profession or farm (attach detailed statement)	$_____	$_____
Income from real property	$_____	$_____
Interest and dividends	$_____	$_____
Alimony, maintenance or support payments payable to the debtor for the debtor's use or that of dependents listed above.	$_____	$_____
Social security or other government assistance (Specify)_____	$_____	$_____
Pension or retirement income	$_____	$_____
Other monthly income	$_____	$_____
(Specify)_____	$_____	$_____
_____	$_____	$_____
TOTAL MONTHLY INCOME	$_____	$_____

TOTAL COMBINED MONTHLY INCOME $_____   (Report also on Summary of Schedules)

Describe any increase or decrease of more than 10% in any of the above categories anticipated to occur within the year following the filing of this document:

FIGURE 8–15 Schedule I—Current Income of Individual Debtor(s)

In re _____, Case No. _____
　　　　　　　Debtor　　　　　　　　　　　　　　　　(If known)

SCHEDULE J- CURRENT EXPENDITURES OF INDIVIDUAL DEBTOR(S)

Complete this schedule by estimating the average monthly expenses of the debtor and the debtor's family. Prorate any payments made bi-weekly, quarterly, semi-annually, or annually to show monthly rate.

☐ Check this box if a joint petition is filed and debtor's spouse maintains a separate household. Complete a separate schedule of expenditures labeled "Spouse."

Rent or home mortgage payment (include lot rented for mobile home)	$_____
Are real estate taxes included?　　Yes _____　No _____	
Is property insurance included?　　Yes _____　No _____	
Utilities Electricity and heating fuel	$_____
Water and sewer	$_____
Telephone	$_____
Other _____	$_____
Home maintenance (repairs and upkeep)	$_____
Food	$_____
Clothing	$_____
Laundry and dry cleaning	$_____
Medical and dental expenses	$_____
Transportation (not including car payment)	$_____
Recreation, clubs and entertainment, newspapers, magazines, etc.	$_____
Charitable contributions	$_____
Insurance (not deducted from wages or included in home mortgage payments)	
Homeowner's or renter's	$_____
Life	$_____
Health	$_____
Auto	$_____
Other _____	$_____
Taxes (not deducted from wages or included in home mortgage payments)	
(Specify)_____	$_____
Installment payments: (in Chapter 12 and 13 cases, do not list payments to be included in the plan)	
Auto	$_____
Other_____	$_____
Other_____	$_____
Alimony, maintenance, and support paid to others	$_____
Payments for support of additional dependents not living at your home	$_____
Regular expenses from operation of business, profession, or farm (attach detailed statement)	$_____
Other_____	$_____

TOTAL MONTHLY EXPENSES (Report also on Summary of Schedules)　　$_____

[FOR CHAPTER 12 AND 13 DEBTORS ONLY]
Provide the information requested below, including whether plan payments are to be made bi-weekly, monthly, annually, or at some other regular interval.

A. Total projected monthly income	$_____
B. Total projected monthly expenses	$_____
C. Excess income (A minus B)	$_____
D. Total amount to be paid into plan each _____	$_____
(interval)	

E·Z Legal Forms•　　　　　　　　　　　　　　　　　　　　　　　　　K100-19

FIGURE 8–16 Schedule J—Current Expenditures of Individual Debtor(s)

United States Bankruptcy Court

DISTRICT OF _____

In re_____, Case No._____
                    Debtor   (If known)

SUMMARY OF SCHEDULES

Indicate as to each schedule whether that schedule is attached and state the number of pages in each. Report the totals from Schedules A,B,D,E,F,I, and J in the boxes provided. Add the amounts from Schedules A and B to determine the total amount of the debtor's assets. Add the amounts from Schedules D,E, and F to determine the total amount of the debtor's liabilities.

NAME OF SCHEDULE	ATTACHED (YES/NO)	NO. OF SHEETS	AMOUNTS SCHEDULED		
			ASSETS	LIABILITIES	OTHER
A - Real Property			$		
B - Personal Property			$		
C - Property Claimed as Exempt					
D - Creditors Holding Secured Claims				$	
E - Creditors Holding Unsecured Priority Claims				$	
F - Creditors Holding Unsecured Non Priority Claims				$	
G - Executory Contracts and Unexpired Leases					
H - Codebtors					
I - Current Income of Individual Debtor(s)					$
J. - Current Expenditures of Individual Debtor(s)					$
Total Number of Sheets of ALL Schedules ->					
Total Assets ->			$		
Total Liabilities ->				$	

FIGURE 8-17 Summary of Schedules

In re _____, Case No. _____
    Debtor   (If known)

DECLARATION CONCERNING DEBTOR'S SCHEDULES

DECLARATION UNDER PENALTY OF PERJURY BY INDIVIDUAL DEBTOR

    I declare under penalty of perjury that I have read the foregoing summary and schedules, consisting of _____ sheets and that they are true and correct to the best of my knowledge, information, and belief.   (Total shown on summary page plus 1)

Date _____   Signature: _____
                                                              Debtor

Date _____   Signature: _____
                                                      (Joint Debtor, if any)
                                            (If joint case, both spouses must sign.)

CERTIFICATION AND SIGNATURE OF NON-ATTORNEY BANKRUPTCY PETITION PREPARER (See 11 U.S.C. § 110)

    I certify that I am a bankruptcy petition preparer as defined in 11 U.S.C. § 110, that I have prepared this document for compensation, and that I have provided the debtor with a copy of this document.

_____   _____
Printed or Typed Name of Bankruptcy Petition Preparer   Social Security Number

_____

Address

Names and Social Security Numbers of all other individuals who prepared or assisted in preparing this document:

If more than one person prepared this document, attach additional signed sheets conforming to the appropriate Official Form for each person.

X_____   _____
Signature of Bankruptcy Petition Preparer   Date

A bankruptcy petition preparer's failure to comply with the provisions of Title 11 and the Federal Rules of Bankruptcy Procedure may result in fines or imprisonment or both. 11 U.S.C. § 110; 18 U.S.C. § 156.

DECLARATION UNDER PENALTY OF PERJURY ON BEHALF OF CORPORATION OR PARTNERSHIP

    I, the _____ [president or other officer or an authorized agent of the corporation or a member or an authorized agent of the partnership] of the _____ [corporation or partnership] named as debtor in this case, declare under penalty of perjury that I have read the foregoing summary and schedules, consisting of _____ sheets (total shown on summary page plus 1), and that they are true and correct to the best of my knowledge, information, and belief.

Date _____

                                            Signature: _____

                                            _____
                                            [Print or type name of individual signing on behalf of debtor.]

[An individual signing on behalf of a partnership or corporation must indicate position or relationship to debtor.]

_____

Penalty for making a false statement or concealing property: Fine of up to $500,000 or imprisonment for up to 5 years or both. 18 U.S.C. § 152 and 3571.

E·Z LEGAL FORMS®   K100-20

FIGURE 8–18 Declaration Concerning Debtor's Schedules

UNITED STATES BANKRUPTCY COURT
DISTRICT OF _____

In re _____ ,

> [Set forth here all names including married. maiden . and trade names used by debtor within last 6 years.]

                           Debtor   Case No. _____

                                           Chapter Seven

Social Security No(s). _____ and all
Employer's Tax Identification Nos. *[If any]* _____

_____

DISCHARGE OF DEBTOR

It appearing that a petition commencing a case under title 11, United States Code, was filed by or against the person named above on _____ , and that an order for relief was entered under chapter 7, and that no complaint objecting to the discharge of the debtor was filed within the time fixed by the court *[or* that a complaint objecting to discharge of the debtor was filed and, after due notice and hearing, was not sustained];

IT IS ORDERED that

1. The above - named debtor is released from all dischargeable debts.

2. Any judgment heretofore or hereafter obtained in any court other than this court is null and void as a determination of the personal liability of the debtor with respect to any of the following:

    (a) debts dischargeable under 11 U.S.C. § 523;

    (b) unless heretofore or hereafter determined by order of this court to be nondischargeable, debts alleged to be excepted from discharge under clauses (2), (4) and (6) of 11 U.S.C. § 523(a);

    (c) debts determined by this court to be discharged.

3. All creditors whose debts are discharged by this order and all creditors whose judgments are declared null and void by paragraph 2 above are enjoined from instituting or continuing any action or employing any process or engaging in any act to collect such debts as personal liabilities of the above - named debtor.

Dated: _____

                                     BY THE COURT

                                  _____

                                  United States Bankruptcy Judge.

FIGURE 8–19 Discharge of Debtor

SUMMARY

- All matters concerning bankruptcy are decided in the Bankruptcy Court, including cases seeking liquidation or reorganization. The bankruptcy laws exist to provide the debtor with relief from unmanageable debt, while benefiting the creditors with an equitable distribution of the debtor's assets. The proceedings may be at the election of either the debtor, in the form of a voluntary bankruptcy, or the creditor, with the filing of an involuntary petition.

- The preparation of the documents required to process any bankruptcy begins with a detailed client interview and checklist preparation. The pleadings involved in the typical bankruptcy are set forth in the Official Forms, which provide the content and appearance of each pleading. The pleadings present the debtor's case before the court and reflect the validity of the creditors' allegations. Once the debts have been proven, the matter is concluded with the discharge, relieving the debtor of the obligation for those debts.

- A business may be reorganized and continue to operate with a provision for the payment of debts from the income of the business. A plan for reorganization must be approved by the court, allowing the business to pay its obligations over time. With the plan, the debtor will not be harassed by creditors while the repayment is made.

IN REVIEW

1. How does a creditor prove his or her claim before a Bankruptcy Court?
2. What is the difference between a voluntary petition and an involuntary petition?
3. How does a Chapter 7 case differ from a Chapter 11 one?
4. What is the purpose of the voluntary petition?
5. What are the "statements and schedules?"
6. What is the function of a statement of financial affairs?
7. What is the purpose of a discharge?

PUTTING IT ALL TOGETHER

Your office has been contacted by Martin "Bub" Brisket, sole owner and proprietor of Bub's Roast & Boast, a local eatery that for years has served the "beef-for-breakfast bunch." Bub has come on hard times with the national awareness of the high cholesterol content of his stock-in-trade. Rather than submit to the pressure to serve fat-free yogurt and wheat germ, Bub has decided to pull up stakes and follow Horace Greeley's advice.

Bub owes the following debts:

B. D. Strangle, rent	$15,000
Brown Chow Food Co., supplies	12,000
Fremont Power & Light, utilities	5,000
No. Bell, telephone	2,000
Four Wheel Finance, truck, secured	10,000
Allhart Savings and Loan, unsecured	50,000
Meltdown Master Charge, unsecured	9,000

Other than the furnishings in his double-wide trailer that he rents from his former brother-in-law and his personal clothing, Bub is without assets. He has approximately $1200 in equity in his truck and does not want to lose the truck. He plans to move to Montana and obtain a fresh start in the beef business, but he cannot make any plans with the creditors breathing down his neck.

Exercises

1. Of the options available to Bub under the Bankruptcy Code, under which chapter would you recommend that he file?
2. Prepare the voluntary petition and the statement and schedules required for the filing of a bankruptcy proceeding.

Federal and State Pleadings

We are not unmindful of the admonition that rules of procedure essential to administer justice should never be permitted to become so technical, fossilized and antiquated that they obscure the justice of the cause and lead to results that bring its administration into disrepute.

SUNDELL V. STATE, 354 SO. 2D 409 (1978)

OBJECTIVES

After completing this chapter, you will be able to:

1. Outline the types and purpose of pleadings
2. Describe the construction of pleadings
3. Prepare a complaint for a federal court case
4. Prepare a summons for a federal court case
5. Prepare an answer
6. Prepare a motion for a federal court case
7. Prepare an order for a federal court judge
8. Discuss pleading special matters in state courts
9. Summarize the filing of amended pleadings

BALLENTINE'S REVIEW

affidavit—Any voluntary statement reduced to writing and sworn to or affirmed before a person legally authorized to administer an oath or affirmation (EXAMPLE: notary public).

answer—A pleading in response to a complaint. An answer may deny the allegations of the complaint, demur to them, agree with them, or introduce affirmative defenses intended to defeat the plaintiff's lawsuit or delay it.

complaint—The initial pleading in a civil action, in which the plaintiff alleges a cause of action and asks that the wrong done him or her be remedied by the court; a formal charge of a crime.

jurisdiction—In a general sense, the right of a court to adjudicate lawsuits of a certain kind; in a specific sense, the right of a court to determine a particular case; in a geographical sense, the power of a court to hear cases only within a specific territorial area.

motion—An application made to a court for the purpose of obtaining an order or rule directing something to be done in favor of the applicant.

§ 9.1 IN GENERAL

The court system of each state is separate and distinct from the federal court system. While the federal courts operate within the borders of the state, they are an independent system with separate jurisdiction. Every state has its own individual court system with general jurisdiction over matters concerning the state, its residents, and their property. The court system is set forth in the rules of civil procedure enacted by each state, commonly called the **rules of court.** Most state rules of court are patterned after the Federal Rules of Civil Procedure, having been enacted by either the state legislature or issued by the state's highest court. Lawsuits are filed in federal court or state court, depending upon various factors that decide proper jurisdiction. A case filed in the wrong court will be dismissed for a lack of proper jurisdiction.

§ 9.2 STATUTES OF LIMITATION

Federal and state laws have established various maximum time limits during which an action may be maintained. Once that maximum time has expired, no lawsuit may be filed regardless of its merit. A law establishing the time limitation to the right of filing an action is called a **statute of limitation,** or *limitation of action.* It serves as a bar to the commencement of a lawsuit, providing the defendant with an affirmative defense that must be pleaded as discussed in the following text.

The statute of limitations begins to run at the time the cause of action arises. For example, with a personal injury claim, the cause of action arises on the day of the accident. For a contract, it arises at the time of the breach or when the first payment is overdue. If the cause of action arises over a period of time or through a series of events, the statute begins to run from the last event. The number of days constituting the statutory period begins the day after the accrual of the cause of action. For instance, if failed payment on a note were due on November 15, the statute of limitations commences running on the following day, November 16.

If the statutory period for limitation expires on a weekend or holiday, the statute does not expire until the next business day. In that case, the statute is said to be **tolled,** which means that it is prevented from expiring until the next business day.

All states have deadlines similar to a statute of limitation for filing certain pleadings set forth in the rules of court. The filing deadlines in the rules of court are of a procedural nature as opposed to a matter of substantive law. The filing of a particular pleading may be prevented by the court rule, thus eliminating a valuable right by a party. In terms of professional responsibility, it is imperative that actions are commenced within the statutory period for filing and that pleadings are filed within the limitations established by the rules of court.

rules of court: Rules promulgated by the court, governing procedure or practice before it.

statute of limitation: A federal or state statute prescribing the maximum period of time during which various types of civil actions and criminal prosecutions can be brought after the occurrence of the injury or the offense.

tolled: Interrupted or suspended; e.g., a statute of limitation is tolled (prevented from expiring) on a weekend or holiday.

§ 9.3 THE NATURE OF FEDERAL PLEADING AND PRACTICE

The Federal Rules of Civil Procedure provide the model from which most states have patterned their respective procedural rules. Most state rules of civil procedure set forth the requirements for matters such as the caption, complaint, counterclaims and cross-claims, service of process, answer, and motions. The federal rules consist of a body of procedural rules governing all civil actions in the federal courts. The United States Supreme Court, with its rule-making power, established the rules in 1938. The rules can now be found in title 28 of the United States Code. Each local district court has its own set of procedural rules that complement the federal rules for the more mechanical issues surrounding procedure. These local rules must be consulted when preparing any federal pleading.

The fundamental rule of pleading in any state court is the same as in the federal system. Pleadings require a short, plain statement about the nature of the relief sought and its grounds. That requirement extends not only to the complaint but also includes any other pleadings filed pursuant to the rules.

The Construction of Pleadings

The preparation of a legal pleading requires attention to the details of form as well as substance. Whereas a legal instrument requires an understanding of the legal principles behind the instrument, the preparation of a pleading involves attention to form to express its content.

There are certain basic guidelines to be followed in the preparation of pleadings. No general form taken from a form book will adequately serve a situation, and care must be taken to tailor the pleading to the individual case. When drafting a pleading, keep in mind the following basic concerns:

- know what you are trying to accomplish
- avoid language that is too broad or too narrow
- eliminate ambiguities in the language
- avoid overuse of legal terminology
- prepare a first draft
- allow for unique circumstances of the individual case
- avoid redundancies such as *due and owing, each and every, null and void*

An attention to detail is of prime importance in the preparation of any legal pleading. It is a skill that is developed through practice over time.

The General Format of Pleadings

The general format of a pleading should be presented in such a way as to state the facts in a clear and orderly manner. Rule 10 of the Federal Rules of Civil Procedure governs the basic format for pleadings.

The Caption. Rule 10 provides that each pleading must have a caption that contains the following:

- the name of the court in which the action is filed
- the title of the action with a designation of the parties
- the name of the pleading, *i.e.,* "COMPLAINT"
- the file number assigned by the clerk of the court

See the sample caption in Figure 9–1.

In state courts, the caption requires basically the same information as that required by the federal rules:

- name of the court
- the file number
- the name of the parties on each side of the case with their proper designations

All pleadings must contain some indication about the nature of the pleading, clearly stating the subject matter of the document. For instance, if the pleading is a complaint, it should clearly so state in its title. (See Figure 9–2.)

Paper Size and Margins. Local federal court rules contain specific requirements relating to paper size, margins, and so on. For example, rule 3 of the Rules of the United States District Court for the Northern District of Florida provides:

> *(A) Form of Pleadings. All pleadings, motions, briefs, applications, and other papers tendered for filing shall be double spaced, if typewritten, and on white letter-sized paper, approximately eight and one-half (8 ½) inches in width and eleven (11) inches in length, with one and one-fourth (1 ¼) inch margins. The first page of every pleading or document filed with the court shall, however, allow a two and one-fourth (2 ¼) inch margin at the bottom of the page where the clerk shall stamp such pleading or document filed; provided, however, that when the pleading or document is on a form approved and furnished by the court, this margin requirement shall not apply, and the clerk will stamp such form on the reverse side of the first page.*

Signatures. Rule 11 of the Federal Rules of Civil Procedure provides an additional requirement that an attorney of record must sign every pleading filed with the court. The attorney's signature represents that he or she has made a reasonable inquiry into the facts and law of the case and that there is a reasonable basis for the court's attention.

Body of Complaint. Rule 10 requires that all allegations and defenses be set forth in a numbered paragraph form. Each paragraph should contain only one set of circumstances and should make a simple plain statement. In the federal courts, if a complaint presents more than one theory of recovery—for example, negligence, contract, breach of warranty—each theory should be set forth in a separate numbered paragraph that alleges those facts that constitute the actionable transaction. These groupings are called **counts.** (See Figure 9–3.)

Each count should be sufficient to state a cause of action alone, without reliance on another count. If one count should be denied by the court, the remaining count will sustain the case.

counts: Statements of causes of action in a complaint.

**IN THE UNITED STATES DISTRICT COURT
FOR THE EASTERN DISTRICT OF MICHIGAN**

OYSTERDENT, INC.,

a Michigan corporation,

        Plaintiff,

            v.   C.A. No. _____

CYBERNET, INC.,

an Ohio corporation,

        Defendant.

_____/

               <u>COMPLAINT</u>

FIGURE 9–1 A sample federal court caption

**STATE OF CALIFORNIA
IN THE CIRCUIT COURT FOR ORANGE COUNTY**

DAVID B. ROUNDSTONE,

        Plaintiff,

            v.   File No: _____

GOLIATH, INC.,

        Defendant.

_____/

               <u>COMPLAINT</u>

FIGURE 9–2 A sample state court caption

COUNT ONE

1. OYSTERDENT, INC., a corporation organized and existing under the laws of the State of Michigan, is the plaintiff herein, with its principal place of business located at 1 Incisor Lane, Detroit, Michigan.

2. CYBERNET, INC., a corporation organized and existing under the laws of the State of Ohio, is the defendant herein, with its principal place of business located at 2 Digital Drive, Cleveland, Ohio.

COUNT TWO

3. The allegations of paragraphs 1 and 2 above are adopted herein by reference.

FIGURE 9–3 A sample of counts

Forms for Pleadings. The forms accompanying the Federal Rules of Civil Procedure found in title 28 of the United States Code provide the necessary format for pleadings pursuant to those rules. Local district court rules should always be consulted for any minor requirements.

§ 9.4 PREPARING THE COMPLAINT

The initial pleading filed in a lawsuit by the plaintiff to commence an action is the **complaint,** sometimes called the *statement* or the *declaration*. Its purpose is to formulate the plaintiff's claim and place the defendant on notice of that claim.

The Checklist

An essential element in the preparation of any pleading is the gathering of the information necessary to formulate the claim. Information must be gathered from the client and any external sources. It is the duty of the preparer to verify the information in the pleading. A checklist is an essential tool in the information-gathering process. Figure 9–4 provides the basic elements of a good personal interview checklist that can be used to prepare the complaint.

The Substance of the Complaint

complaint: The initial pleading in a civil action, in which the plaintiff alleges a cause of action and asks that the wrong done him or her be remedied by the court.

A well-drafted complaint requires the following four elements:

- a proper identification of all parties with names and addresses
- a statement of jurisdiction
- a statement of the claim giving rise to a cause of action
- a prayer for relief

PERSONAL

1. Name
2. Address
3. Date of birth
4. Social Security number
5. Occupation
6. Employment history
7. Education
8. Income
9. Marital status
10. Spousal information
11. Children
12. Assets
13. Liabilities
14. Medical history

FACTS OF THE CASE

1. Date
2. Place
3. Witnesses
4. Addresses/telephone numbers
5. Reports/statements
6. Corporate officers
7. Insurance coverage
8. Narrative of incident(s)

DAMAGES

1. Personal
2. Property
3. Mitigation
4. Preexisting conditions
5. Experts
6. Valuation

RECORDS

1. Tax
2. Banks, brokerages
3. Insurance
4. Police
5. Medical
6. Corporate
7. Contracts
8. Statements

FIGURE 9–4 A sample checklist

There is some variation among local federal district courts as to the specific requirements for any complaint. Local rules *must* be consulted before any pleading is prepared.

The Identification of the Parties. In the opening numbered paragraphs of the complaint, each of the parties should be identified with name and address. For an individual party, it is sufficient to state his or her name along with an address. In the case of a corporate party, its principal place of business along with the address of its corporate headquarters is required. If the party is a public official, the complaint must state his or her official capacity. (See Figure 9–5.)

The proper identification of the parties and their representative capacities and addresses are necessary for purposes of establishing jurisdiction.

The Statement of Jurisdiction. Since jurisdiction exists in federal courts under very specific guidelines, it is necessary to set forth the entitlement to the jurisdiction of the particular court. The caption of the pleading establishes the court for which jurisdiction is deemed proper. The complaint itself must set forth the reason(s) for qualification for federal jurisdiction. If the question arises under a provision of the United States Constitution, the constitutional section must be cited. Where the federal question arises pursuant to a law of the United States, the appropriate statutory citation must be provided. If jurisdiction arises from diversity of citizenship, an appropriate allegation must be made (see Figure 9–6, Exhibit 1).

cause of action:
Circumstances that give a person the right to bring a lawsuit and to receive relief from a court.

The Statement of the Claim. The statement of the claim is a recitation of the facts that entitle the plaintiff to judicial relief. Facts entitling a party to judicial remedy constitute a **cause of action.** A cause of action is frequently based upon negligence, fraud, or breach of contract.

All the facts necessary to amount to a cause of action must be alleged in the complaint. If a material element of the cause of action is omitted, the

---

For an individual:

1. CONRAD P. CROWN resides at 13 Bridge Lane, Detroit, Michigan.

For a corporation:

1. OYSTERDENT, INC., is a Michigan corporation, with its principal place of business located at 1 Incisor Lane, Detroit, Michigan.

For a public official:

1. ALFRED M. CABLE is the Secretary of State of the State of Ohio and resides at 486 Ether Ct., Columbus, Ohio.

FIGURE 9–5 A sample identification of the parties

JURISDICTION

1. Plaintiff is a corporation incorporated under the laws of the State of Michigan having its principal place of business in the State of Michigan, and defendant is a corporation incorporated under the laws of the State of Ohio having its principal place of business in a state other than the State of Michigan. The matter in controversy exceeds, exclusive of interest and costs, the sum of fifty thousand dollars ($50,000).

EXHIBIT 1
A sample allegation of jurisdiction

CLAIM

1. On or about June 31, 1999, in the County of Wayne, State of Michigan, Plaintiff and Defendant entered into an agreement. A copy of the agreement is heretofore attached as Exhibit A and incorporated into this Complaint.

2. Defendant agreed to install a computer network at Plaintiff's place of business as set forth in Exhibit A.

3. Defendant breached said agreement when it failed to perform its obligation under the agreement to install a computer network that would meet the requirements of Plaintiff's business without any loss of existing data.

4. By reason of Defendant's breach, Plaintiff has sustained damages in the sum of Ten Million Dollars ($10,000,000).

EXHIBIT 2
A sample statement of claim

DEMAND FOR JUDGMENT

WHEREFORE, Plaintiff hereby respectfully requests that this Court enter its order as follows:

1. Award judgment against Defendant in the amount of Ten Million Dollars ($10,000,000) plus costs, interest, and attorney fees.

2. Grant the Plaintiff a trial by jury on all issues of fact.

3. Grant the Plaintiff such other and further relief as is just and equitable.

EXHIBIT 3
A sample demand for judgment

CLAUDIA M. WHINE
One Legal Way
Detroit, Michigan 48226
(301) 555-1234
Attorney for Plaintiff

EXHIBIT 4
A sample signature

FIGURE 9–6 Sample elements of a complaint

complaint may be subject to dismissal. For instance, the material elements of a claim for a breach of contract would be:

- the existence of the contract
- a failure without legal excuse to perform the contractual obligation by defendant
- damage as a result of the breach

Thus, a complaint must reflect an allegation of fact as part of its statement of claim that supports each material element of the cause of action.

Assume that Oysterdent, Inc., a Michigan company, and Cybernet, Inc., an Ohio company, had entered into a written agreement under which Cybernet would install a computer network on two hundred computers at Oysterdent's place of business in Detroit. Cybernet's installation of the network resulted in a loss of six years of research data on the use of oyster shells for the manufacture of dentures. In an action in federal district court in Michigan, Oysterdent's claim for damages from Cybernet will be based upon a count of breach of the contract for failure to properly install the network. (See Figure 9–6, Exhibit 2.)

If an additional cause of action arises out of the same set of facts, as in the case of a claim for negligence by Oysterdent, an additional count will need to be added in the complaint.

The Prayer for Relief. The complaint concludes with a request of the court for judicial relief or damages. Such a request is called a **prayer for relief** or **demand for judgment.** Rule 8(a) of the Federal Rules of Civil Procedure refers to the prayer for relief as a demand for judgment that is used by the court as a guide in deciding the nature and extent of the recovery sought (see Figure 9–6, Exhibit 3).

The Signature. Rule 11 of the Federal Rules of Civil Procedure requires that the complaint be signed by an attorney, or by the plaintiff if he or she is unrepresented. The purpose behind the requirement of the attorney's signature is that as an officer of the court, he or she is held to a professional standard that would prevent him or her from filing a frivolous or fraudulent lawsuit. The requirement constitutes a certification by the attorney that the facts are true to the best of his or her knowledge. (See Figure 9–6, Exhibit 4.)

The Demand for Jury Trial

In a civil action in federal court, a jury trial is not a matter of right guaranteed by the United States Constitution. It is a matter that must be specifically requested by the plaintiff at the time of the filing of the complaint or within ten days thereafter. If the demand for a jury trial is requested in the complaint, it can be simply included in the demand for judgment as a separate paragraph. (See Figure 9–6, Exhibit 3.)

The Summons

A form accompanying a complaint used to inform the defendant that an action has been filed and that he or she must answer the complaint within a

prayer for relief: The portion of a complaint or claim for relief that specifies the type of relief to which the plaintiff feels he or she is entitled and for which he or she requests judgment; also called a demand for relief or demand for judgment.

demand for judgment: Another term for a prayer for relief.

specified time is called a **summons.** The summons also informs the defendant that a failure to answer will result in a judgment being entered as requested. The summons in federal district court is a preprinted form that may be obtained from the clerk of the court with the required information supplied by the plaintiff. (See Figure 9–7.)

§ 9.5 SERVICE OF PROCESS

Service of process is similar in most states in its purpose, which is to give the defendant notice of the proceedings against him or her and to provide an opportunity to appear and defend. Reasonable notice to the defendant of the proceedings pending against him or her is accomplished by means of a delivery of the summons and complaint in accordance with rule 4 of the Federal Rules of Civil Procedure. Delivery of the summons and complaint to the defendant is termed **service of process.** The form of process may vary, depending on the state and the nature of the case. Service of process must be accomplished within one hundred and twenty days of the filing of the complaint by:

- personal delivery to the defendant by an authorized individual
- service by mail
- service by publication under specific statutory guidelines

summons: To call or require a person or a group of people to appear or to obey some other command; with a complaint, the summons informs the defendant that an action has been filed and that he or she must answer or have a judgment entered against him or her.

service of process: Delivery of a summons, writ, complaint, or other process to the opposite party, or other person entitled to receive it, in such manner as the law prescribes, whether by leaving a copy at his or her residence, by mailing a copy to the person or his or her attorney, or by publication.

United States District Court

_____ **District** _____

SUMMONS IN A CIVIL ACTION

v.   Case Number:

To: (Name and address of Defendant)

YOU ARE HEREBY SUMMONED and required to file with the clerk of the Court and serve upon Plaintiff's Attorney (Name and Address) an answer to the complaint which is herewith served upon you, within _____ days after service of this summons upon you, exclusive of the day of service. If you fail to do so, judgment by default will be taken against you for the relief demanded in the complaint.

Date _____   _____ Clerk

FIGURE 9–7 A sample summons

- service pursuant to the state's long-arm statute
- service by a United States Marshal

Service of process by a United States Marshal, however, is allowed only in limited circumstances, such as when the United States is the serving party.

Service of process by mail is performed by mailing the summons and complaint to the defendant along with two copies of the notice and acknowledgment form provided in the rules. (See Figure 9–8.)

If the service of process is defective in some manner, the defect may form the basis for a dismissal of the action, resulting in a costly delay or total loss of the action.

§ 9.6 RESPONSIVE PLEADINGS

Once the plaintiff has filed his or her claim in the appropriate court, it is necessary for the defendant to respond to the claim. The response may be in the form of either a motion to dismiss the action, the assertion of certain defenses, or an admission of the claim. The time for filing an answer is always a specified time from the service of the original process, usually twenty days. An extension of time in which to file an answer is frequently granted by the court on motion by the defendant.

The Answer

Rule 8 of the Federal Rules of Civil Procedure governs the defendant's response to a complaint. Allegations that are not denied in response to the complaint are deemed admitted. It is imperative, therefore, that *all* matters requiring a response are addressed in one of the responsive pleadings. The answers of the defendant should be set forth in a clear and plain statement. The defendant may respond with:

- an admission or denial of the allegation
- a combination of an admission in part and a denial in part
- a claim that the defendant is without sufficient knowledge or information to form a belief as to the truth of an averment, having the effect of a denial

The defendant's responses must be drafted without any ambiguity as to the matter being admitted or denied. The answer should contain a caption to the matter, a title designating the nature of the pleading, and numbered paragraphs corresponding to the numbered paragraphs of the complaint. (See Figure 9–9, Exhibit 1.)

affirmative defense: A defense that amounts to more than simply a denial of the allegations the plaintiff's complaint. It sets up new matter which, if proven, could result in a judgment against the plaintiff even if all the allegations of the complaint are true.

Affirmative Defenses

Where the defendant has a defense to the complaint based upon a matter not mentioned in the complaint, the defendant may assert that new matter as an **affirmative defense.** The basis for an affirmative defense may be found in the fact that the plaintiff failed to file the action within a specified length of

(caption)

<u>NOTICE</u>

To: CYBERNET, INC., 2 Digital Drive, Cleveland, Ohio.

The enclosed summons and complaint are served pursuant to Rule 4(c)(2)(ii) of the Federal Rules of Civil Procedure.

You must complete the acknowledgment part of this form and return one copy of the completed form to the sender within 20 days.

You must sign and date the acknowledgment. If you are served on behalf of a corporation, you must indicate under your signature your relationship to that entity. If you are served on behalf of another person and you are authorized to receive process, you must indicate under your signature your authority.

If you do not complete and return the form to the sender within 20 days, you (or the party on whose behalf you are being served) may be required to pay any expenses incurred in serving a summons and complaint in any other manner permitted by law.

If you do not complete and return this form, you (or the party on whose behalf you are being served) must answer the complaint within 20 days. If you fail to do so, judgment by default will be taken against you for the relief demanded in the complaint.

I declare, under penalty of perjury, that this Notice and Acknowledgment of Receipt of Summons and Complaint was mailed on June 30, 1999.

_____
CLAUDIA M. WHINE
June 30, 1999

<u>ACKNOWLEDGMENT OF RECEIPT OF SUMMONS AND COMPLAINT</u>

I declare, under penalty of perjury, that I received a copy of the summons and of the complaint in the above-captioned matter at 2 Digital Drive, Cleveland, Ohio.

_____
VIRGIL RIALITI, President
July 1, 1999

FIGURE 9–8 A sample notice and acknowledgment form

time. Thus, the defendant would have an affirmative defense of the statute of limitations. Rule 8 provides additional affirmative defenses based upon questions of fraud, res judicata, contributory negligence, release and waiver, and discharge in bankruptcy.

Each affirmative defense should be set forth in the answer as a separate matter, with each affirmative defense contained in a separate numbered paragraph (see Figure 9–9, Exhibit 2).

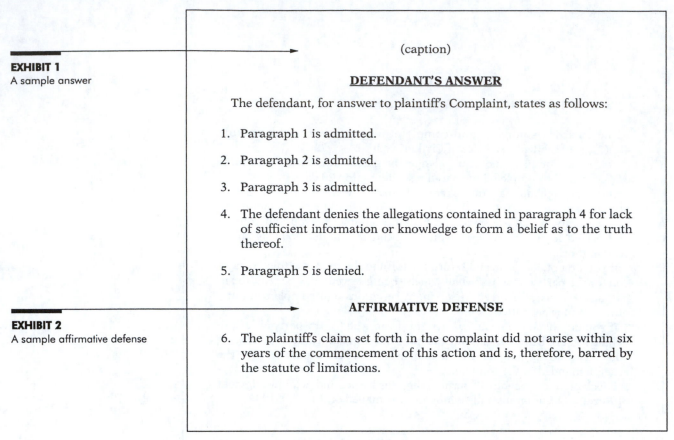

(caption)

DEFENDANT'S ANSWER

The defendant, for answer to plaintiff's Complaint, states as follows:

1. Paragraph 1 is admitted.

2. Paragraph 2 is admitted.

3. Paragraph 3 is admitted.

4. The defendant denies the allegations contained in paragraph 4 for lack of sufficient information or knowledge to form a belief as to the truth thereof.

5. Paragraph 5 is denied.

AFFIRMATIVE DEFENSE

6. The plaintiff's claim set forth in the complaint did not arise within six years of the commencement of this action and is, therefore, barred by the statute of limitations.

FIGURE 9–9 A sample answer containing affirmative defenses

The Motion to Dismiss

Rule 12(b) of the Federal Rules of Civil Procedure provides the defendant with alternatives to the filing of an answer in response to the plaintiff's complaint. Rule 12(b) gives the defendant an opportunity to have the court dismiss the complaint for one of seven different defenses through the filing of a motion pursuant to the rule. Those seven defenses are:

- a lack of jurisdiction over the subject matter
- a lack of jurisdiction over the person
- a lack of proper venue
- a lack of sufficiency of the process (defective summons)
- an insufficiency in service of process
- a failure to state a claim upon which relief can be granted
- a failure to join an essential party to the action

The motion to dismiss can either be made a part of the answer or filed as a separate responsive pleading. If filed as a separate pleading in lieu of filing an answer, it must be filed within the twenty days allowed for the filing of the answer to avoid a judgment on the plaintiff's complaint. The forms in the appendix to the Federal Rules of Civil Procedure, found in title 28 of the United States Code, provide samples for the drafting of the motion to dismiss (see Figure 9–10).

(caption)

DEFENDANT'S MOTION TO DISMISS

Defendant, through its undersigned counsel, hereby moves for dismissal of the complaint pursuant to Federal Rules of Civil Procedure 12(b)(6) on the ground that plaintiffs have failed to state a claim upon which relief can be granted.

I. M. SHARPE
10 Court Ct.
Detroit, Michigan 48226
(301) 555-5678
Attorney for Defendant

FIGURE 9–10 A sample motion to dismiss

The Motion for a More Definite Statement. A situation may arise where a party to an action is unable to frame his or her response to an allegation or defense due to some ambiguity or vagueness in the form of the pleading. It is reasonable that a party be able to understand the nature of an allegation before he or she is required to admit or deny its correctness. The party may request sufficient information upon which to form a response. To facilitate that end, many state court rules provide a procedure for filing a **motion for a more definite statement.** (See Figure 9–11.)

§ 9.7 MOTIONS

The Federal Rules of Civil Procedure provide for certain forms of relief by the order of the court through a process of petition to the court. The oral or written petition to the court for an order directing some act in favor of the applicant is called a **motion.** Rule 7(b)(1) provides:

An application to the court for an order shall be by motion that, unless made during a hearing or trial, shall be made in writing, shall state with particularity the grounds therefor, and shall set forth the relief or order sought. The requirement of writing is fulfilled if the motion is stated in a written notice of the hearing of the motion.

The procedures for bringing a motion before state courts vary greatly. A hearing is not required for every type of motion. There are some forms of motion that are considered to be *ex parte,* which is a hearing by the court attended only by the moving party.

motion for a more definite statement: A motion made by a defendant in response to a vague or ambiguous complaint.

motion: An application made to a court for the purpose of obtaining an order or rule directing something to be done in favor of the applicant.

ex parte: Means "of a side," i.e., from one side or by one party. The term refers to an application made to the court by one party without notice to the other party.

(caption)

MOTION FOR MORE DEFINITE STATEMENT

NOW COMES GOLIATH, INC., by and through its attorney herein, pursuant to Rule 2.68 of the Fremont Rules of Civil Procedure, and moves this Honorable Court:

1. That paragraph 4 of the Complaint alleges that a contract was executed in the calendar year 1988 between plaintiff and defendant.

2. That paragraph 4 of the Complaint is so vague and ambiguous that defendant cannot reasonably frame a response.

WHEREFORE, defendant, GOLIATH, INC., respectfully requests that this Honorable Court order plaintiff to make a more definite statement of its allegation contained in paragraph 4 of the Complaint.
Respectfully submitted,

_____
PHYLLIS STEEN
One Ancient Place
Johns City, California
Attorney for Defendant

FIGURE 9–11 A sample motion for more definite statement

notice of hearing: A notice of the filing of a motion furnished to the nonmoving party to inform them of the time and place of the hearing and to identify the nature of and grounds for the motion.

affidavit: Any voluntary statement reduced to writing and sworn to or affirmed before a person legally authorized to administer an oath or affirmation.

brief: A written statement submitted to a court for the purpose of persuading it of the correctness of one's position. A brief argues the facts of the case and the applicable law, supported by citations of authority.

The motions requiring a hearing for both sides of a dispute are scheduled by the judicial assistant on the court's motion calendar. Certain days or specific times of the week may be set aside for the hearing of motions. The notice of the motion is usually furnished to the nonmoving party through the use of a pleading called a **notice of hearing.** The notice must provide "reasonable" notice of the time and place of the hearing and identify the nature of and grounds for the motion. (See Figure 9–12.)

Motions are required to follow the form of other pleadings. As in the complaint, a caption and title are required. The title of the motion should set forth the nature of the motion itself, for example, "Motion for Summary Judgment." The substance of the motion should be in numbered paragraph form and signed by the attorney. In addition, a certificate of service must be attached reflecting service of the motion on the opposing party.

A motion is frequently accompanied by further documentation to support the allegations or claims upon which the motion is based. The document may be an **affidavit,** which is a sworn statement of facts by the signer acknowledged by a notary. The motion may also be accompanied by a **brief,** or memorandum of law, providing the court with relevant statutory and case law support for the moving party's position. (See Figure 9–13.)

```
                    STATE OF CALIFORNIA
             IN THE CIRCUIT COURT FOR ORANGE COUNTY


DAVID B. ROUNDSTONE,

            Plaintiff,

                  v.          File No: _____

GOLIATH, INC.,

            Defendant.

    _____/


                    NOTICE OF HEARING

TO:  PHYLLIS STEEN
     One Ancient Place
     Johns City, California
     Attorney for Defendant

    PLEASE TAKE NOTICE that the undersigned will bring on for hearing
its Motion for Summary Judgment before the Honorable Moses Army,
Circuit Judge, at the Orange County Court House at 2:00 p.m. on Friday,
November 13, 1999.
    YOU ARE INVITED TO ATTEND.
    I HEREBY CERTIFY that a copy of the foregoing was furnished to the
addressee herein this 1st day of November, 1999, by United States Mail.


                         _____
                         NORMAN SOLOMON
                         2 Old Ave.
                         Johns City, California
                         Attorney for Plaintiff
```

FIGURE 9–12 A sample notice of hearing

Motions must be served upon all parties at least five days before the scheduled hearing, along with all supporting affidavits and briefs. Some motions require a longer notice period. Local district court rules should be consulted.

The nature of the relief sought by motion is frequently procedural, correcting some defect in the form of the action. The relief also may be such that it disposes of the case entirely. If the motion will result in a termination of the lawsuit, the motion is called a **dispositive motion.**

dispositive motion: A motion that, if granted by the court, will dispose of a case entirely, terminating the lawsuit.

**IN THE UNITED STATES DISTRICT COURT
FOR THE EASTERN DISTRICT OF MICHIGAN**

OYSTERDENT, INC.,

a Michigan corporation,

Plaintiff,

v.   C.A. No. _____

CYBERNET, INC.,

an Ohio corporation,

Defendant.

_____/

MOTION FOR SUMMARY JUDGMENT

Defendant, CYBERNET, INC., moves for an order pursuant to Federal Rules of Civil Procedure 56 for summary judgment to be granted against plaintiff in the above-captioned action on the grounds that there is no genuine issue as to any material fact and that defendant, CYBERNET, INC., is entitled to judgment as a matter of law. Defendant attaches its Brief in Support of Motion.

_____
I. M. SHARPE
10 Court Ct.
Detroit, Michigan 48226
(301) 555-5678
Attorney for Defendant

FIGURE 9–13 A sample motion for summary judgment

The rules provide for many motions that control the flow of the litigation in a lawsuit. Figure 9–14 provides a list of many of the forms a motion may take under the rules.

default judgment: A judgment rendered in favor of a plaintiff based upon a defendant's failure to take a necessary step in a lawsuit within the required time.

Default Judgment

If the defendant fails to file an answer within the twenty days prescribed by the rules, the plaintiff is entitled to a judgment on the complaint. The defendant's failure to defend the matter leaves him or her in a state of default, allowing the plaintiff to take a **default judgment** against the defendant.

Motion to Amend	Rule 15
Motion for Amended or Additional Findings of Fact	Rule 52(b)
Motion for Appointment of an Interpreter	Rule 43(f)
Motion to Appoint a Person Before Whom Deposition May Taken	Rule 28(a)
Motion for Appointment of Receiver	Rule 66
Motion for Approval of Dismissal or Compromise of Class Action	Rule 23(e)
Motion to Bring in Third Party	Rule 14
Motion for Continuance	Rule 15(b)
Motion to Correct Clerical Errors	Rule 60(a)
Motion for Declaratory Judgment	Rule 57
Motion for Determination of Class	Rule 23(c)
Action Status Motion for Directed Verdict	Rule 50(a)
Motion for Discovery	Rule 26
Motion to Dismiss	Rule 12(b)
Motion to Drop or Add a Party	Rule 21
Motion for Enforcement of Subpoena	Rule 45(d)
Motion to Enlarge or Shorten Time to Take Deposition	Rule 30(b)
Motion for Enlargement of Time	Rule 6(b)
Motion to Intervene	Rule 24
Motion for Involuntary Dismissal	Rule 41(b)
Motion for Judgment N.O.V.	Rule 50(b)
Motion for Judgment on the Pleadings	Rule 12(c)
Motion for Jury Trial	Rule 39(b)
Motion for Leave to Depose Prisoner	Rule 30(a)
Motion for Leave to Implead	Rule 14(b)
Motion for Leave to Plead Omitted Counterclaim	Rule 13(f)
Motion to Modify or Quash	Rule 45(b)
Motion to Modify Pretrial Order	Rule 16(e)
Motion for More Definite Statement	Rule 12(e)
Motion for New Trial	Rule 59
Motion for Order for Discovery of Documents	Rule 26(b)

FIGURE 9–14 A sample of the types of motions

Motion for Order That Deposition Be Recorded by Nonstenographic Means	Rule 30(b)
Motion for Order to Take Deposition by Phone	Rule 30(b)
Motion for Separate Trials	Rule 42(b)
Motion to Set Aside Entry of Default Judgment	Rule 55(c)
Motion to Set Aside or for Relief from Judgment	Rule 55(c)
Motion for Stay Pending Posttrial Motion	Rule 62(b)
Motion to Strike	Rule 12(f)
Motion to Substitute Party	Rule 25
Motion for Summary Judgment	Rule 56
Motion to Suspend, Modify, Restore, or Grant Injunction Pending Appeal	Rule 62(c)
Motion to Terminate or Limit	Rule 30(d)
Motion to Use Deposition at Trial	Rule 32(a)
Motion for Voluntary Dismissal	Rule 41(a)
Motion for Waiver	Rule 12(h)

FIGURE 9–14 (continued)

Rule 55 provides that the plaintiff must first file a request to enter default supported by an affidavit from the plaintiff's attorney to the effect that service was perfected and that the twenty-day period for response has elapsed. If the documentation is complete, the clerk will enter an entry of default. The three basic pleadings used to file the default judgment are usually prepared simultaneously (see Figure 9–15).

The Motion for Summary Judgment

Rule 56 of the Federal Rules of Civil Procedure provides for a dispositive motion by either party where there exists no genuine issue as to any material fact. If that is the case, the moving party may be entitled to judgment as a matter of law. Such a dispositive motion is called a **motion for summary judgment.** The moving party's entitlement to a grant of the motion is based upon the law as opposed to any question of fact. Once the motion has been granted by the court, there has been a final adjudication on the merits, and the matter is terminated. The burden is on the moving party to show by affidavit or other relevant documents that there is no genuine issue of any material fact. If any doubt exists, resulting in a disputed fact, the matter is resolved against the moving party.

motion for summary judgment: A motion requesting that an action be disposed of without further proceedings.

(caption)

REQUEST TO ENTER DEFAULT

TO THE HONORABLE Melvin Mellow, Clerk of the United States District Court for the Eastern District of Michigan:

You will please enter the default of the defendant, CYBERNET, INC., for failure to plead or otherwise defend as provided by the Federal Rules of Civil Procedure, as appears from the Affidavit of CLAUDIA M. WHINE attached hereto.

This the 31st day of August, 1999.

> CLAUDIA M. WHINE
> One Legal Way
> Detroit, Michigan 48226
> (301) 555-1234
> Attorney for Plaintiff

EXHIBIT 1
A sample request to enter default

(caption)

AFFIDAVIT FOR ENTRY OF DEFAULT

STATE OF MICHIGAN)
COUNTY OF WAYNE)

CLAUDIA M. WHINE, being duly sworn, deposes and says that she is the attorney for plaintiff in the above-entitled action; that the Summons and Complaint in this action were served on defendant, CYBERNET, INC., on July 6, 1999, as appears from the return of service filed in this matter; that the time within which the defendant may answer or otherwise move as to the Complaint has expired; and that defendant has not answered or otherwise moved.

> CLAUDIA M. WHINE
> One Legal Way
> Detroit, Michigan 48226
> (301) 555-1234
> Attorney for Plaintiff

(acknowledgment of notary)

EXHIBIT 2
A sample affidavit for entry of default

(caption)

ENTRY OF DEFAULT

IT APPEARING TO THE COURT that the defendant is in default for failure to plead or otherwise defend as required by law;

EXHIBIT 3
A sample entry of default

FIGURE 9–15 Three pleadings used to file a default judgment

NOW, THEREFORE, DEFAULT is hereby entered against the defendant, CYBERNET, INC.
This 1st day of September, 1999.

_____

MELVIN MELLOW
Clerk of the United States
District Court for the
Eastern District of Michigan

FIGURE 9–15 (continued)

The motion for summary judgment may not be filed by the plaintiff until twenty days have elapsed from the service of the summons and complaint. The defendant may file the motion for summary judgment at any time. The motion is usually accompanied by one or more affidavits regarding the lack of any factual issue and also by a brief or memorandum of law in support of the motion. (See Figure 9–13.)

The Motion for Judgment on the Pleadings

Closely related to a motion for summary judgment is the procedure governed by rule 12(c) of the Federal Rules of Civil Procedure allowing for the entry of judgment by the court solely on the pleadings. Such a judgment is granted only in limited circumstances where the court considers the pleadings in a light most favorable to the nonmoving party and bases its decision on the lack of any disputed fact. If any question of fact exists, the motion will not be granted. (See Figure 9–16.)

The Order

A fundamental rule of pleading is that a court speaks only through its orders. A **court order** is a written direction of the court determining a step in the proceedings. An order is considered *interlocutory* if it decides only some intervening matter but not the ultimate outcome in the case. If the court's order is a ruling that terminates the action, the order is considered a *final order.*

Proposed orders are usually submitted to the court along with the filing of a motion and its supporting documents. Local district court rules should be consulted for both procedure and form for proposed orders, given the wide divergence between court rules. In the matter of Oysterdent against Cybernet, it would appear that Oysterdent's claim may be barred on the pleadings. A procedural tactic to file a motion for a supplemental complaint may forestall the termination of the action. Figure 9–17 provides a sample of the court's order allowing the filing of a supplemental complaint.

court order: An adjudication by a court; a ruling by a court with respect to a motion or any other question before it for determination during the course of a proceeding.

(caption)

MOTION FOR JUDGMENT ON THE PLEADINGS

Pursuant to Rule 12(c) of the Federal Rules of Civil Procedure, defendant, CYBERNET, INC., moves the Court to enter judgment on the pleadings in favor of the defendant. On the undisputed facts in the pleadings, defendant, CYBERNET, INC., is entitled to judgment as a matter of law.
In support of its motion, defendant states:

1. The plaintiff filed the complaint in this action on June 30, 1999.

2. The obligations pursuant to the contract that is the subject of this action expired more than six years prior to the filing of the complaint in this matter.

3. The applicable statute of limitations for such an action is six years, barring plaintiff's recovery.

WHEREFORE, defendant, CYBERNET, INC., requests that the Court enter judgment on the pleadings in favor of defendant.

CLAUDIA M. WHINE
One Legal Way
Detroit, Michigan 48226
(301) 555-1234
Attorney for Plaintiff

FIGURE 9–16 A sample motion for judgment on the pleadings

It is important to recognize the distinction between an *order* and a *judgment*. An order resolves specific issues that are the subject of a motion or request of a party. A judgment provides for a termination of the lawsuit and the granting of the ultimate relief sought.

§ 9.8 AMENDED AND SUPPLEMENTAL PLEADINGS

The need may arise during the course of a lawsuit to change pleadings because some material fact has been discovered or omitted. The Federal Rules of Civil Procedure and the court rules of most states allow a procedure for the filing of amended pleadings, as found in rule 15 of the Federal Rules of Civil Procedure.

The Procedure

A party may amend his or her pleading as a matter of course when there has been no filing of a responsive pleading. If no responsive pleading is

---

**IN THE UNITED STATES DISTRICT COURT
FOR THE EASTERN DISTRICT OF MICHIGAN**

OYSTERDENT, INC.,

a Michigan corporation,

       Plaintiff,

           v.   C.A. No. 12345

CYBERNET, INC.,

an Ohio corporation,

       Defendant.

_____/

ORDER GRANTING LEAVE TO FILE SUPPLEMENTAL COMPLAINT

On the 13th day of September, 1999, plaintiff in the above-captioned matter filed a motion for an order granting leave to file a supplemental complaint. The matter was briefed, argued, and fully heard by this Court on the 25th day of September, 1999.

FOR GOOD CAUSE SHOWN, this Court is of the opinion that leave should be granted for plaintiff to file a supplemental complaint. Such supplemental complaint shall be served no later than the 15th day of October, 1999.

IT IS SO ORDERED.

                              _____
                              Signature of Judge

September 25, 1999

FIGURE 9–17 A sample court order

required and the matter has not been placed on the trial calendar, the plaintiff may amend the complaint within twenty days of service.

In all other circumstances, in most state courts, and in federal court, leave of the court must be obtained before an amended pleading may be filed without the written consent of the opposing party. The rules state that leave of the court shall be freely given when the ends of justice require and the other party is not materially prejudiced. (See Figure 9–18.)

(caption)

MOTION TO AMEND PLEADINGS

NOW COMES the plaintiff, DAVID B. ROUNDSTONE, by and through his attorney, NORMAN SOLOMON, pursuant to Rule 4.3 of the California Rules of Civil Procedure, and moves the Court to allow the amendment of his Complaint for the following reasons:

1. The sling that is the subject of this action was alleged to have been manufactured by defendant within one (1) year of its sale to plaintiff.

2. Records of defendant reflect conclusively that the sling that is the subject of this action was manufactured within ten (10) days of its actual sale to plaintiff and within twenty (20) days of its malfunction, which caused injury to plaintiff.

3. The granting of plaintiff's motion would not surprise defendant or prejudice defendant materially.

4. Denial of plaintiff's motion would result in substantial injustice and prejudice to plaintiff.

5. The ends of justice would be served by granting plaintiff's motion.

WHEREFORE, plaintiff respectfully moves the Court for leave to amend the complaint in this action in the manner and to the extent set forth in the "Amendment to Complaint" attached hereto.
Respectfully submitted,

_____
NORMAN SOLOMON
2 Old Ave.
Johns City, California
Attorney for Plaintiff

FIGURE 9–18 A sample motion to amend the pleadings

SUMMARY

- Pleadings in federal court are designed to introduce the plaintiff's allegations, narrow the issues, place the defendant on notice, and invoke the court's jurisdiction. Regardless of the nature of the document, pleadings should be drafted in language that contains a short, plain statement of the matter.

- A well-drafted complaint contains a proper identification of the parties, a statement of the court's jurisdiction, a statement of the claim, and a prayer for relief. The complaint must state a cause of action upon which relief may be granted and must, therefore, contain all the necessary elements of the cause.

- The preparation of answers, motions, and other responsive pleadings follows the same construction rule in requiring a short, plain statement. Care must be taken to follow the format required by local federal court rule.

- Civil procedure in most state courts is modeled after the Federal Rules of Civil Procedure. The basic procedures from the filing of the complaint through the pretrial pleading stages involve close adherence to the specific court rules of the individual state.

- The preparation of pleadings serves the underlying purpose of adequately framing and narrowing the issues for decision by the court. The goal is the efficient administration of justice. With close adherence to the general rules of pleading and through a careful use of the defenses available to a party, the issues can be significantly narrowed and defined before trial.

IN REVIEW

1. What is the model for the court rules of most states?
2. What are the purposes of a pleading?
3. What is the fundamental rule of pleading in state courts?
4. What basic concerns should be kept in mind when drafting a pleading?
5. What are the four basic elements that must be contained in a complaint?
6. What is the purpose of separate counts?
7. What is the effect of a failure to deny an allegation in a complaint?
8. What is the purpose of the filing of an answer by the defendant?

PUTTING IT ALL TOGETHER

In May 1999, Margaret Mack began her employment with Pitt Bull Freight Lines as an over-the-road driver. In November of that same year, upon review of Marge's personnel file, Pitt Bull's chief dispatcher, Owen "Stretch" Jingo, discovered that he had mistakenly hired a female. From that point on, she hauled only hogs or their by-products. She was steadfastly denied any decent jobs and was even told that no more members of her club, The Gear-Jammin Mommas, would be hired by Pitt Bull. Finally, Marge was forced to quit her employment.

Marge has filed preliminary charges with the Equal Employment Opportunity Commission, and she recently received her right to sue letter from the local office.

Exercises

1. Prepare a complaint for violation of Marge's civil rights for filing in the federal district court. Civil rights complaints are filed pursuant to title VII of the Civil Rights Act of 1964, as amended, 42 United States Code Annotated section 2000 *et seq.*

Discovery

The purpose of our modern discovery procedure is to narrow the issues, to eliminate surprises, and to achieve substantial justice.

———

GREYHOUND LINES, INC. V. MILLER,
402 F.2D 134 (1968)

OBJECTIVES

After completing this chapter, you will be able to:

1. Discuss the use of the various discovery tools

2. Prepare the documents necessary to utilize the various discovery tools

3. Prepare the necessary authorizations for information gathering

BALLENTINE'S REVIEW

admissibility—The quality of being admissible, *i.e.*, of being admitted, allowed, or considered.

deposition—The transcript of a witness's testimony given under oath outside of the courtroom, usually in advance of the trial or hearing, upon oral examination or in response to written interrogatories; in a more general sense, an affidavit, or a statement under oath.

discovery—A means for providing a party, in advance of trial, with access to facts that are within the knowledge of the other side, to enable the party to better try his or her case.

subpoena—A command in the form of written process requiring a witness to come to court to testify.

§ 10.1 IN GENERAL

Preparation for the trial of a lawsuit mandates that each party obtain as much information as possible concerning the opposition's case. The process used to secure the information necessary to prepare for trial is termed **discovery.**

The discovery process is established in each state by its rules of court, which are most frequently patterned after the Federal Rules of Civil Procedure. The rules set forth the procedure for the discovery process and govern its limitations and timing. There may be a wide divergence regarding individual state rules, and these local rules must be consulted before attempting the use of any of the discovery tools.

§ 10.2 THE PURPOSE OF DISCOVERY

The general concept underlying the discovery process is to eliminate surprise. It is the professionally responsible thing to do to learn everything allowed about an opponent's case. To this end, discovery serves the following purposes:

- to narrow the issues
- to obtain facts for trial
- to learn an opponent's contentions
- to reveal the identity of witnesses
- to locate and preserve evidence
- to learn the extent of damages
- to impeach witnesses

Different causes of action will dictate the emphasis on one or more of the purposes of discovery. The identity of witnesses and the preservation of evidence may not be as critical in a breach of contract action as in a personal injury lawsuit.

§ 10.3 THE DISCOVERY TOOLS

There are six discovery tools available to the parties to a lawsuit. The method employed is determined by the need for disclosure of certain information, the time available, and the cost. The discovery tools are:

- the deposition
- the interrogatory
- the request for production
- the request for admission
- the physical and mental examination
- the request to enter land

discovery: A means for providing a party, in advance of trial, with access to facts that are within the knowledge of the other side, to enable the party to better try his or her case.

The nature of the information being sought and the source of that information are also factors that control the particular discovery tool to be employed.

The Deposition

The testimony of a witness taken upon oral examination through the use of question and answer before an officer of the court is called a **deposition.** It is the only discovery tool that may be used to take the testimony of an individual not a party to the action. It may be either written or oral. The most common form is through oral examination, paralleling courtroom testimony. During the deposition, a party's demeanor and veracity may be evaluated for courtroom presentation.

Depositions may be taken before any judicial officer such as a notary public authorized to make an acknowledgment. The officer may not be an employee or relative of any of the parties or attorneys.

In federal court and in most states, permission of the court must be obtained before a deposition may be taken within the first thirty days of service of process. After that time, and during the time allowed by the court rules for discovery, a deposition may be taken upon reasonable notice of the time, place, and the person or persons to be deposed. (See Figure 10–1.)

If the individual being deposed is to make certain documents or records available for examination at the time of the deposition, those documents must be ordered. The production of documents in most states is ordered through the use of a **subpoena,** which is a command to appear at a certain time and place. If the order is for documents or records, a subpoena is termed a **subpoena duces tecum.** The subpoena for records or documents to be examined at the time of the deposition is usually contained within the body of the notice of deposition with language similar to that in Figure 10–2.

Persons not a party to an action must be served with a subpoena before they can be required to appear for a deposition. Any of the witness's documents sought for review should be listed in the subpoena.

Depositions are generally held in an office with all parties to the lawsuit represented by counsel. A transcript of the testimony is made by a court reporter. Objections to questions are reflected in the transcript of the hearing, and exhibits are introduced as in the trial.

The Interrogatories

A pretrial discovery tool consisting of a set of written questions propounded to a party is called an *interrogatory.* **Interrogatories** may be issued to parties only and are a common initial discovery tool to be used to obtain information from an opponent. Interrogatories may be used for any purpose allowed for discovery in general by the court rules of most states and the Federal Rules of Civil Procedure in federal court.

Many states have rules that limit the length of interrogatories or have prescribed sets of interrogatories for various causes of action. If there is to be a deviation from the standardized forms, leave of the court must be obtained.

The original of the interrogatories must be served upon the party to whom the questions are propounded, with copies of both interrogatories and answers to be delivered to all other parties. The answers must be returned to the party propounding the questions.

Preparation of interrogatories involves drafting a set of questions that is clear, concise, and without ambiguity. Questions should be framed to avoid

deposition: The transcript of a witness's testimony given under oath outside of the courtroom, usually in advance of the trial or hearing, upon oral examination or in response to written interrogatories.

subpoena: A command in the form of written process requiring a witness to come to court to testify.

subpoena duces tecum: The Latin term *duces tecum* means "bring with you under penalty." A subpoena duces tecum is a written command requiring a witness to come to court to testify and at that time to produce for use as evidence the papers, documents, books, or records listed in the subpoena.

interrogatories: Written questions put by one party to another or, in limited situations, to a witness in advance of trial. Interrogatories are a form of discovery and are governed by the rules of civil procedure.

IN THE CIRCUIT COURT
FOR THE COUNTY OF MOSQUITO

BELLE BLISS,

      Plaintiff,

              v.   Case No. 34567

THE THIRSTY TURTLE,

      Defendant.

_____/

NOTICE OF TAKING DEPOSITION

TO: Barnwell Boozer
      Attorney for Defendant
      1234 S. Drainage St.
      Orange, Fremont 45091

PLEASE TAKE NOTICE that the undersigned will take the deposition upon oral examination of BUD WISER, at 2:00 p.m. at his office, located at One Harmony Drive, Orange, Fremont, on November 30, 1999, before a notary public or other person authorized by law to take depositions. This deposition is being taken for purposes of discovery, for use at trial, or for any other purpose allowed by law.
    YOU ARE INVITED TO ATTEND.

                            _____
                            WILL PURVALE
                            Attorney for Plaintiff
                            One Harmony Drive
                            Orange, Fremont 45090

FIGURE 10–1 A sample notice of taking deposition

You are required to have with you at that time and place the following:
All books and records pertaining to THE THIRSTY TURTLE.
If you fail to appear, you may be in contempt of court.

FIGURE 10–2 A sample language for a subpoena duces tecum

answers that are not informative, for example, yes or no answers. The document should contain a caption, like any other pleading, must be signed by the attorney for the party, and should be furnished with a certificate of service (see Figure 10–3).

Under oath, the recipient of the interrogatories must answer each question in writing. The answers should be written in the space provided on the original of the interrogatory form. Attachment of records or lengthy documents is permissible.

The Request for Production

The rules of court of all states allow a party to request documents and other things that are relevant to the subject matter and not privileged. This procedure is called a **request for production,** and is available only for use

request for production: The procedure by which parties to a lawsuit request documents and other things that are relevant to the subject matter and not privileged.

**IN THE CIRCUIT COURT
FOR THE COUNTY OF MOSQUITO**

BELLE BLISS,

      Plaintiff,

          v.   Case No. 34567

THE THIRSTY TURTLE,

      Defendant.

_____/

NOTICE OF SERVICE OF INTERROGATORIES

You are notified that BELLE BLISS, Plaintiff herein, has this 30th day of June, 1999, served upon Defendant interrogatories to be answered under oath pursuant to the rules of court.

I HEREBY CERTIFY that a copy was furnished to Barnwell Boozer, attorney for Defendant, this 30th day of June, 1999, by United States Mail.

                          _____
                          WILL PURVALE
                          Attorney for Plaintiff
                          One Harmony Drive
                          Orange, Fremont 45090

FIGURE 10–3 A sample certificate of service

against a party. The request may not be directed toward an individual who is not a party to the action. Rule 34 of the Federal Rules of Civil Procedure forms the model for most state rules for production. It is the intent of the rules that the request encompass more than mere documents. The request may include such things as drawings, graphs, charts, photographs, and data compilations.

The rules permit the production of documents and tangible things to allow their inspection and testing. The material may be examined, copied, sampled, tested, photographed, measured, or preserved. The original of any document or object must be preserved for trial.

In order for a party to request the production of a document or any other tangible thing, the document or object must be in the possession, custody, and control of the party from whom it is requested. The production requested must be reasonable in allowing copies or making something that is not easily transferable available for inspection. In some lawsuits, the physical transfer of voluminous records can be a substantial task requiring cataloging and organization. Some rules provide for reimbursement of the costs involved in the production of documents.

The procedure allowed in most states is the issuance of a subpoena pursuant to notice under the rule. The party to whom the request is made has a set time to respond, typically thirty days, with delivery or objections. The request should list the documents sought with reasonable particularity and without vagueness or ambiguity. (See Figure 10–4.)

Requests for production are usually the next step in the discovery process following the submission of interrogatories. A review of the opposing party's responses to the interrogatories may reveal the existence of documents or other tangible objects that are material and require inspection.

The Request for Admission

The rules of court of each state provide the procedure for a party to request of another party the admission of the truth of any matter within the scope of allowable discovery. The matter sought to be admitted may fall within any of three categories:

- the truth of statements of opinions of fact
- the application of law to facts
- the genuineness of documents

A request for admission serves to narrow the issues to be litigated at the time of trial, eliminating those matters that are not in dispute. The effect of an admission by a party is to conclusively establish that fact for purposes of the present action only, not for any other matter. An admission cannot be used against a party in another lawsuit.

The responding party may admit a fact completely, or the fact may be admitted in part. It is important that the matters sought to be admitted be drafted with as much clarity as possible to avoid any ambiguity in an answer. Vague requests are of no value to the party seeking the admission and are likely to be denied by the responding party.

IN THE CIRCUIT COURT
FOR THE COUNTY OF MOSQUITO

BELLE BLISS,

    Plaintiff,

      v.   Case No. 34567

THE THIRSTY TURTLE,

    Defendant.

_____/

PLAINTIFF'S REQUEST FOR PRODUCTION OF DOCUMENTS

PURSUANT TO Rule 409 of the Fremont Rules of Civil Procedure, BELLE BLISS, plaintiff, requests that defendant, THE THIRSTY TUR- TLE, produce for inspection and copying at the office of BUD WISER, located at One Harmony Drive, Orange, Fremont, or at a time and location to be mutually agreed upon by the parties, the documents requested herein:

1. All records of account of the business of defendant for the years 1998 and 1999 related to premises maintenance and repair.

2. All photographs of the front entrance to Defendant's place of business taken at any time during the years 1998 and 1999.

_____

WILL PURVALE
Attorney for Plaintiff
One Harmony Drive
Orange, Fremont 45090

FIGURE 10–4 A sample request for production of documents

The format for a request for admission is generally similar to the other discovery requests. The caption should be followed by a title designating the nature of the document. The body of the request should contain the matters to be admitted in separately numbered paragraphs. (See Figure 10–5.)

The request for admission is a tool employed in the discovery process after interrogatories, production, and deposition. Once the information from the other tools has been revealed, strategic admissions can be of real value to a party from a tactical standpoint.

IN THE CIRCUIT COURT
FOR THE COUNTY OF MOSQUITO

BELLE BLISS,

Plaintiff,

v.   Case No. 34567

THE THIRSTY TURTLE,

Defendant.

_____/

PLAINTIFF'S REQUEST FOR ADMISSION

PURSUANT TO Rule 503 of the Fremont Rules of Civil Procedure, BELLE BLISS, plaintiff, hereby requests that THE THIRSTY TURTLE, defendant, make the following admissions for purposes of this action only:

1. That each of the documents furnished in response to Plaintiff's Request for Production, and listed in Exhibit A attached hereto, is genuine.

2. That the following statement is true: Defendant knew of the unsafe nature of its premises and failed to undertake any repair prior to the time of plaintiff's injury.

_____
WILL PURVALE
Attorney for Plaintiff
One Harmony Drive
Orange, Fremont 45090

FIGURE 10–5 A sample request for admission

The Physical and Mental Examination

In cases where the physical or mental condition of a party is in controversy, the court rules of every state, as well as the Federal Rules of Civil Procedure, allow for an examination of that condition. Some jurisdictions allow for the examination without leave of the court, while others require an order of the presiding judge. The results of the examination must be forwarded to the opposing party in a report setting forth the physician's findings, diagnosis, and conclusions.

The notice of the examination, or the time and place set by the court, must specify a reasonable time, place, and manner of examination. If costs for travel are involved, many jurisdictions provide for reimbursement of expenses.

In those cases where the physical or mental condition of a party is not in issue but evidence from a party is desired, as in a domestic relation case, the examination must be requested by motion to the court. Good cause must be shown for requiring the examination.

The Request to Enter Land

In many states, it is necessary to file a motion specifically to obtain court permission to enter the land of another. If good cause can be shown to the court for the need to examine land, the court will issue an order allowing the entry. This motion is closely related to the motion for production and, in many states, is covered within the same rule of court.

§ 10.4 THE AUTHORIZATION

In the preparation of most lawsuits, there is a need for documentary evidence to support the claims of a party. Documentary evidence may be secured through the use of any one of the discovery tools above, but it is also obtainable through the use of an authorization provided by either party. An **authorization** is merely the grant of authority to another to do or obtain something. In the case of a lawsuit, an authorization may be used to obtain such information as:

- physician's records
- hospital records
- federal and state income tax records
- employment records

The authorization to obtain these records is usually sent by mail to the custodian of the records, along with a letter of explanation. The letter should also suggest that any costs in the preparation of the records will be reimbursed. (See Figure 10–6.)

The medical authorization form is one that most offices will have already prepared for the client's or party's signature. The authorization is drafted in such general terms as to be flexible enough to cover the particular needs of most situations (see Figure 10–7).

An authorization for the release of income tax records or employment records can be an invaluable tool for the verification of claims related to the action. These records, like medical records, are confidential, and an authorization is required. Employment record authorizations should request the individual's employment application, payroll records, termination status, and any relevant notes. Income tax records may be obtained from the nearest Department of Internal Revenue office or the state capitol of the individual state. (See Figure 10–8.)

authorization: The grant of authority to another to do or obtain something.

WILL PURVALE
Attorney at Law
One Harmony Drive
Orange, Fremont 45090

February 29, 1999

Medical Records Department
Orange Memorial Hospital
P.O. Box 987
Orange, Fremont 45091

Re: Belle Bliss v. The Thirsty Turtle

Case No.: 34567

Dear Records Custodian:
    Please be advised that I represent Ms. Belle Bliss in regard to injuries she sustained in a fall that which occurred on June 30, 1998. I am enclosing herewith a medical authorization form for your records that permits you to furnish all medical records you possess concerning her treatment.
    Please forward copies of the patient's medical chart, nurses' notes, X-ray reports, consultation reports, physicians' notes, laboratory results, and any charges for the treatment. Please do not hesitate to bill me for any charges for this request.
    Thank you very much for your cooperation.

Sincerely,

WILL PURVALE, Esquire

FIGURE 10–6 A sample authorization cover letter

Authorizations are generally used in the early stages of litigation. They may serve to streamline the discovery process and reduce the expense of litigation. The forms may require certain modifications to meet the demands of a particular type of case. If there are going to be substantial costs in the preparation of the records, it may be necessary to make arrangements for payment of those costs.

§ 10.5 THE FEE CONTRACT

Representation by an attorney in a lawsuit is not mandatory but is highly recommended in light of the complexity of the discovery process. Depending on the nature of the case, the client may be asked to sign a contract setting

MEDICAL AUTHORIZATION

This is to authorize you to furnish to WILL PURVALE, Attorney-at-Law, any and all information and records that he may request regarding medical treatment. This authorization hereby cancels any prior authorizations.

DATED this _____ day of _____, 19___.

_____

SUBSCRIBED AND SWORN to before me this _____ day of _____, 19___.

_____
Notary Public

My commission expires: _____

FIGURE 10–7 A sample medical authorization form

WILL PURVALE
Attorney at Law
One Harmony Drive
Orange, Fremont 45090

February 29, 1999

Director
Internal Revenue Service
Cincinnati, OH 47890

Dear Sir:

You are hereby authorized to furnish to WILL PURVALE, Attorney-at-Law, copies of any and all federal income tax returns.

_____
BELLE BLISS
SS# 490-33-1234

FIGURE 10–8 A sample income tax authorization

forth the terms and understanding of the representation. An attorney may work for a client on the basis of an hourly fee for services rendered. As an alternative means of compensation, the attorney may work on the basis of a fee that is dependent on a recovery in the matter, called a **contingent fee.** The contingent fee enables individuals who have a legitimate claim but are unable to afford the hourly fees to be represented by counsel.

The contingent fee agreement usually calls for the payment of costs that are incurred in the development of the case, along with a fee expressed as a graduated percentage of the total recovery. For instance, the fee may be a set percentage of 33 1/3% up to the time of trial and 40% after trial has commenced. (See Figure 10–9.)

The agreement usually provides for a short cancellation period before the fee structure becomes operative to allow for a change of heart, which occasionally occurs. If the agreement is breached in any way, the basic law of contracts applies to the default.

contingent fee: A fee for legal services, calculated on the basis of an agreed-upon percentage of the amount of money recovered for the client by his or her attorney.

CONTINGENT FEE CONTRACT

I, BELLE BLISS, hereby retain and employ WILL PURVALE as my attorney to represent me in my claim for personal injuries sustained in a slip and fall accident against THE THIRSTY TURTLE on June 30, 1999.

I hereby agree to pay for the cost of investigation and other necessary expenses to prosecute this claim, and court costs if it is necessary to institute suit. As for compensation for services, I agree to pay my attorney from the net proceeds the following fee:

Thirty-three and one-third percent (33 1/3%) of any recovery up to the time of the commencement of trial.

Forty percent (40%) of any recovery after the commencement of trial.

I understand this contract may be canceled by written notice to the attorney within ten (10) business days of the signing hereof, and if canceled, I will not be responsible for any fees.

Dated this _____ day of _____, 1999.

_____
BELLE BLISS

_____
WILL PURVALE

FIGURE 10–9 A sample contingent fee agreement

SUMMARY

- Discovery is the process through which each party to a lawsuit is entitled to obtain certain facts, documents, physical evidence, and information to assist in the proof of his or her allegations. Its purpose is to eliminate surprise, narrow the issues, reduce the expense of litigation, and assist the court in its docket. Through the discovery process, a party is entitled to information of any nature as long as it is material to the action and not subject to a privilege.

- It is only through the use of the subpoena and deposition that an individual not a party to the action is subject to the discovery process. Parties may find themselves subject to each of the tools of discovery at various stages of the litigation process. From interrogatories through requests for production and admission and examination, each party attempts to obtain as much information as possible about his or her opponent's case. Through the use of the deposition, that information is further defined and evaluated for purposes of trial. The ultimate goal is to place each party in a posture to try a lawsuit as expeditiously as possible.

IN REVIEW

1. What is the discovery process?
2. What are the six primary discovery tools?
3. How is a deposition different from the other means of discovery?
4. What are the distinctions between depositions and interrogatories?
5. What is the primary concern in the preparation of interrogatories?
6. What is the effect of a request for admission on that fact for purposes of trial?
7. What is the purpose of obtaining authorizations from a party?
8. What is a contingent fee contract?

PUTTING IT ALL TOGETHER

Your office has been retained by the Wet N' Wooly Park, Inc., a water theme park in the state of Fremont, in an action filed by one Purvis Gomer for personal injuries sustained by him resulting from his attempt to ride the "Cracker Barrel." The ride is the park's latest effort to separate the unsuspecting tourist not only from his last dollar, but also from his sanity.

It seemed that Purvis was attempting to impress his best girl, Charlene McSly, with his manhood by riding the Cracker Barrel. The ride involves a trip in an enclosed barrel from a 160-foot waterfall into a small pool at speeds approaching terminal velocity. The result of this folly on Purvis's part left little intact but his stupidity.

The complaint filed by Mr. Gomer alleges that he sustained severe personal injuries from the fall and emotional distress from the loss of Charlene, who apparently was not too impressed. He claims that your client's attempt to create a thrill ride in defiance of Newton's law of gravity and the second law of thermodynamics amounted to a negligent act, causing losses for which he should be reimbursed.

Exercises

1. Prepare the discovery documents appropriate to defend this action, following the filing of the appropriate answer. You may assume that a motion for summary judgment will be entertained by the court once discovery has been completed.

CHAPTER
11

Domestic Relations

Happy and thrice happy are they who enjoy an uninterrupted union, and whose love, unbroken by any complaints, shall not dissolve until the last day.

———

HORACE (65–8 B.C.)

OBJECTIVES

After completing this chapter, you will be able to:

1. Summarize the contractual nature of a marriage
2. Prepare and draft a separation agreement
3. Prepare and draft a complaint for dissolution of marriage
4. Prepare and draft the responsive pleadings in a divorce action
5. Prepare and draft the final judgment for divorce

BALLENTINE'S REVIEW

alimony—Ongoing court-ordered support payments by a divorced spouse, usually payments made by an ex-husband to his former wife.

divorce—A dissolution of the marital relationship between husband and wife.

marriage—The relationship of a man and a woman legally united as husband and wife; a contract binding the parties until one dies or until a divorce or annulment occurs.

postnuptial agreement—A marital agreement entered into after marriage.

prenuptial agreement—An agreement between a man and a woman who are about to be married, governing the financial and property arrangements between them in the event of divorce, death, or even during the marriage. Such an agreement may override obligations or rights provided by statute.

§ 11.1 MARRIAGE

The concept of a marriage between a man and a woman stands at the foundation of social organization in the United States today. Marriages are no longer "arranged" on the basis of property interests or for political reasons. Since the nineteenth century, women have been placed on an equal footing with men in the eyes of the law with the enactment of women's property acts allowing women to own property in their own name. That legal equality allows a freedom of choice in the selection of a mate and continues after the consummation of the marriage.

Marriage is the legal status of a man and woman existing as husband and wife and united for life. It is viewed as a matter of contract for life between a man and a woman to live as husband and wife, and it carries the legally guaranteed freedom of choice regarding such issues as employment, property, and procreation.

§ 11.2 THE DOMESTIC RELATIONS CONTRACTS

The marriage of a man and woman involves a contractual relationship with its attendant requirements of legal capacity, consideration, and offer and acceptance. The enforceability of the contractual relationship has been eroded by the laws of most states abolishing an action for a breach of a covenant to marry, called an **anti–heart balm statute.** Yet, the law of contracts is very much in evidence within the marital framework involving such matters as an agreement before marriage addressing such certain rights and obligations during marriage and upon death or divorce. Contracts may also address the rights and obligations of persons cohabiting, an agreement to separate without a divorce, and an agreement for reconciliation.

The Antenuptial Contract

A contract between prospective spouses in contemplation of marriage is called an **antenuptial agreement.** It is also called a *premarital agreement* or a *prenuptial agreement*. Its purpose is to define the rights, duties, and obligations of the spouses during the marriage and outline any possible divorce. An antenuptial agreement is one that is usually undertaken by individuals with substantial property before marriage.

Antenuptial agreements must be in writing to satisfy the statute of frauds in most states because real property is often a subject of the contract. The agreement must meet the formal requirements for the execution of a contract in that particular state and must contain a full and frank disclosure of all assets. Many states have enacted the Uniform Premarital Agreement Act, a uniform law drafted by the Committee on Uniform Laws of the American Bar Association. The act, in section 3, specifies those matters that may be the subject of the agreement:

- the rights and obligations of each of the parties in any property whenever acquired
- the right to acquire or dispose of any property

marriage: The relationship of a man and a woman legally united as husband and wife. Marriage is a contract binding the parties until one dies or until a divorce or annulment occurs.

anti–heart balm statute: A law that establishes the right to an action for a breach of a covenant to marry. Such laws have been abolished in most states.

antenuptial agreement: An agreement between a man and a woman who are about to be married, governing the financial and property arrangements between them in the event of divorce, death, or even during the marriage. Such an agreement may override obligations or rights provided by statute.

- the disposition of property upon separation, divorce, or death
- spousal support
- child support
- the creation of a will or trust
- life insurance
- choice of law governing the agreement
- any matters not in violation of public policy

It must be kept in mind that not all states permit an antenuptial agreement without some limitation. Some states take the position that an antenuptial agreement is violative of the public policy of that state in that it may encourage or facilitate divorce. Such states are reluctant to uphold certain provisions of the agreement due to the possibility of a change in circumstances between the time of the execution of the agreement and the ultimate divorce.

Figure 11–1 provides a sample antenuptial agreement.

The Separation Agreement

A **separation agreement,** also referred to as a *postnuptial agreement*, is a contract between a husband and wife establishing their respective rights and obligations while they are separated. The agreement is prepared in lieu of the expense of litigation and in those situations where divorce is contemplated but not a certainty. Its purpose is to avoid the uncertainty of an oral understanding on issues such as child support, alimony, and property division.

The separation agreement can be a complex document, depending on the nature of the relationship, the extent of the property interests involved, and the care and support of children and spouse. The development of a thorough checklist can serve to ensure that the parties have considered each topic, as well as provide the preparer with the necessary information to draft the agreement. A checklist should include the following items:

- personal data on the parties
- identification of children
- inventory of real property
- inventory of personal property
- antenuptial agreement
- financial statement
- provision for existing debts and contractual obligations
- alimony considerations
- child custody agreement
- child support understanding
- health insurance and medical provision
- life insurance
- income tax
- attorney fees
- divorce
- reconciliation

separation agreement: An agreement between husband and wife who are about to divorce or to enter into a legal separation, settling property rights and other matters such as custody, child support, visitation, and alimony.

The separation agreement must comply with the requirements of its particular state regarding legality, capacity, and consideration, offer and acceptance.

ANTENUPTIAL AGREEMENT

AGREEMENT made as of this 14th day of June, 1999, between WIN-STON P. BLANSFORD, III ("BLANSFORD"), residing at 1590 West Denton Street, Nelton, New York 10079, and ARCADIA HOLLOWELL ("HOL-LOWELL"), residing at 3898 Georgetown Drive, Geneva, New York 10076.

WITNESSETH:

Whereas, each of the parties has known the other for a period of time, is fully satisfied with the disclosure of the financial circumstances of the other, and desires to make an agreement regarding his and her property rights in consideration of the marriage to each other, and

Whereas, each party acknowledges that the other may hereafter acquire by gift and inheritance, as well as through professional endeavor and from other sources, assets and income of value, and

Whereas, each of the parties has assets and earnings, or earnings potential, sufficient to provide for his or her own maintenance and support in a proper and acceptable standard of living without the necessity of financial contributions by the other, and each of the parties is aware of the hazards and risks of the continuance of earnings and the changes in assets and liabilities of the other and of the possibility of substantially changed financial circumstances of the other with the result that the earnings and/or net worth of one party is or may be substantially different from those of the other party, and

Whereas, except as otherwise herein set forth, each of the parties desires to own, hold, acquire, and dispose of property now and in the future and subsequent to their marriage to each other with the same freedom as though unmarried and to dispose of said property during their respective lifetimes or upon death or upon any other termination of the marriage without restriction or limitation in accordance with his and her own desires, and

Whereas, except as otherwise herein set forth, it is the intention of each of the parties by entering into this agreement to determine unilaterally what property, now and in the future, shall be his or her own separate property and that all of the property of each, however acquired or held, shall be free from any consideration as marital property, community property, quasi-community property, or any other form of marital or community property, as those terms are used and understood in any jurisdiction, including but not limited to the State of New York.

NOW, THEREFORE, in consideration of the marriage of each party to the other and the mutual promises and covenants herein, the parties have mutually agreed as follows:

1. *Present property.* All of the property, real, personal, and mixed, that each party has previously acquired and now holds in his or her name or possession shall be and shall continue to remain the sole and separate property of that person, together with all future appreciation, increases, and other changes in value of that property and irrespective of the contributions (if any) that either party might have made or may hereafter make to said property or to the marriage, directly or indirectly.

FIGURE 11–1 A sample antenuptial agreement

2. *Future property.* All of the property, real, personal, or mixed, that each party may hereafter acquire in his or her own name or possession shall be and shall remain the sole and separate property of that person, together with all future appreciation, increases, and other changes in value of that property and irrespective of the contributions (if any) that either party may make to said property or the marriage, directly or indirectly.

   Notwithstanding the foregoing, any property that is a gift from one party to the other shall remain the sole and separate property of the donee of the gift; and all wedding presents given to both parties shall be deemed jointly owned by the parties wherein each shall hold an undivided one-half interest.

3. *Joint property.* Any property, real, personal, or mixed, that shall now or hereafter be held in the joint names of the parties shall be owned in accordance with the kind of joint ownership as title is held and, if there is no other designation, shall be held equally by the parties with such survivorship rights (if any) as may be specifically designated by the title ownership or as may be implied or be derived by operation of law other than the operation of the so-called equitable distribution law or community property or any similar law of any jurisdiction involving marital property, community property, quasi-community property, or any other form of marital or community property.

4. *Life insurance.* From and after the marriage of the parties, BLANS-FORD shall maintain at his own expenses a policy or policies of life insurance on his life having death benefits payable in the sum of not less than $250,000 for the benefit of HOLLOWELL until the earlier occurrence of the death of either party or the remarriage of HOL-LOWELL (as "remarriage" is hereinafter defined), and he will not encumber said insurance whereby the death benefits that are actually payable shall be less than $250,000. BLANSFORD shall furnish proof of his compliance with this paragraph upon the reasonable request of HOLLOWELL, but not more often than annually; and HOLLOWELL, in addition, is authorized to obtain direct confirmation from any insurance carrier or employer through which said policy or policies are issued and administered.

5. *Estate rights.* Except as otherwise herein set forth, each party hereby releases, waives, and relinquishes any right or claim of any nature whatsoever in the property of the other or otherwise, now or hereafter acquired, and, without limitation, expressly forever waives any right or claim that he or she may have or hereafter acquire, whether as the spouse of the other or otherwise, under the present or future laws of any jurisdiction: (a) to share in the estate of the other party upon the death of the other party; and (b) to act as executor or administrator of the estate of the other or as trustee, personal representative, or in any fiduciary capacity with respect to the estate of the other. All rights that either party may acquire in the other's estate by virtue of the marriage, including but not limited to rights of setoff in New York, all distributive shares in New York, and all rights of election in New York, as such

FIGURE 11–1 (continued)

laws may not exist or hereafter be changed, an any similar or other provision of law in this or any other jurisdiction, are hereby waived by each party.

6. *Wills.* Nothing in this agreement shall prevent or limit either party from hereafter making provisions for the other by Last Will and Testament: (a) to inherit from the estate of the other; and/or (b) to serve in any fiduciary capacity, in which event the provisions thus made in said Last Will and Testament shall control.

7. *Primary residence.* In the event that BLANSFORD should predecease HOLLOWELL during the time when they are married to each other (as "married" is hereinafter defined), HOLLOWELL shall have the right to continue to reside in their primary residence until the occurrence of her remarriage; provided, however, that HOLLOWELL shall pay all expenses of every kind and nature in connection with said residence (including but not limited to all repairs, whether ordinary, extraordinary, structural, or otherwise), except only for the payment of real estate taxes and, if the primary residence is a condominium or cooperative apartment, the maintenance or common charges, as the case may be, which real estate taxes and maintenance charges or common charges, as applicable, shall be paid for by BLANSFORD'S estate as an obligation of the estate. If the primary residence is rented and occupied by the parties under a lease (not a proprietary lease of a cooperative apartment), HOLLOWELL shall have the right to cause said lease to be transferred to her sole name, including any rent security deposited under said lease, without payment to BLANSFORD'S estate, provided that said request is made in writing to BLANSFORD'S estate representatives within ninety days after his death. This paragraph shall apply only to the primary residence of the parties and not to any other residence that they or either of them may own at the time of BLANSFORD'S death.

8. *Support.*

(a) In the event that the parties shall cease to be married for any reason other than BLANSFORD'S death (as "married" is hereinafter defined), BLANSFORD, or his estate, shall pay to HOLLOWELL as and for her support and maintenance the sum of $500 per week, commencing as of the first Friday after the parties shall cease to be married (by reason of death or otherwise) and continuing on each successive Friday thereafter. Said payments shall continue for one week for each full week that the parties were married, but in no event shall said payments continue for a period of more than 260 weeks, whereby said payments shall automatically and without further notice cease. By way of example, if the parties were married for 210 full weeks, a total of 210 weekly payments shall be made; if they were married for 20½ weeks, 20 weekly payments shall be made. Notwithstanding the foregoing, all of said weekly payments shall sooner cease upon the earliest happening of: (i) the death of HOLLOWELL; (ii) the remarriage of HOLLOWELL; or (iii) the fifth anniversary date after the date when payments are required to be commenced. This paragraph

FIGURE 11–1 (continued)

shall not be construed as an indication of any financial need on the part of HOLLOWELL, but rather an expression by BLANSFORD of his desire to make a contribution to the future life of HOLLOWELL under the circumstances and provisions herein set forth.

(b) In the event that BLANSFORD shall die while the parties are married to each other (as "marriage" is hereinafter defined), BLANSFORD'S estate shall pay to HOLLOWELL as and for her support and maintenance the sum of $500 per week, commencing as of the first Friday after his death and continuing on each successive Friday thereafter until the earliest happening of: (i) the death of HOLLOWELL; (ii) the remarriage of HOLLOWELL; or (iii) the fifth anniversary date after the date when payments are required to be commenced.

9. *Definitions.* The following definitions shall apply to the respective expressions whenever used in this agreement:

(a) "Remarriage" as used everywhere in this agreement shall be deemed a remarriage of HOLLOWELL, regardless of whether said remarriage shall be void or voidable or terminated by divorce or annulment or otherwise, and shall also be deemed to include circumstance whereby HOLLOWELL shall live with an unrelated person in a husband-wife relationship (irrespective of whether or not they hold themselves out as such) for a continuous period of 60 days or for a period or periods of time aggregating 120 days or more on a noncontinuous, or interrupted, basis in any 18-month period.

(b) The time during which the parties are "married," or the period of the "marriage" of the parties, as used everywhere in this agreement shall constitute the period of time commencing with the ceremonial marriage of the parties to each other and continuing until the earliest happening of any of the following events: (i) the commencement of a matrimonial action (as "matrimonial action" is presently defined by the State of New York or any similar action or proceeding in any other jurisdiction); (ii) the divorce or legal separation (by decree or judgment or by agreement) of the parties; (iii) the physical separation of the parties wherein either or both of the parties have commenced to live separate and apart from the other with the intent not thereafter to live together, regardless of whether that intent is expressed in writing, orally, or otherwise; or (iv) the death of either party.

10. *Disclosure.* Each party has been apprised of the right to obtain further disclosure of the financial circumstances of the other party and is satisfied with the disclosure made. Each party expressly waives the right to any further financial disclosure and acknowledges that said waiver is made with the full benefit of legal counsel and knowledge of the legal consequences thereof and that neither party properly cannot, and shall not, subsequently assert that this agreement should be impaired or invalidated by reason of any lack of financial disclosure

FIGURE 11–1 (continued)

or lack of understanding or of fraud, duress, or coercion. Without limiting the generality of the foregoing, BLANSFORD represents that his present net worth is in excess of $250,000 and that his annual income is in excess of $63,000, which representation admittedly is not all-inclusive and which is not intended to be relied upon by either party.

11. *General provisions.* This agreement shall be construed as an agreement made and to be performed in the State of New York and cannot be changed, or any of its terms waived, except by a writing signed and acknowledged by both parties. Each party hereby consents to the personal jurisdiction of the State of New York in the event of any dispute or question regarding this agreement. Each party acknowledges receipt of a fully executed copy of this agreement, has had an opportunity to read it, and understands the same after consultation with independent counsel and is fully satisfied with the disclosure made of all the financial circumstances of the other party. The paragraph captions in this agreement are for the purpose of convenience only and are not a part of this agreement.

12. Each party has been separately represented by an attorney of his or her choice. HOLLOWELL has been represented by Fishburn, Durst and Knowell, P.A., 4986 East Churchill Road, New York, New York 10024, and BLANSFORD has been represented by Billings and Brown, P.A., 38979 Washington Avenue, New York, New York 10024 in connection with the negotiation, making, and execution of this agreement.

IN WITNESS WHEREOF the parties, for themselves and their heirs, next-of-kin, representatives, and assigns, have executed these presents prior to their marriage to each other on the day and year first above written.

_____

ARCADIA HOLLOWELL

_____

WINSTON P. BLANSFORD, III

FIGURE 11–1 (continued)

It is also subject to individual state law on questions such as fraud, duress, or undue influence, which are particularly sensitive questions in a separation where emotions play a significant role.

The custom and rules regarding the form and content of the separation agreement vary significantly from state to state due to the ever-changing landscape of domestic relations theory. The specific matters to be addressed in a basic separation agreement should consist of:

- caption and identification of the parties
- separation clause
- provision for alimony

- property division
- custody and child support
- responsibility for debts
- insurance
- wills
- modification

The format for the agreement should consist of numbered paragraphs similar to a formal contract. Subheadings are advisable for individual topics.

The Caption and Identification of the Parties. The introductory provisions of the agreement should reflect those matters under state law that provide for the validity of the agreement. The agreement must conform with the public policy of the state, must not be collusive in nature, and must not be in contemplation of a divorce. Since all contracts require a recitation of consideration, the separation agreement should reflect the mutual exchange of promises as fulfilling that requirement. Figure 11–2, Exhibit 1, provides a sample caption and introduction for a marital separation agreement.

The Separation Clause. In order to satisfy the public policy of most jurisdictions, which states that it will tolerate nothing that fosters divorce, the separation agreement must reflect that the marriage is best served by a permanent separation. A timely effort on the part of the marriage partners avoids judicial interference. The parties must, in fact, be living separated and must express an intent to so remain, electing to not act as husband and wife. (See Figure 11–2, Exhibit 2.)

The Provision for Alimony Clause. At common law a wife had a right to be supported by her husband. The modern state of the law is to view that obligation of support to be mutual, thus complying with the Fourteenth Amendment avoiding discrimination on the basis of sex. The duty of spousal support in the form of an allowance for maintenance is called **alimony.** That allowance may take the form of a lump sum, or it may be in periodic payments. A lump-sum alimony payment must be clearly designated as such to avoid any confusion with a property division, which may have certain tax consequences.

The amount of alimony provided, if any, depends on the level of need and the ability to pay. The Uniform Marriage and Divorce Act, section 308, provides guidelines to be considered in determining alimony in both separation situations and divorce:

> (a) In a proceeding for dissolution of marriage, legal separation, or maintenance following a decree of dissolution of the marriage by a court which lacked personal jurisdiction over the absent spouse, the court may grant a maintenance order for either spouse only if it finds that the spouse seeking maintenance:
>> (1) lacks sufficient property to provide for his reasonable needs; and
>> (2) is unable to support himself through appropriate employment or is the custodian of a child whose condition or circumstances make it appropriate that the custodian not be required to seek employment outside the home.

alimony: Ongoing court-ordered support payments by a divorced spouse, usually payments made by an ex-husband to his former wife.

MARITAL SEPARATION AGREEMENT

THIS AGREEMENT, entered into this 30th day of November, 1999, between FOSTER SPLITT, hereinafter referred to as Husband, residing at 14 Freedom Circle, Johnstown, Fremont, and WANDA SPLITT, hereinafter referred to as Wife, residing at 1 Limbo Lane, Johnstown, Fremont.

WHEREAS, the parties were married on June 30, 1990, and a daughter, FAITH, was born on July 4, 1991, as a result of irreconcilable differences, the parties have been living apart since February 29, 1999. The parties wish to enter into this agreement to settle all custody, support, and property rights between them. Both parties have had independent advice of legal counsel and have not been coerced into entering into this agreement.

NOW THEREFORE, in consideration of the promises and the mutual obligations contained in this agreement, the parties agree as follows:

Husband and Wife shall continue to live separate and apart, each free from interference, authority, and control, either direct or indirect, of the other, except as may expressly be in this Agreement, and intend to do so permanently.

ALIMONY

Husband shall pay to Wife as alimony or separate maintenance payments the sum of One Thousand Five Hundred Dollars ($1500.00) per month on the first day of each month commencing on the first month following the date of the execution of this Agreement. Payments shall terminate upon death of Husband or upon the remarriage of Wife. All payments shall be made in cash. Husband shall have the obligation to make alimony or separate maintenance payments for a period of thirty-six months following the execution of this agreement.

Husband and Wife intend that all payments made pursuant to this paragraph shall be included as income on Wife's income tax returns and shall be a deduction on Husband's income tax returns pursuant to the Internal Revenue Code beginning in the year of the execution of this agreement.

PROPERTY

Husband and Wife hereby agree to divide equitably between them their marital property vested during their marriage, as follows:

(a) *Residence.* Husband and Wife are co-owners of real property located at 1 Limbo Lane, Johnstown, Fremont, and agree to sell the property as soon as practicable and to divide the net proceeds therefrom equally.

(b) *Personal Property.* Husband and Wife have amicably divided their personal property and each shall be the owner of any such property in their custody and control.

FIGURE 11–2 A sample marital separation agreement

CHILD CUSTODY AND VISITATION ◄────────────

(a) Wife shall have the permanent custody and control of the minor children subject only to the rights of visitation hereunder vested in Husband.

(b) (optional provisions regarding the exact nature of visitation agreed upon)

CHILD SUPPORT ◄────────────

Husband shall pay to Wife for the support and maintenance of the child the sum of One Hundred Fifty ($150.00) per week on the first day of each month, commencing on the first day of August, 1999, and continuing until said child marries, dies, or attains the age of majority or until custody of said child is awarded.

LIFE INSURANCE ◄────────────

Husband agrees to maintain the life insurance policies listed in Exhibit A attached hereto and made a part of this Agreement, and to pay all premiums thereon due until the child support obligations under this Agreement are fully performed. The insurers will be instructed to change the beneficiaries of each policy to the minor child.

LAST WILL AND TESTAMENT ◄────────────

Husband and Wife agree that each will maintain a Last Will and Testament which provides that his or her estate be divided and distributed, at the time of death, in such manner that the full value of the estate be placed in trust for the use and benefit of the minor child until such time as the minor child shall attain the age of majority (18). The parties' heirs, administrators, executors, trustees, and assigns shall be bound by this agreement whether or not such Last Will and Testament is, in fact, executed.

EXHIBIT 5
A sample child custody clause

EXHIBIT 6
A sample child support clause

EXHIBIT 7
A sample insurance clause

EXHIBIT 8
A sample wills clause

FIGURE 11–2 (continued)

(b) The maintenance order shall be in amounts and for periods of time the court deems just, without regard to marital misconduct, and after considering all relevant factors, including:
(1) the financial resources of the party seeking maintenance, including marital property apportioned to him, his ability to meet his needs independently, and the extent to which a provision for support of a child living with the party includes a sum for that party as custodian;
(2) the time necessary to acquire education or training to enable the party seeking maintenance to find appropriate employment;
(3) the standard of living established during the marriage;
(4) the duration of the marriage;

(5) the age and the physical and emotional condition of the spouse seeking maintenance; and
(6) the ability of the spouse from whom maintenance is sought to meet his needs while meeting those of the spouse seeking maintenance.

In drafting the maintenance provisions of the agreement, it is necessary to consider the periodic nature of the payments, the dollar amount, termination upon death, and any limitations on the period or amount. Modification should also be considered (see Figure 11–2, Exhibit 3).

The Property Division Clause. Any property division must be fair and equitable, but not necessarily equal. The division of the property must concern itself with the nature of the property, its source, and how it is currently held.

The property that may be subject to division can be either real property or personal property. The source of the property, whether real or personal, may vary, as in a gift or bequest to or a purchase by one spouse or both spouses jointly. The property may be held in the name of one of the spouses, or it may be held jointly with rights of survivorship, as in the marital home.

The general rule for property division in most states that base their law on the common law is that property acquired by a spouse before the marriage is deemed separate property and is not subject to division. Property acquired solely by one spouse as through a gift or bequest is similarly treated as not divisible. Property acquired in this manner is considered **nonmarital property.** If such property gains in value during the period of the marriage, that **appreciation** is subject to division.

Any other property, whether real or personal, acquired during the marriage is subject to division upon separation or divorce and is considered **marital property.** The general rule is the division must be equitable, even if not equal. The separation agreement should reflect a fair distribution of marital property mutually agreed upon by the parties. (See Figure 11–2, Exhibit 4.)

The Custody Clause. In a divorce or dissolution matter, the court determines all matters relative to child custody. In a separation agreement, the issue of custody is a matter of agreement between the parties regarding what form is in the best interests of the child. The agreement cannot contravene the public policy of each state, which is to ensure that each minor child has frequent contact with both parents and that those parents share the responsibilities of childraising, called **shared parental responsibility.** Those issues that form the focus of the court in awarding child custody in a contested matter do not appear in this clause of the separation agreement. (See Figure 11–2, Exhibit 5.)

The Child Support Clause. Children are entitled to be maintained by law until they reach the age of majority. In a separation agreement, the maintenance of a child is the burden of the noncustodial parent. The amount of the child support payment is one that has received attention by most state legislatures through the adoption of child support guidelines. Those guidelines form the basis for an equitable means of determining the amount of support and should be considered by the parties in formulating the separation agreement.

nonmarital property: Property acquired by a spouse before marriage or through a gift or bequest; such separate property is not subject to division in a dissolution of the marriage.

appreciation: An increase in the value of something.

marital property: Property acquired by the parties during the marriage, which a court will divide between the former spouses upon dissolution of the marriage if the parties have not themselves made disposition by marital agreement.

shared parental responsibility: A situation in which both parents have frequent contact with their children and share the responsibilities of childraising, even after a divorce.

The agreement should also maintain a provision for health insurance for the child where it is reasonably available through a group insurance plan. (See Figure 11–2, Exhibit 6.)

The options available to the parties are solely a matter of agreement and may depend upon:

- the amount of support
- the method of payment
- the time of payment
- the termination of payment

The well-drafted agreement anticipates the changing needs of the child, including the payment for a college education if that is contemplated by the parties.

The Responsibility for Debts Clause. In any separation, there will be joint financial obligations that must be met by one party or the other. The responsibility for the debts should be addressed in the agreement in a separate paragraph that addresses the following issues:

- identity of the creditors
- account or loan numbers
- balances owed
- payments
- party responsible

The debts should each be listed in the agreement or made the subject of an exhibit to be attached to the agreement. Each creditor should be notified by the parties regarding from whom the payment will be forthcoming.

The Insurance Clause. The preparer of the agreement may want to consider the necessity of maintaining the existence of life, health, and disability policies at the time of separation. A separate clause should provide for the continuation of premium payments and an obligation to keep the policies in effect. The beneficiary designation may change, depending on the agreement of the parties. A child may be specifically designated as the beneficiary, with the proceeds of the insurance held in trust for the child until the age of majority. (See Figure 11–2, Exhibit 7.)

The Wills Clause. The separation agreement should concern itself with the matter of the Last Will and Testament of each of the parties. Because of the unlikelihood of either party wishing to benefit the other, and with the intention to provide for the children, the wills clause is necessary to provide for the distribution of property should either party die. It is incumbent upon the husband and wife to decide how the property is to be held until the children reach the age of majority, and then to implement that decision with the necessary instruments. Whatever the decision may be, it is necessary to incorporate those concerns in the agreement. A sample wills clause may begin like the one shown in Figure 11–2, Exhibit 8.

The Modification Clause. Provisions of a separation agreement providing for periodic changes in the amount of alimony or child support may be incorporated. The parties may wish to provide for an increase in the amount of support based upon changes in the consumer price index or a reduction if the noncustodial parent should become unable to earn a living because of a disability. The variations in the way a modification is handled depends upon the desires of the parties and the creativity of the preparer.

§ 11.3 DISSOLUTION/DIVORCE

The termination of the legal status of marriage, whereby a man and woman no longer coexist as husband and wife, is known as **divorce.** The term *dissolution* means the same thing and is found in the statutes of many states in an attempt to soften the impact of disruption of the social institution.

The Nature and Types of Divorce

Most divorces in the United States are uncontested, which means that the parties are in agreement as to the necessity of the termination of the marital relationship. They are also in agreement on the issues of child custody, support, alimony, and property division. The form of the divorce varies with the circumstances, giving rise to various types of divorce. Some of those types are:

- **Default divorce:** A divorce where no appearance is made by the defendant, so that the plaintiff is granted the dissolution without contest.
- *Ex parte* **divorce:** A divorce where the court does not have jurisdiction over the defendant and only one party is present in court.
- **Migratory divorce:** A divorce where the husband and wife travel to another state to obtain a divorce because of the laxity of the laws in that state.
- **Foreign divorce:** A divorce obtained in a state other than the current state where enforcement is being sought.

In these types of divorce, the procedure is merely one of formality, involving none of the issues surrounding the grounds for divorce or the questions of property, custody, and support.

§ 11.4 THE PROCEDURE

The preliminary step to the filing of any pleading in a dissolution of marriage is to obtain as much information as possible. The development of a good checklist facilitates the process. Most law offices that specialize in domestic relations matters have interview forms and checklists available for the information-gathering process.

The Complaint

The complaint in a domestic relations matter, in some states referred to as a petition, is the initial pleading filed to commence the cause of action. As in

---

divorce: A dissolution of the marital relationship between husband and wife.

default divorce: A divorce in which no appearance is made by the defendant, so that the plaintiff is granted the dissolution without contest.

ex parte **divorce:** A divorce proceeding in which only one spouse participates. If the failure to participate is due to inadequate notice, any divorce decree granted is invalid.

migratory divorce: A divorce obtained by a person who changed his or her residence or domicile to another state for the length of time required to secure a divorce in that state, but with no intention of remaining there.

foreign divorce: A divorce granted in a state or country other than the couple's state of residence.

any other civil matter, it must state a claim upon which relief may be granted. It must contain a statement of the jurisdiction of the court, the grounds for granting the divorce, and the relief being sought. Other matters of the court's consideration—such as child custody, child support, alimony, and property division—must be pleaded if in issue.

A complaint for dissolution of marriage should contain the following:

- a caption
- an identification of the nature of the cause of action
- the jurisdiction of the court
- the details of the marriage
- an identification of the children of the marriage, if any
- allegations regarding child custody
- allegations regarding child support
- allegations regarding alimony
- allegations regarding property division
- the grounds for the divorce

See Figure 11–3 for a sample of a divorce complaint.

The Answer

The responsive pleading filed by the defendant or respondent in a divorce action is his or her first appearance of record in the matter. In all cases, the defendant has a specified period of time in which to file his or her answer, typically twenty days after service of the complaint. The answer either admits, denies, or pleads insufficient knowledge regarding each element of the complaint and may contain a counterclaim for any matter deemed necessary. For instance, if the plaintiff is seeking child custody and the defendant is also seeking child custody, allegation sufficient to warrant the granting of custody to the defendant must be pleaded. The answer contains the following:

- the caption
- an identification of the parties
- an admission or denial of the allegations in the complaint
- any counterclaims to be asserted
- a prayer for relief

If only a portion of any specific allegation is to be denied, the answer must state with specificity the portion to be admitted.

The Simplified Divorce

In many states, the domestic relations procedural rules contain provisions for the submission of a "simple" divorce to the court for dissolution. Usually, a simple divorce is available in a situation where there are no minor children involved and the property of the parties, if any, is not an issue. In such cases, the complaint is a simplified version of the full complaint, and the proceedings are shortened to the scheduling of a quick hearing to enter the decree. The complaint should contain the following:

**IN THE CIRCUIT COURT
FOR BOONE COUNTY, FLORIDA**

IN RE: The Marriage of

FLORENCE LAURENCE,

      Petitioner,

and

LAWRENCE LAURENCE,

      Respondent.

_____/

**PETITION FOR DISSOLUTION
OF MARRIAGE**

Petitioner, FLORENCE LAURENCE, petitions for the dissolution of the marriage between herself and LAWRENCE LAURENCE, and in support thereof, states:

1. This is an action for dissolution of marriage between Petitioner and LAWRENCE LAURENCE.

2. Petitioner has been a resident of the State of Florida for more than six (6) months.

3. Petitioner and Respondent were married to each other on November 12, 1989, at Boone Valley, Florida, and lived together as husband and wife until June 30, 1999.

4. There was one child born of this marriage: PATIENCE LAURENCE, born April 25, 1991.

5. Petitioner has not participated as a party, witness, or in any other litigation or custody proceeding, in this or any other state, concerning custody of the child subject to this proceeding.

6. Petitioner has no information of any custody proceeding pending in a court of this or any other state concerning the child subject to this proceeding.

7. Petitioner does not know of any person not a party to this proceeding who has physical custody or claims to have visitation rights with respect to the child subject to this proceeding.

8. Petitioner says that she is a fit and proper person to have permanent care, custody, and control of the minor child, PATIENCE LAURENCE.

9. Respondent is well and able to provide for, and Petitioner requires financial support of, the minor child of the parties.

10. There is personal property to be divided equitably between the parties.

FIGURE 11-3 A sample complaint for dissolution

11. There are debts and obligations owing by the parties that should be equitably divided by the Court.

12. The marriage between the parties is irretrievably broken.

WHEREFORE, Petitioner, FLORENCE LAURENCE, requests that this Court enter a Final Judgment dissolving the marriage between the parties and grant to Petitioner:

1. Take jurisdiction of this cause and enter an order dissolving her marriage to Respondent.

2. Temporary and permanent care, custody, and control of PATIENCE LAURENCE.

3. Temporary and permanent support money for PATIENCE LAURENCE.

4. An equitable division of the personal property owned by the parties.

5. Enter any order that the Court deems proper and just in this matter.

_____
FLORENCE LAURENCE,
Petitioner

_____
MAVIS MAVEN
Attorney at Law
1234 Marvin Place
Boone, Florida 54890
(309) 555-1212

FIGURE 11–3 (continued)

- a caption
- an identification of the nature of the cause of action
- the jurisdiction of the court
- the details of the marriage
- allegations regarding property division
- the grounds for the divorce

See Figure 11–4 for a sample of a simplified divorce complaint.

The Final Judgment

The final judgment is the order of the court granting the divorce along with any other relief sought by the parties and deemed appropriate by the court after hearing the facts. The final decision of the court addresses the matter of

**IN THE CIRCUIT COURT
FOR BOONE COUNTY, FLORIDA**

IN RE: The Marriage of

FLORENCE LAURENCE,

        Petitioner,

and

LAWRENCE LAURENCE,

        Respondent.

_____/

**PETITION FOR DISSOLUTION
OF MARRIAGE**

Petitioner, FLORENCE LAURENCE, petitions for the dissolution of the marriage between herself and LAWRENCE LAURENCE, and in support thereof, states:

1. This is an action for dissolution of marriage between Petitioner and LAWRENCE LAURENCE.

2. Petitioner has been a resident of the State of Florida for more than six (6) months.

3. Petitioner and Respondent were married to each other on November 12, 1989, at Boone Valley, Florida, and lived together as husband and wife until June 30, 1999.

4. There are no minor children born as a result of this marriage, and none are expected to be born.

5. The property of the parties has been equitably divided pursuant to the attached agreement of the parties.

6. The marriage is irretrievably broken.

  WHEREFORE, petitioner, FLORENCE LAURENCE, respectfully prays the court to enter a judgment to:

1. Dissolve the marriage of the two parties.

2. Grant such other and further relief as may appear proper.

_____
FLORENCE LAURENCE, Petitioner

FIGURE 11–4 A sample complaint for simplified dissolution

jurisdiction over the parties and the subject matter of the litigation. The court orders the dissolution of the marital relationship, child custody, support, alimony, and property division. (See Figure 11–5.)

The final decision of the court may be rendered after a hearing, after a trial on the merits, or as the result of an agreement by the parties.

**IN THE CIRCUIT COURT
FOR BOONE COUNTY, FLORIDA**

IN RE: The Marriage of

FLORENCE LAURENCE,

      Petitioner,

and

LAWRENCE LAURENCE,

      Respondent.

_____/

FINAL JUDGMENT OF DISSOLUTION OF MARRIAGE

From the evidence, the Court finds:
The Court has jurisdiction of the parties and the subject matter of this action, and
The marriage of the parties FLORENCE LAURENCE and LAWRENCE LAURENCE is irretrievably broken.

    IT IS ORDERED AND ADJUDGED:

1. The marriage of FLORENCE LAURENCE and LAWRENCE LAURENCE is dissolved and each spouse is restored to the status of being single and unmarried.

2. The property of the parties is hereby divided pursuant to the agreement of the parties attached to the complaint herein.

    DONE AND ORDERED at Boone, Florida, this ____ day of _____, 1999.

                                _____
                                  CIRCUIT JUDGE

FIGURE 11–5 A sample judgment of dissolution

SUMMARY

- The marital union is considered a matter of contract between the spouses, yet it is treated in a manner unlike the typical contractual agreement in the eyes of the court. Each state has a public policy interest in preserving the marital union. If a breakdown of that marital union occurs, the state has a vested interest in securing the procedural safeguards for each spouse.

- The primary concern of the laws surrounding domestic relations is to equitably divide the property, provide for the welfare of minor children, and present an opportunity for the spouses to proceed on an even footing. The legal documents necessary to ensure these values from a procedural standpoint are governed by the rules of procedure for domestic relations of each state. The form and content of the documents are governed by court rule or statute. The preparer of the documents must consult local and state rules where available.

IN REVIEW

1. What is an antenuptial agreement?
2. What is a separation agreement?
3. What are the elements of a good checklist to be used before drafting a separation agreement?
4. What are the various types of divorce?
5. What are the elements of a complaint for divorce?
6. What should be included in an answer to a complaint for divorce?
7. What matters are stated in the final judgment for divorce?

PUTTING IT ALL TOGETHER

The law firm of Elliott & Ness has retained your paralegal firm to assist in the handling of a recently acquired domestic relations matter. The heavenly bonds of matrimony between Bonnie and Clyde Barker have broken down irretrievably due to the excessive stress placed upon their relationship as a result of years of pursuit by law enforcement authorities throughout the southern Midwest. The Barkers have been "on the lam" for the better part of six years, having dragged their son Junior on their odyssey since his birth on April 1, 1990. They had recently settled in your community, only to be ratted out by Bonnie's hairdresser, Bruce Phlough, a material witness at their trial. The Barkers are now serving twenty years to life in the state penitentiary, and Junior has been temporarily living with Clyde's mother, Ma.

The Barkers want to end their years of marital bliss on as peaceful a note as possible and are desirous of Junior being raised by Ma, since she seems to have done so well with Clyde. Their property consists of one 1984 Ford Bronco II 4x4 with air-conditioning, courtesy of the arresting officers, and an unspecified amount of cash and securities hidden in an unknown location to be divided equally.

Exercises

1. Prepare a complaint for divorce reflecting the grounds for dissolution, the custody of Junior, and the property settlement. In addition, since the matter will be heard expeditiously, prepare an order for entry by the court.

Appellate Procedure

Law never is, but is always about to be.

—

JUSTICE BENJAMIN CARDOZO (1921)

OBJECTIVES

After completing this chapter, you will be able to:

1. Define an appeal
2. Describe the nature of the appellate process
3. Classify the basic elements of an appellate brief
4. Identify the content of each section of the appellate brief

BALLENTINE'S REVIEW

appeal—The process by which a higher court is requested by a party to a lawsuit to review the decision of a lower court

appellant—A party who appeals from a lower court to a higher court.

appellate court—A higher court to which an appeal is taken from a lower court.

appellee—A party against whom a case is appealed from a lower court to a higher court.

§ 12.1 THE APPEAL

A challenge to the judgment of a trial court is called an **appeal.** The appeal takes place once there has been a final disposition of the case at the trial court level. The court to which an appeal is taken is called an **appellate court.** Appellate courts do not retry the case but merely review the issues raised by the parties to determine the existence of any errors of law. The party filing the appeal is called the **appellant,** and the party against whom the appeal is filed (usually the prevailing party at the trial court level) is called the **appellee.** In some courts, the parties are referred to, respectively, as petitioner and respondent.

§ 12.2 THE APPELLATE PROCESS

The appellate process is one of review of the action of a lower court to decide whether or not there has been an error of law. Some types of appeal are discretionary with the appellate court, and appeal is not granted as a matter of right. Other types of appeal are a matter of right and must be heard by the appellate court. Questions of fact that were decided by the trial court are not presented as issues on appeal. If the appellate court is convinced that there has been an error of law, the court may reverse the decision of the trial court. If there has been no error of law, the appellate court merely affirms the decision of the trial court.

An appeal is taken to the court of appeals in the district in which the case was tried. In federal courts, appeals from the United States District Court are appealed to the United States Circuit Court of Appeals. Appeals from that court are then taken to the United States Supreme Court if accepted. At the state level, appeals are taken from the trial court to a court of appeals and then to the state's supreme court. Court rules must be carefully reviewed in all questions of appellate procedure.

In all appeals, the appellate court is limited to the record of the case made at the time of trial, called the **record below.** The record consists of:

- case docket
- transcripts of the proceedings
- exhibits
- pleadings
- motions and briefs

Almost without exception, the appellate court will refuse to hear any "new" evidence that was not submitted to the trial court for its decision. In addition, the appellate court limits its consideration of the case to only those issues that were presented at the trial court level. The theory is that the trial court must have had a specific issue presented for decision before it can be considered to have made an error. For instance, if a particular piece of damaging evidence against a party was introduced at the time of trial and a party failed to object to its introduction, that party may not raise the objection for the first time on appeal. The scope of appellate review is limited to those questions before the trier of fact in the trial court.

appeal: The process by which a higher court is requested by a party to a lawsuit to review the decision of a lower court. Such reconsideration is normally confined to a review of the record from the lower court, with no new testimony taken nor new issues raised.

appellate court: A higher court to which an appeal is taken from a lower court.

appellant: A party who appeals from a lower court to a higher court.

appellee: A party against whom a case is appealed from a lower court to a higher court.

record below: The papers a trial court transmits to the appellate court, on the basis of which the appellate court decides the appeal. The record below includes the pleadings, all motions made before the trial court, the official transcript, and the judgment or order appealed from.

The appellate court will not disturb a ruling of a trial court unless there has been an error of law that has materially affected the outcome of the trial. The scope of appellate review is limited to **material error,** that is, error that may have influenced the decision of the court in a particular direction. If the error is harmless or supported by other competent evidence, the decision will remain undisturbed.

Unless a decision of the trial court is final and all matters before the trial court have been completed, the appellate court will refuse to hear the appeal. This rule allows the appellate court to hear *all* the issues at one time, rather than in a piecemeal manner. There are certain limited exceptions where a party may appeal an interim decision of a court, but these are rare. The court rules set out the grounds for such appeals.

An appeal is started with the filing of a **notice of appeal** by the appellant. The notice of appeal is a formal request for a hearing before the appellate court. In most cases, the notice must be filed within a specified period of time, such as thirty days, with service on all parties. Local court rules determine the form, although most notices contain the following information:

- the identity of the appealing party
- the identity of the appellee
- the judgment or order appealed from
- the court to which the appeal is taken

In some courts, the appealing party must also file a bond to provide security to ensure payment of costs on appeal. Figure 12–1 is a sample notice of appeal.

§ 12.3 THE APPELLATE BRIEF

An **appellate brief** is a lengthy written legal document submitted to an appellate court to persuade the court that an error has occurred in a lower court. The preparation of the appellate brief is both an art and a science. The artistic aspect of the appellate brief is beyond the scope of this text, but the scientific side of the brief is one that lends itself to analysis. The appellate brief is structured in a similar manner in both federal courts and state courts, although court rules must be consulted before preparation. The brief consists of the following components:

- cover page
- table of contents
- index of authorities
- statement of jurisdiction
- statement of questions involved
- statement of facts
- argument
- conclusion
- relief
- appendix

material error: Reversible error; judicial error that causes a miscarriage of justice.

notice of appeal: The process by which appellate review is initiated; specifically, written notice to the appellee advising him or her of the appellant's intention to appeal.

appellate brief: A written statement submitted to an appellate court that argues the facts of the case, supported by citations of authority, in order to persuade the court that an error has occurred in a lower court.

**UNITED STATES DISTRICT COURT
FOR THE EASTERN DISTRICT OF FREMONT**

I. M. HURT,

    Plaintiff,

                    v.   File No.

H. E. DIDDITT,

    Defendant.

_____/

NOTICE OF APPEAL

Notice is hereby given that H. E. Didditt, defendant above named, hereby appeals to the United States Court of Appeals for the First Circuit from the final judgment entered in this action on June 31, 1999.

Dated:

                                    _____
                                    M. N. SHURRED
                                    Attorney for Defendant
                                    12 Fortune Place
                                    Orange, FR 22330

FIGURE 12–1 A sample notice of appeal

The court rules of both the state and federal courts are very specific about the form and contents of the brief. Rule 28 of the Federal Rules of Appellate Procedure provides:

(a) *BRIEF OF THE APPELLANT. The brief of the appellant shall contain under appropriate headings and in the order here indicated:*
   (1) *A table of contents, with page references, and a table of cases (alphabetically arranged), statutes and other authorities cited, with references to the pages of the brief where they are cited.*
   (2) *A statement of the issues presented for review.*
   (3) *A statement of the case. The statement shall first indicate briefly the nature of the case, the course of the proceedings, and its disposition in the court below. There shall follow a statement of the facts relevant to the issue presented for review, with appropriate references to the record. . . .*
   (4) *An argument. The argument may be preceded by a summary. The argument shall contain the contentions of the appellant with respect to the issues presented and the reasons therefore,*

> *with citations to the authorities, statutes and parts of the record relied on.*
>
> *(5) A short conclusion stating the precise relief sought.*
>
> (b) *BRIEF OF THE APPELLEE. The brief of the appellee shall conform to the requirements of subdivision (a)(1)–(4), except that a statement of the issues of the case need not be made unless the appellee is dissatisfied with the statement of the appellant.*
>
> (c) *REPLY BRIEF. The appellant may file a brief in reply to the brief of the appellee, and if the appellee has cross-appealed, the appellee may file a brief in reply to the response of the appellant to the issues presented by the cross appeal. No further briefs may be filed except with leave of the court.*

The Cover Page

The cover page of the brief is similar to the headings and captions on pleadings, identifying the court and the matter before it. It should contain:

- identity of the court
- identity of the parties
- case number assigned
- name of the lower court
- name of the brief
- name of the attorney

A sample cover page is presented in Figure 12–2.

The Table of Contents

The table of contents of the appellate brief sets out the sections of the brief and their locations, providing the court with convenient access to any component. It is usually one of the final steps in the preparation of the brief due to the fact that the contents and their locations are not known until completion. A table of contents is shown in Figure 12–3.

The Index of Authorities

Most jurisdictions require that the appellate brief contain a list of the citations of the legal authorities relied on to support arguments made on behalf of a party. The index of authorities, sometimes called a table of authorities, provides the appellate court with a list of authorities arranged by category, including the following:

- case law
- constitutional provisions
- statutes
- regulations
- secondary authority

Cases are listed in alphabetical order, and statutes are listed in their order of appearance in the brief. (See Figure 12–4.)

**IN THE
SUPREME COURT OF THE STATE OF
FREMONT**

No. 95-6749

MAJOR GASTROCNEMIUS,

Petitioner,

v.

PUMP-U-UP HEALTH SPAS, INC.,

Respondent.

ON APPEAL TO THE SUPREME COURT
OF THE STATE OF FREMONT FROM
THE COURT OF APPEALS

BRIEF OF PETITIONER

MARLIN MILQUETOAST
Attorney for Petitioner
Suite 40
1122 Garden Lane
Walden, FR 22334

FIGURE 12–2 A sample cover page

Table of Contents

FIGURE 12–3 A sample table of contents

The Statement of Jurisdiction

The statement of jurisdiction section of the brief is a short statement of the court's jurisdiction of the appeal. The purpose is to advise the court that all the preliminary appellate steps have been satisfied for jurisdiction and that the court has jurisdiction to render an opinion. The statement may be as succinct as:

This Honorable Court has jurisdiction pursuant to 12 U.S.C.A. § 1290.

The statement of facts will include a recitation of the procedural steps involved in the appeal.

The Statement of Questions Presented

This section of the brief, also referred to as the statement of issues or statement of questions involved, provides the statement of the issues of law involved in the appeal. The manner of the phrasing of the questions involves some degree of advocacy and has a significant impact on how the court views the arguments. It is a statement of questions of law phrased in the best light for the party submitting the brief and constitutes a valuable tool of persuasion.

The Statement of Facts

The statement of facts, also called the statement of the case, presents the factual picture of the case to the appellate court. The facts should include:

- a narrative of the essential facts as disclosed at trial
- a statement of the prior proceedings
- a short summary of the lower court's decision

The facts and summary of proceedings must be based on the record below. They must be set forth in a clear, concise, and unbiased manner. Accuracy and

---

Index of Authorities

Cases

Carson v. Johnson, 660 F.2d 1042 (3d Cir. 1980). 9
Hardy v. Smith, 490 F. Supp 10 (D. Fla. 1984). 13

Statutes

15 U.S.C.A. § 1368. 15
15 U.S.C.A. § 1370. 17

FIGURE 12–4 A sample index of authorities

comprehensiveness are of utmost importance, while advocacy should be avoided.

The Argument

The **argument** is the advocacy portion of the brief devoted to a discussion of the issues and their legal support. The party offering the argument is seeking to have the court adopt its reasoning in holding for that position, offering case law and statutory authority in support. Counsel for a party argue in a well-reasoned and logical manner, using the authorities in support of the position, citing legislative history and custom and usage, and making a direct attack on the opponent's authorities. The argument is the bulk of the brief and should be of sufficient length as to thoroughly present the authorities without being laborious.

The Conclusion

The **conclusion** is the section of the brief summarizing the party's position and arguments. It should be a short, concise, and direct statement of the party's position, without rearguing the case, and may consist of nothing more than a single sentence on each issue.

The Relief

The **relief** section of the brief is the request by the proponent of an argument that the court hold in a certain manner on behalf of that party. The relief is a statement of the remedy sought from the appellate court. It should not include any argument or advocacy and should not address any of the specific issues. (See Figure 12–5.)

The Appendix

In most courts, the appellant must file an appendix with the brief to provide the court with the relevant procedural documents from the lower court. The appendix portion of the brief should include:

argument: An attorney's effort, either by written brief or oral argument, to persuade a court or administrative agency that his or her client's claim should prevail; reason put forward in an effort to convince.

conclusion: A summary of a party's position and arguments.

relief: A person's object in bringing a lawsuit; the function or purpose of a remedy.

Relief

WHEREFORE, Petitioner respectfully requests that this Honorable Court reverse the decision of the Court of Appeals and remand this matter for further proceedings consistent with its opinion.

FIGURE 12–5 A sample relief section

- relevant docket entries from the lower court
- relevant pleadings
- orders, judgments, decisions, or rulings
- relevant portions of the record

The appendix is a matter of agreement between the parties pursuant to most court rules. If the parties cannot agree, each may submit a proposed appendix for consideration and ruling. If exhibits are to be included in the appendix, they should be so designated.

§ 12.4 THE MOTIONS ON APPEAL

Any application for relief or order from the appellate court must be made by motion with service upon all parties. The motion must contain the grounds for relief and be supported by briefs. Motions are filed for such matters as:

- motion for extension of time
- motion for procedural orders
- motion for costs
- motion for emergency relief

The motion form and the allowable grounds are dictated by court rule. Local court rules should be consulted prior to the preparation and filing of any motion. (See Figure 12–6.)

**UNITED STATES COURT OF APPEALS
FOR THE FIRST CIRCUIT**

I. M. HURT

        Petitioner,

                    v.   File No. 99-1234

H. E. DIDDITT,

        Respondent.

_____/

<u>MOTION FOR EXTENSION OF TIME</u>

    NOW COMES H. E. DIDDITT, Petitioner herein, and moves this Court for a 30-day extension for the filing of his brief in the above-captioned matter.

    This motion is made pursuant to Local Circuit Rule 11-2(a), and an affidavit in support thereof is attached hereto.

    Dated:

                                    _____
                                    M. N. SHURRED
                                    Attorney for Defendant
                                    12 Fortune Place
                                    Orange, FR 22330

FIGURE 12–6 A sample motion for extension of time

SUMMARY

- From the standpoint of the legal document, the appellate process is relatively simple. After the filing of the notice of appeal, the preparation of the brief is the most significant effort for the appellant, and the responsive brief is the appellee's greatest task.

- The motion practice on appeal is quite limited in most states and in the federal courts. The substantive issues of law forming the grounds for appeal and providing the basis for reversible error in the eyes of the appellant are the focus of the appeal. The entire process is one of an emphasis on substance more than form.

IN REVIEW

1. What is an appeal?
2. What are the documents that form the record below?
3. What are the main sections of an appellate brief?
4. What material is presented in the statement of facts?
5. What are the motions typically filed during an appeal?

PUTTING IT ALL TOGETHER

When Ernest Winter, Sr., contracted for his subscription to *The Liver Spot*, he did so in response to representations in the advertising campaign of its publisher, Senectitude Press, that he would be provided with health tips designed to lengthen his "golden years." In his nineties at the time his first issue arrived, Ernest was ready to believe anything that this literary Ponce de Leon had to serve up. Therefore, when the article appeared in the travel section describing the "Liver Spot of the Month" travel designation, Ernest was ready.

The "Spot" turned out to be a hot springs near Ocala, Florida. Instead of the enjoyment of a proverbial pool of Bethesda-like healing waters, the only thing Ernest received was second- and third-degree burns over forty percent of his already decrepit body. The resulting medical treatment ran into the tens of thousands, leading him to the United States District Court for the Middle District of Florida in an action against *The Liver Spot* and its publisher, Senectitude Press.

Alas, the jury felt that our modern-day Don Quixote was merely jousting at windmills and found his action to be without merit. Ernest is now seeking to appeal the lower court judgment to the United States Court of Appeals.

Exercises

1. Prepare the notice of appeal and provide Ernest's attorney with an outline of the proper sections for an appellate brief, along with a notation about the content of each.

APPENDIX
A
Canons of Ethics

NATIONAL ASSOCIATION OF LEGAL ASSISTANTS CODE OF ETHICS AND PROFESSIONAL RESPONSIBILITY

Preamble

It is the responsibility of every legal assistant to adhere strictly to the accepted standards of legal ethics and to live by general principles of proper conduct. The performance of the duties of the legal assistant shall be governed by specific canons as defined herein in order that justice will be served and the goals of the profession attained.

The canons of ethics set forth hereafter are adopted by the National Association of Legal Assistants, Inc., as a general guide, and the enumeration of these rules does not mean there are not others of equal importance although not specifically mentioned.

Canon 1

A legal assistant shall not perform any of the duties that lawyers only may perform nor do things that lawyers themselves may not do.

Canon 2

A legal assistant may perform any task delegated and supervised by a lawyer so long as the lawyer is responsible to the client, maintains a direct relationship with the client, and assumes full professional responsibility for the work product.

Canon 3

A legal assistant shall not engage in the practice of law by accepting cases, setting fees, giving legal advice or appearing in court (unless otherwise authorized by court or agency rules).

Canon 4

A legal assistant shall not act in matters involving professional legal judgment as the services of a lawyer are essential in the public interest whenever the exercise of such judgment is required.

Canon 5

A legal assistant must act prudently in determining the extent to which a client may be assisted without the presence of a lawyer.

Canon 6

A legal assistant shall not engage in the unauthorized practice of law and shall assist in preventing the unauthorized practice of law.

Canon 7

A legal assistant must protect the confidences of a client, and it shall be unethical for a legal assistant to violate any statute now in effect or hereafter to be enacted controlling privileged communications.

Canon 8

It is the obligation of the legal assistant to avoid conduct which would cause the lawyer to be unethical or even appear to be unethical, and loyalty to the employer is incumbent upon the legal assistant.

Canon 9

A legal assistant shall work continually to maintain integrity and a high degree of competency throughout the legal profession.

Canon 10

A legal assistant shall strive for perfection through education in order to better assist the legal profession in fulfilling its duty of making legal services available to clients and the public.

Canon 11

A legal assistant shall do all other things incidental, necessary, or expedient for the attainment of the ethics and responsibilities imposed by statute or rule of court.

Canon 12

A legal assistant is governed by the American Bar Association Model Code of Professional Responsibility and the American Bar Association Model Rules of Professional Conduct.

Adopted May, 1975
Revised November, 1979
Revised September, 1988

APPENDIX
B

A Consultation Contract

CONSULTATION AGREEMENT

This Agreement is made this 31st day of February, 1999, between **OVERNIGHT CONSTRUCTION COMPANY**, a Michigan corporation, hereinafter referred to as "Builder," and **LES THANADAY**, a business development consultant, hereinafter referred to as "Consultant."

In consideration of their mutual promises and for their mutual benefit, Builder and Consultant agree as follows:

1. Appointment of Consultant

Builder hereby appoints Consultant to perform to the best of his abilities such consultation services as may be necessary to facilitate the sale, purchase, construction, and completion of homes developed by Builder.

2. Compensation

In consideration for such consultation services, the Builder agrees to pay Consultant an amount equal to two percent (2%) of the purchase price of said home, said amount to be paid at the time of the closing of the sale of said home.

3. Status of Consultant

This Agreement does not constitute a hiring by either party. It is the parties' intention that Consultant shall be an independent contractor and not Builder's employee for all purposes. Consultant shall retain sole and absolute discretion in the judgment and means of carrying out Consultant's activities and responsibilities hereunder. Consultant shall be entitled to engage in any activities which are not expressly prohibited by this Agreement. This Agreement shall not be construed as a partnership, and neither party shall be liable for any obligation incurred by the other. The consultation services provided by Consultant shall not be construed to be those of one acting in the capacity of a real estate broker.

4. Assignability

The interest of Consultant under this Agreement shall not be assignable or subject to the claims of any of his creditors, except that Consultant may designate a beneficiary to receive upon his death any amounts due and owing under this Agreement.

5. Attorney Fees and Litigation Costs

If any legal action or other proceeding is brought for the enforcement of this Agreement, the successful or prevailing party shall be entitled to recover reasonable attorneys' fees and other costs incurred in that action or proceeding, in addition to any other relief to which that party would be entitled.

6. Termination of Agreement

This Agreement will terminate two (2) years from the date hereof, unless terminated sooner as provided herein. Either party may terminate this Agreement upon thirty (30) days written notice of termination to the other party, at which time the Agreement shall terminate immediately.

7. Entire Agreement

This Agreement constitutes the entire Agreement of the parties and supersedes all prior agreements, understandings and negotiations, whether written or oral, between the parties. This Agreement may not be changed orally but only by an agreement in writing signed by both parties and stated to be an amendment hereto.

8. Provisions Severable

In case any one or more of the provisions of this Agreement shall be invalid, illegal or unenforceable in any respect, the validity, legality and enforceability of the remaining provisions contained herein shall not be in any way affected or impaired thereby.

9. Headings

Headings set forth herein are for the convenience of the parties only and are not a part of the Agreement.

10. Interpretation

This Agreement shall be construed and interpreted under the laws of the State of Michigan.

11. Notices

All notices herein shall be in writing and may be delivered personally, or by mail, postage prepaid. Any notice sent by mail, postage prepaid, will be deemed received three days after it is mailed.

IN WITNESS WHEREOF, the parties hereto have executed this Agreement at Detroit, to be effective as of the 31st day of February, 1999.

OVERNIGHT CONSTRUCTION CO.

BY: _____
HUGH BILDITT, President

AND: _____
LESS THANADAY

APPENDIX
C

An Employment Contract

AGREEMENT OF EMPLOYMENT

THIS AGREEMENT OF EMPLOYMENT ("Agreement") is made on February 30, 1999 by and between ACADEMIC COMICS, INC., an Ohio corporation, having its principal office at 10 Varsity Blvd., Columbia, Ohio 42212, the "Publisher," and BLANTON B. BUFFOON, the "Employee," as follows:

1. <u>Effectiveness</u>. This Agreement shall become effective on June 31, 1999.

2. <u>Employment</u>. The Publisher hereby agrees to employ the Employee, and the Employee, in consideration of such employment, hereby accepts employment as a Creator upon the terms and conditions set forth herein. During the term of his employment, the Employee shall do all things necessary and incident to the above position. The Employee shall be responsible to the Board of Directors and appropriate officers of the Publisher, and the Publisher reserves the right from time to time to make any and all changes in the Employee's scope of employment which the Publisher deems to be necessary or appropriate.

3. <u>Term</u>. The term of such employment shall commence on the Effective Date and shall continue for a period of one year or the earlier of: (a) the death or permanent disability of the Employee; or (b) such employment is terminated by Publisher by serving written notice to that effect on the other party at least two weeks prior to the effective date of said termination.

Nothing in this Agreement shall be construed to prevent the Publisher from immediately terminating the Employee's employment hereunder at any time for good cause, which shall include, but not be limited to, neglect of duty, misconduct, fraud, misappropriation, embezzlement, or violation of any of the provisions of this Agreement. Such termination of the Employee's employment shall not constitute a breach of this Agreement by the Publisher.

4. <u>Compensation</u>. Subject to such modifications as may be approved from time to time by the Board of Directors or officers of the Publisher, the Employee shall receive as compensation an annual salary of seventy-five thousand dollars ($75,000).

5. <u>Outside Employment</u>. The Employee shall devote full time and attention to the performance of the duties incident to the Employee's position with the Publisher, and shall not have any other employment, or responsibility for the operation of any other profit-seeking enterprise, which may tend to adversely affect the Publisher or the performance of the Employee's duties.

6. <u>Confidential Information</u>. The Employee recognizes and acknowledges that information gained by the Employee while in the Publisher's employ, including without limitation that concerning the Publisher's customers and suppliers, and the methods, techniques, devices, and operations of the Publisher, as they may exist from time to time, are of a confidential nature and are valuable, special and unique assets of the Publisher's business. The Employee shall not during the term of, or after the termination of employment, disclose in any way any such confidential information to any person, firm, corporation or any other operation or entity, or use the same on the Employee's own behalf, for any reason or purpose. Upon termination of

employment, the Employee shall deliver up to the Publisher all lists of the Publisher's customers and suppliers and all copies thereof, and all notes, records, memoranda, complete correspondence files and other papers, and all copies thereof, relating to the methods, techniques, devises, and operations of the Publisher, and the Employee does not have nor can the Employee acquire any property right therein or claim thereto or in the underlying confidential information.

7. <u>Diversion of Business</u>. The Employee shall not, during the period of employment by the Publisher and following termination of employment (whether such termination be with or without cause) either for the Employee or on behalf of any person, firm, corporation or any other operation or entity, directly or indirectly:

> 7.1 Divert or attempt to divert from the Publisher any business whatsoever by influencing or attempting to influence, or soliciting or attempting to solicit any of the customers of the Publisher with whom Employee may have dealt at any time or who were customers of the Publisher on the date of termination of the Employee's employment or had been customers of the Publisher prior thereto; or

> 7.2 Divert or attempt to divert from the Publisher any person employed by the Publisher by influencing or attempting to influence such person to leave the Publisher's employ.

8. <u>Non-Compete Clause</u>. For a period of three years from the termination of employment, the Employee shall not, either for the Employee or on behalf of any person, firm corporation or any other operation or entity, directly or indirectly own, control, or participate in the ownership or control of, or be employed by or on behalf of, any business which is similar to and is competitive with the business of the Publisher within the markets serviced by the Publisher.

9. <u>Remedies</u>. The Employee recognizes that a breach of any of the restrictive covenants herein set forth will cause irreparable harm to the Publisher and that actual damages may be difficult to ascertain and in any event may be inadequate. Accordingly, the Employee agrees that in the event of such breach, the Publisher shall be entitled to injunctive relief in addition to such other legal or equitable remedies as may be available, and the Publisher, at its option, may seek to enforce its remedies through binding arbitration or any court of competent jurisdiction.

10. <u>Severability of Clauses</u>. Each of the Sections of this Agreement shall stand independently and severally, and the invalidity of any one Section or portion thereof shall not affect the validity of any other provision. In the event any provision shall be construed to be invalid, no other provision of this Agreement shall be affected thereby. Furthermore, it is agreed that any period of restriction or covenant hereinabove stated shall not include any period of violation or period of time required for litigation or arbitration to enforce such restrictions or covenants.

11. <u>Property of Publisher</u>. All ideas, inventions, discoveries, proprietary information, know-how, processes and other developments and, more specifically, improvements to existing inventions conceived by the Employee, alone or with others, during the term of the Employee's employment, whether or not during working hours and whether or not while working on a specific project, that are within the scope of the Publisher's business operations or that relate to any Publisher work or projects, are and shall remain the exclusive property of the Publisher. Inventions, improvements and discoveries relating to the business of the Publisher conceived or made by the Employee, whether alone or with others, while employed by or within one year following termination of employment with the Publisher are conclusively and irrefutably presumed to have been made during the period of employment and are the sole property of the Publisher. The Employee shall promptly disclose in writing any such matters to the Publisher but to no other person without the Publisher's consent. The Employee hereby assigns and agrees to assign all rights, title, and interest in and to such matters to the Publisher. The Employee will, upon request of the Publisher, execute such assignments or other instruments and assist the Publisher in the obtaining, at the Publisher's sole expense, of any patents, trademarks or similar protection, if available, in the name of the Publisher.

12. <u>Applicable Law</u>. This Agreement shall be governed in all respects by the law of the State of Ohio, shall be binding upon the Employee's assigns, heirs, and legal representatives and shall inure to the benefit of the Publisher, its successors and assigns.

IN WITNESS WHEREOF, the parties hereto have executed this Agreement at Columbia, Ohio, to be effective as of the 30th day of February, 1999.

ACADEMIC COMICS, INC.

BY: _____
     CLARK K. MARVEL, President

AND: _____
     BLANTON B. BUFFOON

APPENDIX
D

Corporate Bylaws

BYLAWS OF CYBERSPACE, INC.

Article I—Offices

The principal office of the corporation in the State of Fremont, shall be located in the City of Cascade, County of Tad. The corporation may have such other offices, either within or without the State of incorporation as the board of directors may designate or as the business of the corporation may from time to time require.

Article II—Stockholders

1. ANNUAL MEETING. The annual meeting of the stockholders shall be held on the 32nd day of July in each year, beginning with the year 1999 at the hour 2:00 o'clock P.M., for the purpose of electing directors and for the transaction of such other business as may come before the meeting. If the day fixed for the annual meeting shall be a legal holiday such meeting shall be held on the next succeeding business day.

2. SPECIAL MEETINGS. Special meetings of the stockholders, for any purpose or purposes, unless otherwise prescribed by statute, may be called by the president or by the directors, and shall be called by the president at the request of the holders of not less than fifty-one percent (51%) of all the outstanding shares of the corporation entitled to vote at the meeting.

3. PLACE OF MEETING. The directors may designate any place, either within or without the State unless otherwise prescribed by statute, as the place of meeting for any annual meeting or for any special meeting called by the directors. A waiver of notice signed by all stockholders entitled to vote at a meeting may designate any place, either within or without the state unless otherwise prescribed by statute, as the place for holding such meeting. If no designation is made, or if a special meeting be otherwise called, the place of meeting shall be the principal office of the corporation.

4. NOTICE OF MEETING. Written or printed notice stating the place, day and hour of the meeting and, in case of a special meeting, the purpose or purposes for which the meeting is called, shall be delivered not less than five (5) nor more than fifteen (15) days before the date of the meeting, either personally or by mail, by or at the direction of the president, or the secretary, or the officer or persons calling the meeting, to each stockholder of record entitled to vote at such meeting. If mailed, such notice shall be deemed to be delivered when deposited in the United States mail, addressed to the stockholder at his address as it appears on the stock transfer books of the corporation, with postage thereon prepaid.

5. CLOSING OF TRANSFER BOOKS OF FIXING OF RECORD DATE. For the purpose of determining stockholders entitled to notice of or to vote at any meeting of stockholders or any adjournment thereof, or stockholders entitled

to receive payment of any dividend, or in order to make a determination of stockholders for any other proper purpose, the directors of the corporation may provide that the stock transfer books shall be closed for a stated period but not to exceed, in any case, thirty (30) days. If the stock transfer books shall be closed for the purpose of determining stockholders entitled to notice of or to vote at a meeting of stockholders, such books shall be closed for at least fifteen (15) days immediately preceding such meeting. In lieu of closing the stock transfer books, the directors may fix in advance a date as the record date for any such determination of stockholders, such date in any case to be not more than thirty (30) days and, in case of a meeting of stockholders, not less than fifteen (15) days prior to the date on which the particular action requiring such determination of stockholders is to be taken. If the stock transfer books are not closed and no record date is fixed for the determination of stockholders entitled to notice of or to vote at a meeting of stockholders, or stockholders entitled to receive payment of a dividend, the date on which notice of the meeting is mailed or the date on which the resolution of the directors declaring such dividend is adopted, as the case may be, shall be the record date for such determination of stockholders. When a determination of stockholders entitled to vote at any meeting of stockholders has been made as provided in this section, such determination shall apply to any adjournment thereof.

6. VOTING LISTS. When requested to do so, the officer or agent having charge of the stock transfer books for shares of the corporation shall make, at least thirty (30) days before each meeting of stockholders, a complete list of the stockholders entitled to vote at such meeting, or any adjournment thereof, arranged in alphabetical order, with the address of and the number of shares held by each, which list, for a period of fifteen (15) days prior to such meeting, shall be kept on file at the principal office of the corporation and shall be subject to inspection by any stockholder at any time during usual business hours. Such list shall also be produced and kept open at the time and place of the meeting and shall be subject to the inspection of any stockholder during the whole time of the meeting. The original stock transfer book shall be prima facie evidence as to who are the stockholders entitled to examine such list or transfer books or to vote at the meeting of stockholders.

7. QUORUM. At any meeting of stockholders fifty-one percent (51%) of the outstanding shares of the corporation entitled to vote, represented in person or by proxy, shall constitute a quorum at a meeting of stockholders. If less than said number of the outstanding shares are represented at a meeting, a majority of the shares so represented may adjourn the meeting from time to time without further notice. At such adjourned meeting at which a quorum shall be present or represented, any business may be transacted which might have been transacted at the meeting as originally notified. The stockholders present at a duly organized meeting may continue to transact business until adjournment, notwithstanding the withdrawal of enough stockholders to leave less than a quorum.

8. PROXIES. At all meetings of stockholders, a stockholder may vote by proxy executed in writing by the stockholder or by his duly authorized attorney in fact. Such proxy shall be filed with the secretary of the corporation before or at the time of the meeting.

9. VOTING. Each stockholder entitled to vote in accordance with the terms and provisions of the certificate of incorporation and these bylaws shall be entitled to one vote, in person or by proxy, for each share of stock entitled to vote held by such stockholders. Upon the demand of any stockholder, the vote for directors and upon any question before the meeting shall be by ballot. All elections for directors shall be decided by plurality vote; all other questions shall be decided by majority vote except as otherwise provided by the Certificate of Incorporation or the laws of this State.

10. ORDER OF BUSINESS. The order of business at all meetings of the stockholders, shall be as follows:

1. Roll Call.
2. Proof of notice of meeting or waiver of notice.
3. Reading of minutes of preceding meeting.
4. Reports of Officers.
5. Reports of Committees.
6. Election of Directors.
7. Unfinished Business.
8. New Business.

11. INFORMAL ACTION BY STOCKHOLDERS. Unless otherwise provided by law, any action required to be taken at a meeting of the shareholders, or any other action which may be taken at a meeting of the shareholders, may be taken without a meeting if a consent in writing, setting forth the action so taken, shall be signed by all of the shareholders entitled to vote with respect to the subject matter thereof.

Article III—Board of Directors

1. GENERAL POWERS. The business and affairs of the corporation shall be managed by its board of directors. The directors shall in all cases act as a board, and they may adopt such rules and regulations for the conduct of their meetings and the management of the corporation as they may deem proper, not inconsistent with these bylaws and the laws of this State.

2. NUMBER, TENURE AND QUALIFICATIONS. The number of directors of the corporation shall be not less than three (3) and not more then seven (7). Each director shall hold office until the next annual meeting of stockholders and until his successor shall have been elected and qualified.

3. REGULAR MEETINGS. A regular meeting of the directors, shall be held without other notice than this bylaw immediately after, and at the same place as, the annual meeting of stockholders. The directors may provide, by resolu-

tion, the time and place for the holding of additional regular meetings without other notice than such resolution.

4. SPECIAL MEETINGS. Special meetings of the directors may be called by or at the request of the president or any two directors. The person or persons authorized to call special meetings of the directors may fix the place for holding any special meeting of the directors called by them.

5. NOTICE. Notice of any special meeting shall be given at least five (5) days previously thereto by written notice delivered personally, or by telegram or mailed to each director at his business address. If mailed, such notice shall be deemed to be delivered when deposited in the United States mail so addressed, with postage thereon prepaid. If notice be given by telegram, such notice shall be deemed to be delivered when the telegram is delivered to the telegraph company. The attendance of a director at a meeting shall constitute a waiver of notice of such meeting, except where a director attends a meeting for the express purpose of objecting to the transaction of any business because the meeting is not lawfully called or convened.

6. QUORUM. At any meeting of the directors, two (2) shall constitute a quorum for the transaction of business, but if less than said number is present at a meeting, a majority of the directors present may adjourn the meeting from time to time without further notice.

7. MANNER OF ACTING. The act of the majority of the directors present at a meeting at which a quorum is present shall be the act of the directors.

8. NEWLY CREATED DIRECTORSHIPS AND VACANCIES. Newly created directorships resulting from an increase in the number of directors and vacancies occurring in the board for any reason except the removal of directors without cause may be filled by a vote of a majority of the directors then in office, although less than a quorum exists. Vacancies occurring by reason of the removal of directors without cause shall be filled by vote of the stockholders. A director elected to fill a vacancy caused by resignation, death or removal shall be elected to hold office for the unexpired term of his predecessor.

9. REMOVAL OF DIRECTORS. Any or all of the directors may be removed for cause by vote of the stockholders or by action of the board. Directors may be removed without cause only by vote of the stockholders.

10. RESIGNATION. A director may resign at any time by giving written notice to the board, the president or the secretary of the corporation. Unless otherwise specified in the notice, the resignation shall take effect upon receipt thereof by the board or such officer, and the acceptance of the resignation shall not be necessary to make it effective.

11. COMPENSATION. No compensation shall be paid to directors, as such, for their services, but by resolution of the board a fixed sum and expenses for actual attendance at each regular or special meeting of the board may be authorized. Nothing herein contained shall be construed to preclude any

director from serving the corporation in any other capacity and receiving compensation therefor.

12. PRESUMPTION OF ASSENT. A director of the corporation who is present at a meeting of the directors at which action on any corporate matter is taken shall be presumed to have assented to the action taken unless his dissent shall be entered in the minutes of the meeting or unless he shall file his written dissent to such action with the person acting as the secretary of the meeting before the adjournment thereof or shall forward such dissent by registered mail to the secretary of the corporation immediately after the adjournment of the meeting. Such right to dissent shall not apply to a director who voted in favor of such action.

13. EXECUTIVE AND OTHER COMMITTEES. The board, by resolution, may designate from among its members and executive committee and other committees, each consisting of three or more directors. Each such committee shall serve at the pleasure of the board.

Article IV—Officers

1. NUMBER. The officers of the corporation shall be a president, a vice-president, a secretary and a treasurer, each of whom shall be elected by the directors. Such other officers and assistant officers as may be deemed necessary may be elected or appointed by the directors.

2. ELECTION AND TERM OF OFFICE. The officers of the corporation to be elected by the directors shall be elected annually at the first meeting of the directors held after each annual meeting of the stockholders. Each officer shall hold office until his successor shall have been duly elected and shall have qualified or until his death or until he shall resign or shall have been removed in the manner hereinafter provided.

3. REMOVAL. Any officer or agent elected or appointed by the directors may be removed by the directors whenever in their judgment the best interests of the corporation would be served thereby, but such removal shall be without prejudice to the contract rights, if any, of the person so removed.

4. VACANCIES. A vacancy in any office because of death, resignation, removal, disqualification or otherwise, may be filled by the directors for the unexpired portion of the term.

5. PRESIDENT. The president shall be the principal executive officer of the corporation and, subject to the control of the directors, shall in general supervise and control all of the business and affairs of the corporation. He shall, when present, preside at all meetings of the stockholders and of the directors. He may sign, with the secretary or any other proper officer of the corporation thereunto authorized by the directors, certificates for shares of the corporation, and deeds, mortgages, bonds, contracts, or other instruments which the directors have authorized to be executed, except in cases where the signing

and execution thereof shall be expressly delegated by the directors or by these bylaws to some other officer or agent of the corporation, or shall be required by law to be otherwise signed or executed; and in general shall perform all duties incident to the office of president and such other duties as may be prescribed by the directors from time to time.

6. VICE-PRESIDENT. In the absence of the president or in event of his death, inability or refusal to act, the vice-president shall perform the duties of the president, and when so acting, shall have all the powers of and be subject to all the restrictions upon the president. The vice-president shall perform such other duties as from time to time may be assigned to him by the President or by the directors.

7. SECRETARY. The secretary shall keep the minutes of the stockholders' and of the directors' meetings in one or more books provided for that purpose, see that all notices are duly given in accordance with the provisions of these bylaws or as required, be custodian of the corporate records and of the seal of the corporation and keep a register of the post office address of each stockholder which shall be furnished to the secretary by such stockholder, have general charge of the stock transfer books of the corporation and in general perform all duties incident to the office of secretary and such other duties as from time to time may be assigned to him by the president or by the directors.

8. TREASURER. If required by the directors, the treasurer shall give a bond for the faithful discharge of his duties in such sum and with such surety or sureties as the directors shall determine. He shall have charge and custody of and be responsible for all funds and securities of the corporation; receive and give receipts for monies due and payable to the corporation from any source whatsoever, and deposit all such monies in the name of the corporation in such banks, trust companies or other depositories as shall be selected in accordance with these bylaws, and in general perform all of the duties incident to the office of treasurer and such other duties as from time to time may be assigned to him by the president or by the directors.

9. SALARIES. The salaries of the officers shall be fixed from time to time by the directors and no officer shall be prevented from receiving such salary by reason of the fact that he is also a director of the corporation.

Article V—Contracts, Loans, Checks and Deposits

1. CONTRACTS. The directors may authorize any officer or officers, agent or agents, to enter into any contract or execute and deliver any instrument in the name of and on behalf of the corporation, and such authority may be general or confined to specific instances.

2. LOANS. No loans shall be contracted on behalf of the corporation and no evidences of indebtedness shall be issued in its name unless authorized by a

resolution of the directors. Such authority may be general or confined to specific instances.

3. CHECKS, DRAFTS, ETC. All checks, drafts or other orders for the payment of money, notes or other evidences of indebtedness issued in the name of the corporation, shall be signed by such officer or officers, agent or agents of the corporation and in such manner as shall from time to time be determined by resolution of the directors.

4. DEPOSITS. All funds of the corporation not otherwise employed shall be deposited from time to time to the credit of the corporation in such banks, trust companies or other depositories as the directors may select.

Article VI—Certificates for Shares and Their Transfer

1. CERTIFICATES FOR SHARES. Certificates representing shares of the corporation shall be in such form as shall be determined by the directors. Such certificates shall be signed by the president and by the secretary or by such other officers authorized by law and by the directors. All certificates for shares shall be consecutively numbered or otherwise identified. The names and addresses of the stockholders, the number of shares and date of issue, shall be entered on the stock transfer books of the corporation. All certificates surrendered to the corporation for transfer shall be canceled and no new certificate shall be issued until the former certificate for a like number of shares shall have been surrendered and canceled, except that in case of a lost, destroyed or mutilated certificate a new one may be issued therefor upon such terms and indemnity to the corporation as the directors may prescribe.

2. TRANSFERS OF SHARES.

(a) Upon surrender to the corporation or the transfer agent of the corporation of a certificate for shares duly endorsed or accompanied by proper evidence of succession, assignment or authority to transfer, it shall be the duty of the corporation to issue a new certificate to the person entitled thereto, and cancel the old certificate; every such transfer shall be entered on the transfer book of the corporation which shall be kept at its principal office.

(b) The corporation shall be entitled to treat the holder of record of any share as the holder in fact thereof, and, accordingly, shall not be bound to recognize any equitable or other claim to or interest in such share on the part of any other person whether or not it shall have express or other notice thereof, except as expressly provided by the laws of this state.

Article VII—Fiscal Year

The fiscal year of the corporation shall begin on the 1st day of July in each year.

Article VIII—Dividends

The directors may from time to time declare, and the corporation may pay, dividends on its outstanding shares in the manner and upon the terms and conditions provided by law.

Article IX—Seal

The directors shall provide a corporate seal which shall be circular in form and shall have inscribed thereon the name of the corporation, the state of incorporation, year of incorporation and the words, "Corporate Seal."

Article X—Waiver of Notice

Unless otherwise provided by law, whenever any notice is required to be given to any stockholder or director of the corporation under the provisions of these bylaws or under the provisions of the articles of incorporation, a waiver thereof in writing, signed by the person or persons entitled to such notice, whether before or after the time stated therein, shall be deemed equivalent to the giving of such notice.

Article XI—Amendments

These bylaws may be altered, amended or repealed and new bylaws may be adopted by a vote of the stockholders representing a majority of all the shares issued and outstanding, at any annual stockholders' meeting or at any special stockholders' meeting when the proposed amendment has been set out in the notice of such meeting.

APPENDIX
E

A General Partnership Agreement

KING, QUEEN & SQUIRE
PARTNERSHIP AGREEMENT

Agreement made November 31, 1999, between REX KING, of 1044 Hastings, City of Orange, County of York, State of Fremont; COURTNEY QUEEN, of 1215 Bayeaux Street, City of Orange, County of York, State of Fremont; and MARSHALL SQUIRE, of 1100 Norman Drive, City of Orange, County of York, State of Fremont; herein referred to as partners.

Recitals

1. Partners desire to join together for the pursuit of common business goals.

2. Partners have considered various forms of joint business enterprises for their business activities.

3. Partners desire to enter into a partnership agreement as the most advantageous business form for their mutual purposes.

In consideration of the mutual promises contained herein, partners agree as follows:

Article One
Name, Purpose, and Domicile

The name of the partnership shall be KING, QUEEN & SQUIRE. The partnership may engage in any all activities as may be necessary, incidental or convenient to carry out the business of providing paralegal services. The principal place of business shall be at 10 Court Street, City of Orange, County of York, State of Fremont, unless relocated by majority consent of partners.

Article Two
Duration of Agreement

The term of this agreement shall be for twenty (20) years, commencing on November 31, 1999, and terminating on November 30, 2019, unless sooner terminated by mutual consent of the parties or by operation of the provisions of this agreement.

Article Three
Classification and Performance by Partners

1. Partners shall be classified as active partners, advisory partners or estate partners.

An active partner may voluntarily become an advisory partner, may be required to become one irrespective of age, and shall automatically become one after attaining the age of sixty-five (65) years, and in each case shall continue as such for two (2) years unless he sooner withdraws or dies.

If an active partner dies, his estate will become an estate partner for two (2) years. If an advisory partner dies within one (1) year of having become an advisory partner, his estate will become an estate partner for the balance of the two-year period.

Only active partners shall have any vote in any partnership matter.

At the time of the taking effect of this partnership agreement, all the partners shall be active partners.

2. An active partner, after attaining the age of sixty-five (65) years, or prior thereto if the executive committee with the approval of two-thirds of all the other active partners determines that the reason for the change in status is bad health, may become an advisory partner at the end of any calendar month upon giving one (1) calendar month's prior notice in writing of his intention so to do. Such notice shall be deemed to be sufficient if sent by registered mail addressed to the partnership at its principal office at 10 Court Street, Orange, Fremont 00001 not less than one (1) calendar month prior to the date when such change is to become effective.

3. Any active partner may at any age be required to become an advisory partner at any time if the executive committee with the approval of two-thirds of the other active partners shall decide that such change is for any reason in best interests of the partnership, provided notice thereof shall be given in writing to such partner. Such notice shall be signed by the chairman of the executive committee or, in the event of his being unable to sign at such time, by another member of such executive committee and shall be served personally upon such partner required to change his status, or mailed by registered mail to his last known address and thereupon such change shall become effective as of the date specified in such notice.

4. Every active partner shall automatically and without further act become an advisory partner at the end of the fiscal year in which his sixty-fifth (65th) birthday occurs.

5. In the event that an active partner becomes an advisory partner or dies, he or his estate shall be entitled to payments to be agreed upon.

Each active partner shall apply all of his experience, training, and ability in discharging his assigned functions in the partnership and in the performance of all work that may be necessary or advantageous to further the business interests of the partnership.

Article Four
Contribution

Each partner shall contribute Ten Thousand Dollars ($10,000) on or before November 31, 1999, to be used by the partnership to establish its capital position. Any additional contribution required of partners shall only be determined and established in accordance with Article Nineteen herein.

Article Five
Business Expenses

The rent of the buildings where the partnership business shall be carried on, and the cost of repairs and alterations, all rates, taxes, payments for insurance, and other expenses in respect to the buildings used by the partnership, and the wages for all persons employed by the partnership are all to become payable on the account of the partnership. All losses incurred shall be paid out of the capital of the partnership business, or, if both shall be deficient, by the partners on a pro rata basis, in proportion to their original contributions, as provided in Article Nineteen.

Article Six
Authority

No partner shall buy any goods or articles or enter into any contract exceeding the value of One Hundred Dollars ($100.00) without the prior consent in writing of the other partners. If any partner exceeds this authority, the other partners shall have the option to take the goods or accept the contract on account of the partnership or to let the goods remain the sole property of the partner who shall have obligated himself.

Article Seven
Separate Debts

No partner shall enter into any bond or become surety, security, bail or cosigner for any person, partnership or corporation, or knowingly condone anything whereby the partnership property may be attached or taken in execution, without the written consent of the other partners.

Each partner shall punctually pay his separate debts and indemnify the other partners and the capital and property of the partnership against his separate debts and all expenses relating thereto.

Article Eight
Books and Records

Books of accounts shall be maintained by the partners, and proper entries made therein of all sales, purchases, receipts, payments, transactions, and property of the partnership, and the books of accounts and all records of the partnership shall be retained at the principal place of business as specified in Article One herein. Each partner shall have free access at all times to all books and records maintained relative to the partnership business.

Article Nine
Accounting

The fiscal year of the partnership shall be from January 1 to December 31 of each year. On the 31st day of January, commencing in 2001, and on the 31st day of January in each succeeding year, a general accounting shall be made and taken by the partners of all sales, purchases, receipts, payments, and transactions of the partnership during the preceding fiscal year, and of all the capital property and current liabilities of the partnership. The general accounting shall be written in the partnership account books and signed in each book by each partner immediately after it is completed. After the signature of each partner is entered, each partner shall keep one of the books and shall be bound by every account, except that if any manifest error is found therein by any partner and shown to the other partners within one (1) month after the error shall have been noted by all of them, the error shall be rectified.

Article Ten
Division of Profits and Losses

Each partner shall be entitle to thirty three and one-third percent (33 1/3%) of the net profits of the business, and all losses occurring in the course of the business shall be borne in the same proportion, unless the losses are occasioned by the willful neglect or default, and not the mere mistake or error, of any of the partners, in which case the loss so incurred shall be made good by the partner through whose neglect or default the losses shall arise. Distribution of profits shall be made on the 31st day of January each year.

Article Eleven
Advance Draws

Each partner shall be at liberty to draw out of the business in anticipation of the expected profits any sums that may be mutually agreed on, and the sums are to be drawn only after there has been entered in the books of the partnership the terms of agreement, giving the date, the amount to be drawn by the respective partners, the time at which the sums shall be drawn, and any other conditions or matters mutually agreed on. The signatures of each partner shall be affixed thereon. The total sum of the advanced draw for each partner shall be deducted from the sum that partner is entitled to under the distribution of profits as provided for in Article Ten of this agreement.

Article Twelve
Salary

No partner shall receive any salary from the partnership, and the only compensation to be paid shall be as provided in Articles Ten and Eleven herein.

Article Thirteen
Retirement

In the event any partner shall desire to retire from the partnership, he shall give three (3) months' notice in writing to the other partners and the continuing partners shall pay to the retiring partner at the termination of the three (3) months' notice the value of the interest of the retiring partner in the partnership. The value shall be determined by a closing of the books and a rendition of the appropriate profit and loss, trial balance, and balance sheet statements. All disputes arising therefrom shall be determined as provided in Article Twenty.

Article Fourteen
Rights of Continuing Partners

On the retirement of any partner, the continuing partners shall be at liberty, if they so desire, to retain all trade names designating the firm name used, and each of the partners shall sign and execute any assignments, instruments, or papers that shall be reasonably required for effectuating an amicable retirement.

Article Fifteen
Death of Partner

In the event of the death of one partner, the legal representative of the deceased partner shall remain as a partner in the firm, except that the exercising of the right on the part of the representative of the deceased partner shall not continue for a period in excess of three (3) months, even though under the terms hereof a greater period of time is provided before the termination of this agreement. The original rights of the partners herein shall accrue to their heirs, executors, or assigns.

Article Sixteen
Employee Management

No partner shall hire or dismiss any person in the employment of the partnership without the consent of the other partners, except in cases of gross misconduct by the employee.

Article Seventeen
Release of Debts

No partner shall compound, release, or discharge any debt that shall be due or owing to the partnership, without receiving the full amount thereof, unless that partner obtains the prior written consent of the other partners to the discharge of the indebtedness.

Article Eighteen
Covenant Against Revealing Trade Secrets

No partner shall, during the continuance of the partnership or for five (5) years after its determination by any means, divulge to any person not a member of the firm any trade secret or special information employed in or conducive to the partnership business and, which may come to his knowledge in the course of this partnership, without the consent in writing of the other partners, or of the other partners' heirs, administrators, or assigns.

Article Nineteen
Additional Contributions

The partners shall not have to contribute any additional capital to the partnership to that required under Article Four herein, except as follows: (1)

each partner shall be required to contribute a proportionate share in additional contributions if the fiscal year closes with an insufficiency in the capital account or profits of the partnership to meet current expenses, or (2) the capital account falls below Thirty Thousand Dollars ($30,000.00) for a period of six (6) months.

Article Twenty
Arbitration

If any difference shall arise between or among the partners as to their rights or liabilities under this agreement, or under any instrument made in furtherance of the partnership business, the difference shall be determined and the instrument shall be settled by LANCE L. KNIGHT, acting as arbitrator, and the decision shall be final as to the contents and interpretations of the instrument and as to the proper mode of carrying the provision into effect.

Article Twenty-One
Additions, Alterations, or Modifications

Where it shall appear to the partners that this agreement, or any terms and conditions contained herein, are in any way ineffective or deficient, or not expressed as originally intended, and any alteration or addition shall be deemed necessary, the partners will enter into, execute, and perform all further deeds and instruments as their counsel shall advise. Any addition, alteration, or modification shall be in writing, and no oral agreement shall be effective.

IN WITNESS WHEREOF, the parties have executed this agreement at Orange, Fremont the day and year first above written.

_____
REX KING

_____
COURTNEY QUEEN

_____
MARSHALL SQUIRE

APPENDIX
F

A Limited Partnership Agreement

AGREEMENT OF PARTNERSHIP

Agreement of limited partnership made September 31, 1999, between ARNOLD NICKLAUS, INC., of 18 Long Drive, City of Orange, State of Fremont, herein referred to as general partner, and PALMER B. HOGAN, of 21 Putts, City of Orange, State of Fremont, herein referred to as limited partner.

Recitals

1. General and limited partner desire to enter into the business of putt-putt golf.
2. General partner desires to manage and operate the business.
3. Limited partner desires to invest in the business and limit his liabilities.

In consideration of the mutual covenants contained herein, the parties agree as follows:

1. General Provisions. The limited partnership is organized pursuant to the provisions of The Uniform Partnership Act of the State of Fremont, and the rights and liabilities of the general and limited partners shall be as provided therein, except as herein otherwise expressly stated.

2. Name of Partnership. The name of the partnership shall be NICKLAUS AND HOGAN, LTD., herein referred to as the partnership.

3. Business of partnership. The purpose of the partnership is to engage in the business of putt-putt golf.

4. Principal Place of Business. The principal place of business of the partnership shall be at 2122 Ironwood Circle, Suite 4A, City of Orange, State of Fremont. The partnership shall also have other places of business as from time to time shall be determined by general partner.

5. Capital Contribution of General Partner. General partner shall contribute Six Hundred Fifty Thousand Dollars ($650,000.00) to the original capital of the partnership. The contribution of general partner shall be made on or before September 31, 1999. If general partner does not make his entire contribution to the capital of the partnership on or before that date, this agreement shall be void. Any contributions to the capital of the partnership made at that time shall be returned to the partners who have made the contributions.

6. Capital Contribution of Limited Partners. The capital contributions of limited partners shall be as follows:

Name	Amount
PALMER B. HOGAN	$500,000.00

Receipt of the capital contribution from each limited partner as specified above is acknowledged by the partnership. No limited partner has agreed to contribute any additional cash or property as capital for use of the partnership.

7. Duties and Rights of Partners. General partner shall diligently and exclusively apply himself in and about the business of the partnership to the utmost of his skill and on a full-time basis.

General partner shall not engage directly or indirectly in any business similar to the business of the partnership at any time during the term hereof without obtaining the written approval of all other partners.

General partner shall be entitled to ten (10) days' vacation and five (5) days' sick leave in each calendar year, commencing with the calendar year 2000. If general partner uses sick leave or vacation days in a calendar year in excess of the number specified above, the effect on his capital interest and share of the profits and losses of the partnership for that year shall be determined by a majority vote of limited partners.

No limited partners shall have any right to be active in the conduct of the partnership's business, nor have power to bind the partnership in any contract, agreement, promise, or undertaking.

8. Salary of General Partner. General partner shall be entitled to a monthly salary of Two Thousand Dollars ($2,000.00) for the services rendered by him. The salary shall commence on November 1, 1999, and be payable on the 15th day of each month thereafter. The salary shall be treated as an expense of the operation of the partnership business and shall be payable irrespective of whether or not the partnership shall operate at a profit.

9. Limitations on Distribution of Profits. General partner shall have the right, except as hereinafter provided, to determine whether from time to time partnership profits shall be distributed in cash or shall be left in the business, in which event the capital account of all partners shall be increased.

In no event shall any profits be payable for a period of six (6) months until seventy-five percent (75%) of those profits have been deducted to accumulate a reserve fund of Fifteen Thousand Dollars ($15,000.00) over and above the normal monthly requirements of working capital. This accumulation is to enable the partnership to maintain a sound financial operation.

10. Profits and Losses for Limited Partners. Limited partners shall be entitled to receive a share of the annual net profits equivalent to their share in the capitalization of the partnership.

Limited partners shall bear a share of the losses of the partnership equal to the share of profits to which limited partners are entitled. The share of losses of limited partners shall be charge against the limited partners' capital contribution.

Limited partners shall at no time become liable for any obligations or losses of the partnership beyond the amounts of their respective capital contributions.

11. Profits and Losses for General Partner. After provisions have been made for the shares of profits of limited partners, all remaining profits of the partnership shall be paid to general partner. After giving effect to the share of losses chargeable against the capital contributions of limited partners, the remaining partnership losses shall be borne by general partner.

12. Books of Accounts. There shall be maintained during the continuance of this partnership an accurate set of books of accounts of all transactions, assets, and liabilities of the partnership. The books shall be balanced and closed at the end of each year, and at any other time on reasonable request of the general partner. The books are to be kept at the principal place of business of the partnership and are to be open for inspection by any partner at all reasonable times. The profits and losses of the partnership and its books of accounts shall be maintained on a fiscal year basis, terminating annually on December 31, unless otherwise determined by general partner.

13. Substitutions, Assignments, and Admission of Additional Partners. General partner shall not substitute a partner in his place, or sell or assign all or any part of his interest in the partnership business without the written consent of limited partners.

Additional limited partners may be admitted to this partnership on terms that may be agreed on in writing between general partner and the new limited partners. The terms so stipulated shall constitute an amendment to this partnership agreement.

No limited partner may substitute an assignee as a limited partner in his place; but the person or persons entitled by rule or by intestate laws, as the case may be, shall succeed to all the rights of limited partner as a substituted limited partner.

14. Termination of Interest of Limited Partner; Return of Capital Contribution. The interest of any limited partner may be terminated by (1) dissolution of the partnership for any reason as provided herein, (2) the agreement of all partners, or (3) the consent of the personal representative of a deceased limited partner and the partnership.

On the termination of the interest of a limited partner there shall be payable to that limited partner, or his estate, as the case may be, a sum to be determined by all partners, which sum shall not be less than two (2) times the capital account of the limited partner as shown on the books at the time of the termination, including profits or losses from the last closing of the books of the partnership to the date of the termination, when the interest in profits and losses terminated. The amount payable shall be an obligation payable only out of partnership assets, and at the option of the partnership, may be paid within three (3) years after the termination of the interest, provided that interest at the rate of ten percent (10%) shall be paid on the unpaid balance.

15. Borrowing by Partner. In case of necessity as determined by a majority vote of all partners, a partner may borrow up to Five Thousand Dollars ($5,000.00) from the partnership. Any such loan shall be repayable at twenty-five percent (25%) per year, together with interest thereon at the rate of ten percent (10%) per year.

16. Term of Partnership and Dissolution. The partnership term commences September 31, 1999, and shall end on (1) the dissolution of the partnership by operation of law, (2) dissolution at any time designated by general partner, or (3) dissolution at the close of the month following the qualification and appointment of the personal representative of deceased general partner.

17. Payment for Interest of Deceased General Partner. In the event of the death of general partner there shall be paid out of the partnership's assets to decedent's personal representative for decedent's interest in the partnership, a sum equal to the capital account of decedent as shown on the books at the time of his death, adjusted to reflect profits or losses from the last closing of the books of the partnership to the day of his death.

18. Amendments. This agreement, except with respect to vested rights of partners, may be amended at any time by a majority vote as measure by the interest and the sharing of profits and losses.

19. Binding Effect of Agreement. This agreement shall be binding on the parties hereto and their respective heirs, executors, administrators, successors, and assigns.

IN WITNESS WHEREOF, the parties have executed this agreement at Orange, Fremont the day and year first above written.

GENERAL PARTNER:

_____

ARNOLD NICKLAUS

LIMITED PARTNER:

_____

PALMER B. HOGAN

APPENDIX
G

A Last Will
and
Testament

LAST WILL AND TESTAMENT
OF ALVIN B. ALERT

I, ALVIN B. ALERT, a resident of the County of Osceola, State of Fremont, being of sound and disposing mind, memory and understanding, do hereby make, publish and declare this to be my Last Will and Testament, hereby revoking all wills and codicils at any time heretofore made by me.

Article I

For information purposes, at the time of this Will, I am married to ALICE B. ALERT, and have natural born children, namely: AMANDA B. ALERT, born August 31, 1956; ARTHUR B. ALERT, born November 15, 1961.

Article II

I direct that all my legally enforceable debts, funeral expenses, expenses of my last illness and administrative expenses, be paid by my Personal Representative from the assets of my estate as soon as practicable after my death.

I direct that all inheritance, transfer, succession and other death taxes, which may be payable with respect to any property includable as a part of my gross estate, shall be paid from my residuary estate, without any apportionment thereof.

Article III

All the rest, residue and remainder of my estate, of every nature and kind, which I may own at the time of my death, real, personal, and mixed, tangible and intangible, of whatsoever nature and wheresoever situated, I give, devise and bequeath to my spouse, ALICE B. ALERT, providing she survives me.

In the event that my spouse shall predecease me, I give and devise all the rest, residue and remainder of my estate, as aforesaid, to my children, namely: AMANDA B. ALERT and ARTHUR B. ALERT, equally, share and share alike or to their issue, in equal share per stirpes.

Article IV

If any part or principal of my estate shall become distributable to any beneficiary hereunder who is then under the age of eighteen (18) years, my Personal Representative named hereinafter is hereby granted a power of trust, without bond or other undertaking, to hold and administer such property for the benefit of such person until such person shall attain the age of eighteen (18) years, to invest or reinvest such property, to collect the property allocable thereto, to pay to or apply to the use and benefit of such person so much of the net income as, in my Trustee's sole discretion, is deemed appropriate and to accumulate for the benefit of such person any income not so paid or applied. My Trustee is authorized to pay to or apply to the use and benefit of such person so much of the principal amount of such person's property and accumulation as deemed appropriate in the sole discretion of my

Trustee. Any remaining principal and income shall be paid to such person when he or she attains the age of eighteen (18) years.

Article V

I appoint my spouse, ALICE B. ALERT, as Personal Representative of this Will, with full power and authority to sell, transfer and convey any and all property, real or personal, which I may own at the time of my death, at such time and place and upon such terms and conditions as my Personal Representative may determine, without necessity of obtaining a court order. If my spouse does not survive me or if she fails to qualify for or, if having qualified should die, resign or become incapacitated, then in that event I nominate and appoint VIRGIL B. VIGILANT as successor Personal Representative of this Will and as trustee of any trusts created by this will, with all the powers and duties afforded my Personal Representative herein.

I direct that no Personal Representative nominated and appointed by me shall be required to furnish any bond or other security for the faithful performance of his or her duties, notwithstanding any provision of law to the contrary.

IN WITNESS WHEREOF, I have hereunto subscribed my name and affixed my seal at the City of Orange, State of Fremont, this 31st day of June, 1999, in the presence of the subscribing witnesses who I have requested to attest hereto.

_____

ALVIN B. ALERT

This instrument was, on the date hereof, signed, published and declared by ALVIN B. ALERT, to be his Last Will and Testament, and we, at the same time, at his request, in his presence and in the presence of each other, have hereunto signed our names and addresses as attesting witnesses.

_____

MARK M. MARK   of   23 Endorser Pl.
Orange, FR 39901

_____

SALLY S. SEAL   of   410 Affixer Way
Orange, FR 39901

STATE OF FREMONT
COUNTY OF OSCEOLA

WE, ALVIN B. ALERT, MARK M. MARK and SALLY S. SEAL, the Testator and the witnesses, respectively, whose names are signed to the attached and foregoing instrument, being first duly sworn, do hereby declare to the under-signed officer that the Testator signed the instrument as his Last Will and Testament and that he signed voluntarily and that each of the witnesses, in the presence of the Testator, at his request, and in the presence of each other, signed the Will as a witness and that to the best of the knowledge of each witness the Testator was at that time eighteen or more years of age, of sound mind and under no constraint or unique influence.

_____

ALVIN B. ALERT, Testator

_____

MARK M. MARK, Witness

_____

SALLY S. SEAL, Witness

Subscribed and acknowledged before me by ALVIN B. ALERT, the Testator, and subscribed and sworn to before me by MARK M. MARK and SALLY S. SEAL, the witnesses on the 31st day of June, 1999.

_____

Notary Public

A
Testamentary
Trust

⚖

LAST WILL AND TESTAMENT
OF ARTEMUS LONGREACH

With a Testamentary Trust

I, ARTEMUS LONGREACH, a resident of the County of Citrus, State of Fremont, being of sound and disposed mind, memory and understanding, do hereby make, publish and declare this to be my last will and testament, hereby revoking all wills and codicils at any time heretofore made by me.

Item I

For information purposes, at the time of this Will, I am single, and have one natural born child, namely: ALENE LONGREACH.

Item II

I direct that all my legally enforceable debts, funeral expenses, expenses of my last illness and administrative expenses, be paid by the Personal Representative from the assets of my estate as soon as practicable after my death.

I direct that all my inheritance, transfer, succession and other death taxes, which may be payable with respect to any property includable as a part of my gross estate, shall be paid from my residuary estate, without any apportionment thereof.

Item III

All the rest, residue and remainder of my estate, of every nature and kind, which I may own at the time of my death, real, personal and mixed, tangible and intangible, of whatsoever nature and wheresoever situated, I give, devise and bequeath to my Trustee, IN TRUST NEVERTHELESS, to be held under the terms and conditions hereinafter set forth, for the following purposes:

(A) My Trustee shall divide this property into as many equal parts as there are children of mine living and children of mine who shall have previously died leaving descendants then living and in respect to such parts my Trustee is directed as follows:

(1) To pay over one of such parts to the then living descendants of each of my children who shall have theretofore died leaving descendants then living, in equal shares, per stripes.

(2) To hold one of such equal parts in trust for the benefit of each of my children then living, to invest and reinvest the same, to collect and receive the income therefrom, until such time as such child for which such part shall be held in trust shall attain the age of twenty-five (25) years, and then to pay such child the entire principle of the trust created for the benefit of such child absolutely, together with all undistributed income, to be the property of such child absolutely.

(3) In the event that any of my children shall die while a beneficiary under a trust created under this paragraph, that child's trust shall then terminate and the principle thereof, together with any accumulated income thereon, shall be paid in equal shares to such deceased child's descendants then living, per stripes. If such deceased child shall not be survived by any descendants as shall then be living, in equal shares, per stripes.

(B) As to any of my children entitled to the benefit of a trust created hereunder, but who shall then be under the age of twenty-five (25) years, my Trustee shall pay to or apply so much of the income from the trust for such child, or if such income is not sufficient, then such portions of the principle of that child's trust, as in the discretion of my Trustee may be necessary for the care, protection, support, maintenance and education of such child, and to accumulate the remainder until he or she attains the age of twenty-five (25) years, and thereupon my Trustee shall pay over and distribute all such accumulations of income and all principle as herein above directed.

Item IV

If any part or principle of my estate shall become distributable to any beneficiary hereunder who is then under the age of twenty-five (25) years, my Personal Representative and Trustee named hereinafter is hereby granted a power of trust, without bond or other undertaking, to hold and administer such property for the benefit of such person until such person shall attain the age of twenty-five (25) years, to invest or reinvest such property, to collect the income therefrom, and, after deducting therefrom all charges properly allocable thereto, to pay to or apply to the use and benefit of such person so much of the net income as, in my Trustee's sole discretion, is deemed appropriate and to accumulate for the benefit of such person any income not so paid or applied. My Trustee is authorized to pay to or apply to the use and benefit of such person so much of the principle amount of such person's property and accumulations as is deemed appropriate in the sole discretion of my Trustee. Any remaining principle and income shall be paid to such when he or she attains the age of twenty-five (25) years.

Item V

In the investment, administration and distribution of my estate and any trusts created hereby, expect where otherwise restricted, my Personal Representative and Trustee may perform every act in the management of my estate or of the trusts which individuals may perform in the management of like property owned by them free of any trust, without authorization of any court, even though any such act would not be authorized or appropriate for fiduciaries but for this power under any statutory or other rule of law, including in this grant, without impairing its plenary nature, power; to acquire by purchase or otherwise and to retain, temporarily or permanently, any and all kinds of realty and personalty, including corporate shares and unsecured obligations, without diversification as to kind or amount; to sell or otherwise dispose of any such property, publicly or privately, wholly or partly on credit;

to delegate discretion; and to distribute in kind or in money, or partly in each, even if shares be composed differently.

Item VI

I nominate and appoint OSWOLD COSMOLD as my Personal Representative of this Will. If he does not survive me or, if he fails to qualify, or, if having qualified should die, resign or become incapacitated, then in that event I nominate and appoint SABAL BANK AND TRUST COMPANY as successor Personal Representative and as Trustee of any trusts created by this Will. I direct that no Personal Representative or Trustee nominated and appointed by me shall be required to furnish any bond or other security for the faithful performance of his/her duties, notwithstanding any provision of law to the contrary.

IN WITNESS WHEREOF, I have hereunto set my hand and affixed my seal at the City of Orange, State of Fremont, this 31st day of June, 1999, in the presence of the subscribing witness who I have requested to become attesting witness hereto.

_____
ARTEMUS LONGREACH

This instrument was, on the date hereof, signed, published and declared by ARTEMUS LONGREACH, to be his Last Will and Testament, in our presence and in the presence of each of us and we, at the same time, at his request, in his presence and in the presence of each other, have hereunto signed our names and addresses as attesting witnesses.

_____
DAVID SCOTT   of   10 Pathlane
Boulder, FR 56932

_____
SCOTT DAVID   of   567 Rocky Rd.
Boulder, FR 56932

STATE OF FREMONT
COUNTY OF CITRUS

We, ARTEMUS LONGREACH, DAVID SCOTT, and SCOTT DAVID, the Testator, and the witnesses, respectively, whose names are signed to the attached and foregoing instrument, being first duly sworn, do hereby declare to the undersigned officer that the Testator signed the instrument as his Last Will and Testament and that he signed voluntarily and that such of the witnesses, in the presence of the Testator, at his request, and in the presence of each other, signed the Will as a witness and that to the best of the knowledge of each witness the Testator was at that time eighteen or more years of age, of sound mind and under no constraint or undue influence.

_____
ARTEMUS LONGREACH

_____
SCOTT DAVID

_____
DAVID SCOTT

Subscribed and acknowledged before me by _____, the Testator, and subscribed and sworn to before me by _____ and _____, the witnesses, on the _____ day of _____, 19___.

_____
(SEAL)   Notary Public

INTERROGATORIES

IN THE CIRCUIT COURT
FOR THE COUNTY OF MOSQUITO

BELLE BLISS,

      Plaintiff,

v.   Case No. 34567

THE THIRSTY TURTLE,

      Defendant.

_____/

Interrogatories to Plaintiff

Defendant, THE THIRSTY TURTLE, through his undersigned attorney, propounds the following interrogatories to Plaintiff pursuant to court rules, to be answered within thirty (30) days from the date hereof.

As used herein "person" means the full name, present or last-known residence address (designating which). Any reference to the singular person, place, thing, or entity, including but not limited to any partnership, corporation, firm, proprietorship, association, or governmental body, shall include the plural, as well as the singular, and the feminine as well as the masculine or neuter.

The term "accident" means that certain accident between the automobiles of plaintiff and defendant.

If answering for another person or entity, answer with respect to that person or entity, unless otherwise stated.

1. What is the name and address of the person answering these interrogatories, and, if applicable, the person's official position or relationship with the party to whom the interrogatories are directed?

2. List the names, business addresses, dates of employment and rates of pay regarding all employers, including self-employment, for whom you have worked in the past ten years.

3. List all former names and when you were known by those names. State all addresses where you have lived for the past ten years, the dates you lived at each address, your social security number, your date of birth, and if you are or have ever been married, the name of your spouse or spouses.

4. Do you wear glasses, contact lenses, or hearing aids? If so, who prescribed them; when were they prescribed; when were your eyes or ears last examined; and what is the name and address of the examiner?

5. Have you ever been convicted of a crime, other than any juvenile adjudication, where the law under which you were convicted was punishable by

death or imprisonment in excess of one year, or that involved dishonesty or a false statement regardless of the punishment? If so, state as to each conviction, the specific crime, the date and place of conviction.

6. Were you suffering from physical infirmity, disability, or sickness at the time of the accident described in the complaint? If so, what was the nature of the infirmity, disability, or sickness?

7. Did you consume any alcoholic beverages or take any drugs or medications within twelve hours before the time of the incident described in the complaint? If so, state the type and amount of alcoholic beverages, drugs, or medication which were consumed and when and where you consumed them.

8. Describe in detail how the incident described in the complaint happened, including all actions taken by you to prevent the accident.

9. Describe in detail each act or omission on the part of any party to this lawsuit that you contend constituted negligence that was a contributing legal course of the incident in question.

10. Were you charged with any violation of law (including any regulations or ordinances) arising out of the incident described in the complaint? If so, what was the nature of the charge; what plea, or answer, if any, did you enter to the charge; what court or agency heard the charge; was any written report prepared by anyone regarding this charge, and, if so, what is the name and address of the person or entity that prepared the report; do you have a copy of the report; and was the testimony at any trial, hearing, or other proceeding on the charge recorded in any manner, and, if so, what was the name and address of the person who recorded the testimony?

11. Describe each injury for which you are claiming damages in this case, specifying the part of your body that was injured, the nature of the injury, and, as to any injuries you contend are permanent, the effects on you that you claim are permanent.

12. List each item of expense or damage, other than loss of income or earning capacity, that you claim to have incurred as a result of the incident described in the complaint, giving for each item: the date incurred, the name and business address to whom each was paid or is owed, and the goods or services for which each was incurred.

13. Do you contend that you have lost any income, benefits, or earning capacity in the past or future as a result of the incident described in the complaint? If so, state the nature of the income, benefits, or earning capacity, and the amount and the method that you used in computing the amount.

14. Has anything been paid or is anything payable from any third party for the damages listed in your answers to these interrogatories? If so, state the amounts paid or payable, the name and business address of the person or entity who paid or owes said amounts, and which of those third parties have or claim a right of subrogation.

15. List the names and business addresses of each physician who has treated or examined you, and each medical facility where you have received any treatment or examination for the injuries for which you seek damages in this case; and state as to each the date of treatment or examination and the injury or condition for which you were examined or treated.

16. List the names and business addresses of all other physicians, medical facilities, or other health care providers by whom or at which you have been examined or treated in the past ten years; and state as to each the dates of examination or treatment and the condition or injury for which you were examined or treated.

17. List the names and addresses of all persons who are believed or known by you, your agents or attorneys to have any knowledge concerning any of the issues in this lawsuit; and specify the subject matter about which the witness has knowledge.

18. Have you heard or do you know about any statement or remark made by or on behalf of any party to this lawsuit, other than yourself, concerning any issue in this lawsuit? If so, state the name and address of each person who made the statement or statements, the name and address of each person who heard it, and the date, time, place, and substance of each statement.

19. State the name and address of every person known to you, your agents, or attorneys, who has knowledge about, or possession, custody or control of any model, plat, map, drawing, motion picture, video tape, or photograph pertaining to any fact or issue involved in this controversy; and describe as to each, what such person has, the name and address of the person who took or prepared it, and the date it was taken or prepared.

20. Do you intend to call any expert witnesses at the trial of this case? If so, state as to each such witness the name and business address of the witness, the witness's qualifications as an expert, the subject matter upon which the witness is expected to testify, and a summary of the grounds for each opinion.

21. Have you made an agreement with anyone that would limit that party's liability to anyone for any of the damages sued upon in this case? If so, state whether you were plaintiff or defendant, the nature of the action, and the date and court in which such suit was filed.

BELLE BLISS

BEFORE ME, the undersigned authority, personally appeared BELLE BLISS, known to me and known by me to be the Plaintiff in the above-mentioned lawsuit and who executed the foregoing Answers to Interrogatories, under oath, stated that she is the person who executed the same and that according to her best knowledge and belief the answers are true and correct. BELLE BLISS was under oath.

Form of Identification _____.

Sworn to and subscribed before me, this _____ day of _____, 19___.

_____

Printed name _____
Notary Public, State of Fremont at Large

My Commission expires:

I HEREBY CERTIFY that the original and one copy of the foregoing Interrogatories to Plaintiff were furnished to WILL PURVALE, Attorney for Plaintiff, One Harmony Drive, Orange, Fremont 45090, this _____ day of _____, 19___, by U.S. Mail.

_____
BARNWELL BOOZER
Attorney for Defendant
1234 S. Drainage St.
Orange, Fremont 45091

I HEREBY CERTIFY that the original interrogatories with answers were furnished to BARNWELL BOOZER, Attorney for Defendant, 1234 S. Drainage St., Orange, Fremont 45091, this _____ day of _____, 19___, by U.S. Mail.

_____
WILL PURVALE
Attorney for Plaintiff
One Harmony Drive
Orange, Fremont 45090

GLOSSARY

A

abatement: The process by which fixed assets of an estate are liquidated in order to cover payments requiring cash for which the estate has insufficient liquid assets.

abstract of title: A short account of the state of the title to real estate, reflecting all past ownership and any interests or rights, such as a mortgage or other liens, that any person might currently have with respect to the property.

acknowledgment: The signing of a document, under oath, whereby the signer certifies that he or she is, in fact, the person who is named in the document as the signer; the certificate of the person who administered the oath. EXAMPLES: clerk of court; justice of the peace; notary.

adjustable rate mortgage: A mortgage in which the rate of interest is not absolute but is adjusted from time to time based upon conditions in the money market; often referred to as an ARM.

admissibility: The quality of being admissible, *i.e.*, of being admitted, allowed, or considered.

affidavit: Any voluntary statement reduced to writing and sworn to or affirmed before a person legally authorized to administer an oath or affirmation.

affirmative defense: A defense that amounts to more than simply a denial of the allegations the plaintiff's complaint. It sets up new matter which, if proven, could result in a judgment against the plaintiff even if all the allegations of the complaint are true.

alimony: Ongoing court-ordered support payments by a divorced spouse, usually payments made by an ex-husband to his former wife.

annual report: A report issued yearly by a corporation, informing its stockholders, the government, and the public, in some detail, of its operations, particularly its fiscal operations, during the year.

answer: A pleading in response to a complaint. An answer may deny the allegations of the complaint, demur to them, agree with them, or introduce affirmative defenses intended to defeat the plaintiff's lawsuit or delay it.

antenuptial agreement: An agreement between a man and a woman who are about to be married, governing the financial and property arrangements between them in the event of divorce, death, or even during the marriage. Such an agreement may override obligations or rights provided by statute.

anti–heart balm statute: A law that establishes the right to an action for a breach of a covenant to marry. Such laws have been abolished in most states.

appeal: The process by which a higher court is requested by a party to a lawsuit to review the decision of a lower court. Such reconsideration is normally confined to a review of the record from the lower court, with no new testimony taken nor new issues raised.

appellant: A party who appeals from a lower court to a higher court.

appellate brief: A written statement submitted to an appellate court that argues the facts of the case, supported by citations of authority, in order to persuade the court that an error has occurred in a lower court.

appellate court: A higher court to which an appeal is taken from a lower court.

appellee: A party against whom a case is appealed from a lower court to a higher court.

appreciation: An increase in the value of something.

arbitration: A method of settling disputes by submitting a disagreement to a person (an arbitrator) or a group of individuals (an arbitration panel) for decision instead of going to court.

arbitrator: A person who conducts an arbitration; primary considerations in choosing the person are impartiality and familiarity with the type of matter in dispute.

argument: An attorney's effort, either by written brief or oral argument, to persuade a court or administrative agency that his or her client's claim should prevail; reason put forward in an effort to convince.

articles of incorporation: The charter or basic rules that create a corporation and by which it functions.

attestation: The act of witnessing the signing of a document, including signing one's name as a witness to that fact.

attestation clause: A clause, usually at the end of a document such as a deed or a will, that provides evidence of attestation.

attorney's opinion letter: A summary of an attorney's examination of an abstract of title, providing an opinion as to the legal effect of the matters of record.

authorization: The grant of authority to another to do or obtain something.

automatic stay: A halt to any proceedings that may be pending in another court, which is effected by the filing of a petition in bankruptcy.

B

---

balloon payment mortgage: A mortgage whose final payment is considerably higher than any of the previous regular payments, the final payment representing much if not all of the entire principal.

bankruptcy: The circumstances of a person who is unable to pay his or her debts as they come due; the system under which a debtor may come into court or be brought into court by his or her creditors, either seeking to have his or her assets administered and sold for the benefit of his or her creditors and to be discharged from his or her debts, or to have his or her debts reorganized.

beneficiary: A person for whom property is held in trust.

bequests: Technically, gifts of personal property by will, *i.e.*, legacies, although the term is often loosely used in connection with testamentary gifts of real estate as well.

bona fide purchaser: A person who purchases something in good faith for what it is worth, without knowing that anyone else has any legal interest in it.

breach of contract: Failure, without legal excuse, to perform any promise that forms a whole or a part of a contract, including the doing of something inconsistent with its terms.

brief: A written statement submitted to a court for the purpose of persuading it of the correctness of one's position. A brief argues the facts of the case and the applicable law, supported by citations of authority.

bylaws: Regulations adopted by a group or organization.

C

capacity: A person's ability to understand the nature and effect of the act in which he or she is engaged.

capitalization: The total value of the stocks, bonds, and other securities issued by a corporation.

caption: A heading or title; in legal practice, it generally refers to the heading of a court paper.

cause of action: Circumstances that give a person the right to bring a lawsuit and to receive relief from a court.

certificate of stock: An instrument issued by a corporation stating that the person named is the owner of a designated number of shares of its stock.

closing: Completing a transaction, particularly a contract for the sale of real estate.

closing statement: A document prepared in connection with a real estate closing that details the financial aspects of the transaction.

codicil: An addition or supplement to a will, which adds to or modifies the will without replacing or revoking it.

complaint: The initial pleading in a civil action, in which the plaintiff alleges a cause of action and asks that the wrong done him or her be remedied by the court.

conclusion: A summary of a party's position and arguments.

conditions precedent: Conditions that must first occur for a contractual obligation (or a provision of a will, deed, or the like) to attach.

confession of judgment: The entry of a judgment upon the admission and at the direction of the debtor, without the formality, time, or effort involved in bringing a lawsuit.

contingent fee: A fee for legal services, calculated on the basis of an agreed-upon percentage of the amount of money recovered for the client by his or her attorney.

contract: An agreement entered into, for adequate consideration, to do, or refrain from doing, a particular thing. In addition to adequate consideration, the transaction must involve an undertaking that is legal to perform, and there must be mutuality of agreement and obligation between at least two competent parties.

conventional mortgage: A mortgage granted by a conventional lender, that is, a bank or a savings and loan institution rather than the FHA or VA.

corporate minute book: The corporate record of the actions of the shareholders and directors of a corporation.

corporation: An artificial person, existing only in the eyes of the law, to whom a state or the federal government has granted a charter to become a legal entity, separate from its shareholders, with a name of its own, under which its shareholders can act and contract and sue and be sued.

counts: Statements of causes of action in a complaint.

court order: An adjudication by a court; a ruling by a court with respect to a motion or any other question before it for determination during the course of a proceeding.

covenant: In a deed, a promise to do or not to do a particular thing, or an assurance that a particular fact or circumstance exists or does not exist.

creditor: A person to whom a debt is owed by a debtor.

D

damages: The sum of money that may be recovered in the courts as financial reparation for an injury or wrong suffered as a result of breach of contract or a tortious act.

debt: An unconditional and legally enforceable obligation for the payment of money; that which is owing under any form of promise, including obligations arising under contract, *e.g.*, mortgage or installment sale contract, and obligations imposed by law without contract, *e.g.*, judgment or unliquidated damages.

debtor: A person who owes another person money; a person who owes another person anything.

debtor in possession: A debtor who continues to operate his or her business while undergoing a business reorganization under the jurisdiction of the Bankruptcy Court.

deed: A document by which real property, or an interest in real property, is conveyed from one person to another.

default divorce: A divorce in which no appearance is made by the defendant, so that the plaintiff is granted the dissolution without contest.

default judgment: A judgment rendered in favor of a plaintiff based upon a defendant's failure to take a necessary step in a lawsuit within the required time.

demand for judgment: Another term for a prayer for relief.

deposition: The transcript of a witness's testimony given under oath outside of the courtroom, usually in advance of the trial or hearing, upon oral examination or in response to written interrogatories.

devises: Gifts of real property by will, although the term is often loosely used to mean testamentary gifts of either real property or personal property.

discovery: A means for providing a party, in advance of trial, with access to facts that are within the knowledge of the other side, to enable the party to better try his or her case.

dispositive motion: A motion that, if granted by the court, will dispose of a case entirely, terminating the lawsuit.

dissolution: The change in the relation of partners caused by any partner's ceasing to be associated in the carrying on of the business.

dissolution agreement: A formal contractual agreement between the partners to wind up the partnership business and terminate its existence.

divorce: A dissolution of the marital relationship between husband and wife.

document: Anything with letters, figures, or marks recorded on it. EXAMPLES: printed words; photographs; pictures; maps.

domicile: The relationship that the law creates between a person and a particular locality or country.

E

elite: A typewriter providing twelve characters to the linear inch.

equitable title: Title recognized as ownership in equity, even though it is not legal title or marketable title; title sufficient to give the party to whom it belongs the right to have the legal title transferred to him or her.

equity: A system for ensuring justice in circumstances where the remedies customarily available under conventional law are inadequate; a system of jurisprudence less formal and more flexible than the common law, available in particular types of cases to better ensure a fair result.

estate planning: The creation of a method for the orderly handling, disposition, and administration of an estate when the owner dies.

execution: The signing of a document or instrument; the completion of any transaction.

executor: A person designated by a testator to carry out the directions and requests in the testator's will and to dispose of his or her property according to the provisions of his or her will.

executrix: A term used to describe a female executor.

ex parte: Means "of a side," *i.e.*, from one side or by one party. The term refers to an application made to the court by one party without notice to the other party.

ex parte **divorce:** A divorce proceeding in which only one spouse participates. If the failure to participate is due to inadequate notice, any divorce decree granted is invalid.

express contract: A contract, whether written or oral, whose terms are stated by the parties.

express warranty: A warranty created by the seller in a contract for sale of goods, in which the seller, orally or in writing, makes representations regarding the quality or condition of the goods.

F

FHA mortgage: A mortgage in which the loan is insured by the Federal Housing Administration, which is an agency of the United States that supports the availability of housing and a sound mortgage market by insuring bank mortgages granted to borrowers who meet its standards.

fiduciary duty: The duty to act loyally and honestly with respect to the interests of another.

first meeting of creditors: The first meeting of creditors of a bankrupt, required for the purpose of allowing the claims of creditors, questioning the bankrupt under oath, and electing a trustee in bankruptcy.

fixed rate mortgage: A mortgage in which the rate of interest is absolute, that is, not adjusted from time to time.

font: An assortment or set of type all of one size and style; a typeface.

footer: A line containing page numbers that appears at the bottom of each page of a legal document.

foreign corporation: A corporation incorporated under the laws of one state, doing business in another.

foreign divorce: A divorce granted in a state or country other than the couple's state of residence.

G

general partnership: An ordinary partnership, as distinguished from a limited partnership; synonymous with partnership.

general revocatory clause: A clause in a will that shows that it is the testator's intent that the document supersede any previously published will or codicil.

general warranty deed: A deed in which the grantor, or seller, guarantees the title against any defects.

H

heading: The title of a legal document that indicates exactly what the document claims to be.

heirs at law: Persons who are entitled to inherit real or personal property of a decedent who dies intestate; persons receiving property by descent.

I
---

implied contract: A contract that the law infers from the circumstances, conduct, acts, or the relationship of the parties rather than from their spoken words.

implied warranty: In the sale of personal property, a warranty by the seller, inferred by law (whether or not the seller intended to create the warranty), as to the quality or condition of the goods sold.

incorporators: Persons who form a corporation.

indemnification: Payment made by way of compensation for a loss.

instrument: Any formal legal document evidencing an agreement or the granting of a right. EXAMPLES: contract; deed; mortgage; will.

intent: Purpose; the plan, course, or means a person conceives to achieve a certain result.

interrogatories: Written questions put by one party to another or, in limited situations, to a witness in advance of trial. Interrogatories are a form of discovery and are governed by the rules of civil procedure.

intestate: Pertaining to a person, or to the property of a person, who dies without leaving a valid will.

involuntary petition: A bankruptcy petition that is filed by a creditor to force the debtor into a bankruptcy proceeding.

irrevocable living trust: A trust created and executed during the settlor's lifetime that cannot be revoked by him or her at any time.

J
---

judgment creditor: A creditor who has secured a judgment against his or her debtor that has not been satisfied.

jurat: The certification that an affidavit has been duly sworn by the affiant before a duly authorized person. EXAMPLES: notary public.

jurisdiction: In a general sense, the right of a court to adjudicate lawsuits of a certain kind; in a specific sense, the right of a court to determine a particular case; in a geographical sense, the power of a court to hear cases only within a specific territorial area.

justification: The process or result of justifying lines of text so that the right margin is aligned from the right side of the paper at a preset dimension.

L

law: The entire body of rules of conduct created by government and enforced by the authority of government. EXAMPLES: constitutions; statutes; ordinances; regulations; judicial decisions.

laws of descent and distribution: The laws determining the manner of distribution of a deceased's property when there is no valid will concerning that particular property.

laws of intestate succession: The laws through which an individual's property is distributed when an individual dies intestate, *i.e.*, without leaving a valid will.

lease: A contract for the possession of real estate in consideration of payment of rent, ordinarily for a term of years or months, but sometimes at will. The person making the conveyance is the landlord or lessor; the person receiving the right of possession is the tenant or lessee.

legal cap: The preprinted left margin of paper that was once used for legal documents; paper with a legal cap is now prohibited by many court rules.

legal document: The written, physical embodiment of information conforming to the principles of law enacted by the government through the legislative process and reviewed by the judicial system.

legal size: Paper that measures 8 ½ x 14 inches; the paper on which legal documents have historically been presented.

limited partnership: A partnership in which the liability of one or more of the partners is limited to the amount of money they have invested in the partnership.

liquidated damages: A sum agreed upon by the parties at the time of entering into a contract as being payable by way of compensation for loss suffered in the event of a breach of contract; a sum similarly determined by a court in a lawsuit resulting from breach of contract.

living trust: A trust that is effective during the lifetime of the creator of the trust. Also known as an *inter vivos trust*.

M

margin: A border; a boundary ("the margin of the page").

marital property: Property acquired by the parties during the marriage, which a court will divide between the former spouses upon dissolution of the marriage if the parties have not themselves made disposition by marital agreement.

marriage: The relationship of a man and a woman legally united as husband and wife. Marriage is a contract binding the parties until one dies or until a divorce or annulment occurs.

material error: Reversible error; judicial error that causes a miscarriage of justice.

migratory divorce: A divorce obtained by a person who changed his residence or domicile to another state for the length of time required to secure a divorce in that state, but with no intention of remaining there.

modification: A change, alteration, or amendment.

mortgage: A pledge of real property to secure a debt.

mortgagee: The person to whom a mortgage is made; the lender.

mortgagor: A person who mortgages his or her property; the borrower.

motion: An application made to a court for the purpose of obtaining an order or rule directing something to be done in favor of the applicant.

motion for a more definite statement: A motion made by a defendant in response to a vague or ambiguous complaint.

motion for summary judgment: A motion requesting that an action be disposed of without further proceedings.

N

N/A: Not applicable; used in legal documents to signify that the space has been considered and the information that should go in that space is not available or does not exist.

nonmarital property: Property acquired by a spouse before marriage or through a gift or bequest; such separate property is not subject to division in a dissolution of the marriage.

notice: The method and necessity of the conveyance of any information called for by the terms of a contract.

notice of appeal: The process by which appellate review is initiated; specifically, written notice to the appellee advising him or her of the appellant's intention to appeal.

notice of hearing: A notice of the filing of a motion furnished to the nonmoving party to inform them of the time and place of the hearing and to identify the nature of and grounds for the motion.

numeric designation: Numbers that express amounts that can also be expressed with words; used in legal documents along with word forms to further clarify text.

O

organizational meeting: The final act of the incorporators to complete the process of establishing a corporation.

P

pagination: The numbers or marks used to indicate the sequence of pages.

partial release of mortgage: A satisfaction, or payment, of a debt secured by part of an affected property.

partnership: An undertaking of two or more persons to carry on, as coowners, a business or other enterprise for profit; an agreement between or among two or more persons or entities to put their money, labor, and skill into commerce or business and to divide the profit in agreed-upon proportions.

partnership at will: A partnership that is intended to continue as long as the partners do business together, *i.e.*, until the partnership is dissolved according to the agreement or until the death or resignation of one of the partners.

par value: The value of a share of stock or of a bond, according to its face; the named or nominal value of an instrument.

personal property: All property other than real property, including stocks, bonds, and mortgages. EXAMPLES: money; goods; evidence of debt. Personal property can be further categorized as tangible or intangible property.

petition: A formal request in writing, addressed to a person or body in a position of authority, signed by a number of persons or by one person; the name given in some jurisdictions to a complaint or other pleading that alleges a cause of action.

pica: Twelve-point type; a typewriter type providing ten characters to the linear inch and six lines to the vertical inch.

pleadings: Formal statements by the parties to an action setting forth their claims or defenses. EXAMPLES: complaint; cross-complaint; answer; counterclaim.

postnuptial agreement: A marital agreement entered into after marriage.

prayer for relief: The portion of a complaint or claim for relief that specifies the type of relief to which the plaintiff feels he or she is entitled and for which he or she requests judgment; also called a demand for relief or demand for judgment.

preferential transfer: Under the Bankruptcy Code, a transfer of property by an insolvent debtor to one or more creditors to the exclusion of others, enabling such creditors to obtain a greater percentage of their debt than other creditors of the same class.

preincorporation agreement: An agreement that contains the basic understanding between two or more persons who associate themselves for the purpose of forming a corporaiton.

prenuptial agreement: An agreement between a man and a woman who are about to be married, governing the financial and property arrangements between them in the event of divorce, death, or even during the marriage. Such an agreement may override obligations or rights provided by statute.

private express trust: A trust created by an individual expressly for the purposes of estate planning.

probate: The judicial act whereby a will is adjudicated to be valid; a term that describes the functions of the probate court, including the probate of wills and the supervision of the accounts and actions of administrators and executors of decedents' estates.

promissory note: A written promise to pay a specific sum of money by a specified date or on demand.

promoters: Persons who organize a business venture or are major participants in organizing the venture.

proof of claim: In bankruptcy, a statement in writing, signed by a creditor, setting forth the amount owed and the basis of the claim.

prove: To establish a fact by the required degree of evidence.

purchase money mortgage: A mortgage executed by a purchaser of real property to secure his or her obligation to pay the purchase price.

Q

quitclaim deed: A deed that conveys whatever interest the grantor has in a piece of real property, as distinguished from the more usual deed which conveys a fee and contains various covenants, particularly title covenants.

R

real property: Land, including things located on it or attached to it directly (EXAMPLE: buildings) or indirectly (EXAMPLE: fixtures). In the technical sense, the interest a person has in land.

record below: The papers a trial court transmits tot eh appellate court, on the basis of which the appellate court decides the appeal. The record below includes the pleadings, all motions made before the trial court, the official transcript, and the judgment or order appealed from.

recording: The act of making a record.

registered agent: That individual appointed by a corporation and required by statute for the purpose of receiving service of process.

release of mortgage: A satisfaction, or payment in full, of a mortgage.

relief: A person's object in bringing a lawsuit; the function or purpose of a remedy.

reorganization: Chapter 11 of the Bankruptcy Code allows a debtor to restructure the debt of a business in order to remain in business and preserve ongoing operations while the debt is resolved.

request for production: The procedure by which parties to a lawsuit request documents and other things that are relevant to the subject matter and not privileged.

residuary: Pertaining to the residue; pertaining to that which is left over.

revocable living trust: A trust created by a settlor during his or her lifetime that reserves the right of revocation of the trust, *i.e.*, the settlor can change, alter, or amend the terms of the agreement during his or her lifetime.

rules of court: Rules promulgated by the court, governing procedure or practice before it.

S

satisfaction of mortgage: The payment of a mortgage in full.

schedules: Pages attached to a document listing additional details relating to the matter contained in the main document.

"S" corporation: A corporation electing to be taxed under subchapter S of the Internal Revenue Code. Its income is taxed to the shareholders rather than at the corporate level.

seal: An imprint made upon an instrument by a device such as an engraved metallic plate, or upon wax affixed to the instrument; symbolizes authority or authenticity.

self-proving: A document that establishes its own authenticity through the acknowledgment by a notary public or other such official authorized by statute to administer oaths attached to the document proper.

separation agreement: An agreement between husband and wife who are about to divorce or to enter into a legal separation, settling property rights and other matters such as custody, child support, visitation, and alimony.

service of process: Delivery of a summons, writ, complaint, or other process to the opposite party, or other person entitled to receive it, in such manner as the law prescribes, whether by leaving a copy at his or her residence, by mailing a copy to the person or his or her attorney, or by publication.

settlor: The creator of a trust; the person who conveys or transfers property to another (the trustee) to hold in trust for a third person (the beneficiary).

severability: The divisibility of the terms or clauses in a contract, with the result that a breach of one promise is not a breach of the contract as a whole.

shared parental responsibility: A situation in which both parents have frequent contact with their children and share the responsibilities of childraising, even after a divorce.

sole proprietorship: Ownership by one person, as opposed to ownership by more than one person or by a corporation or partnership.

solid caps: Uppercase letters used in a legal document to give certain words and names emphasis.

special warranty deed: A deed in which the grantor only covenants to defend the title against people making a claim or demand by, through, and under the grantor.

statute of limitation: A federal or state statute prescribing the maximum period of time during which various types of civil actions and criminal prosecutions can be brought after the occurrence of the injury or the offense.

stock: Shares in a corporation or a joint-stock company owned by shareholders; the sum of all the rights and duties of the shareholders.

stock subscription agreement: The agreement of incorporators or promotors to purchase a set number of shares of stock in a new corporation at a stated price.

stock transfer ledger: A corporation's record of the identity of each owner of the shares of the corporation, the date of his or her purchase, and any transfer of those shares.

subpoena: A command in the form of written process requiring a witness to come to court to testify.

subpoena duces tecum: The Latin term *duces tecum* means "bring with you under penalty." A subpoena duces tecum is a written command requiring a witness to come to court to testify and at that time to produce for use as evidence the papers, documents, books, or records listed in the subpoena.

subrogation: The substitution of one person for another with respect to a claim or right against a third person; the principle that when a person has been required to pay a debt that should have been paid by another person, he or she becomes entitled to all of the remedies that the creditor originally possessed with respect to the debtor.

summons: To call or require a person or a group of people to appear or to obey some other command; with a complaint, the summons informs the defendant that an action has been filed and that he or she must answer or have a judgment entered against him or her.

T

---

testamentary trust: A trust created by will.

testate: Pertaining to a person, or to the property of a person, who dies leaving a valid will.

testator: A person who dies leaving a valid will.

testimonium clause: A clause at the end of a deed, which recites that the parties have "set their hands and seals" to the deed on the date specified.

title: The rights of an owner with respect to real or personal property, *i.e.*, possession and the right of possession. A document that evidences the rights of an owner. EXAMPLES: deed; bill of sale.

title examination: A search of all documents of record relating to the status or condition of the title to a given piece of real estate (including deeds reflecting past ownership and outstanding mortgages and other liens) in order to verify title.

titles: Portions of a legal instrument or pleading designating its identity and purpose.

tolled: Interrupted or suspended; *e.g.*, a statute of limitation is tolled (prevented from expiring) on a weekend or holiday.

trust: A fiduciary relationship involving a trustee who holds trust property for the benefit or use of a beneficiary.

trustee: The person who holds the legal title to trust property for the benefit of the beneficiary of the trust, with such powers and subject to such duties as are imposed by the terms of the trust and the law.

trustee in bankruptcy: A person appointed by a bankruptcy court to collect any amounts owed the debtor, well the debtor's property, and distribute the proceeds among the creditors.

trust property: Property that is the subject of a trust. It is also referred to as the *trust res*, the *res of the trust*, or the *corpus* of the trust.

V

VA mortgage: A mortgage in which the loan is insured by the Veterans Administration, which is the federal agency that administers federal statutes providing for the welfare of military veterans and their dependents.

venue: The county or judicial district in which a case is to be tried; in bankruptcy, it is the district in which the debtor resides or has a place of business or in which the debtor's principal assets are located.

voidable transfer: A transfer that is made by a debtor, within one year of the filing of a petition for bankruptcy, with the intention and for the purpose of defrauding creditors.

voluntary petition: A bankruptcy petition that is initiated by the debtor under one of the provisions of the Bankruptcy Code.

W

warranty: With respect to a contract for sale of goods, a promise, either express or implied by law, with respect to the fitness or merchantability of the article that is the subject of the contract.

will: An instrument by which a person (the testator) makes a disposition of his or her property, to take effect after his or her death.

wraparound mortgage: Secondary financing with a new mortgagee/lender, whereby the lender refinances the property by assuming the first mortgage and lending additional money above the existing mortgage balance, that is used where there is a low interest rate on older financing with a substantial difference between the amount owed on the original mortgage and the value of the property.

Index

$$\triangle\!|\!\triangle$$

INDEX